Demographic Techniques

DEMOGRAPHIC TECHNIQUES

A H Pollard

M.Sc., M.Sc.(Econ.), Ph.D., F.I.A., F.A.S.S.A.
Emeritus Professor, formerly
Professor of Economic Statistics, Director of
Actuarial Studies, Head of the School of
Economic and Financial Studies, Macquarie University

Farhat Yusuf

B.Sc.(Hons.), M.A., Ph.D.
Senior Lecturer in Statistics, Macquarie University

G N Pollard

M.Sc., A.I.A.
Senior Lecturer in Statistics, Macquarie University

Pergamon Press
SYDNEY · OXFORD · NEW YORK · TORONTO · PARIS · FRANKFURT

Pergamon Press (Australia) Pty Ltd
19a Boundary Street, Rushcutters Bay, NSW 2011, Australia

Pergamon Press Ltd
Headington Hill Hall, Oxford OX3 0BW, England

Pergamon Press Inc.
Fairview Park, Elmsford, NY 10523, USA

Pergamon of Canada
Suite 104, 150 Consumers Road, Willowdale, Ontario M2J 1P9, Canada

Pergamon Press GmbH
6242 Kronberg/Taunus, Hammerweg 6, Postfach 1305,
Federal Republic of Germany

Pergamon Press SARL
24 rue des Ecoles, 75240 Paris, Cedex 05, France

First published 1974, reprinted 1975
Second edition 1981
Cover design by Vane Lindesay
Typeset in Hong Kong by Asco Trade Typesetting Limited
Printed in Singapore by Kyodo-Shing Loong Printing Industries (Pte) Ltd

National Library of Australia Cataloguing in Publication Data

Pollard, Alfred Hurlstone, 1916-
    Demographic techniques.

    2nd ed.
    Index
    Bibliography
    ISBN 0 08 024817 9

    1. Demography – Methodology.   I. Yusuf, Farhat, joint
    author.   II. Pollard, G. N., joint author.   III. Title.

304.6′01′8

Contents

Preface to second edition

This book has been prepared as an introduction to demographic techniques for students who have a general interest in population studies. The authors have been teaching demography at Macquarie University and elsewhere for many years and the material in this book has been used for that purpose. Although Macquarie University remains the only Australian university teaching demography at both undergraduate and graduate level, an increasing number of universities are realizing the importance of population studies and are introducing demographic components into their courses. The chapters on sources of demographic statistics, basic demographic measures, the life table, mortality, fertility and population projections have been found suitable for these short basic courses. The other chapters, in association with some social demography, have been used for more advanced students. For example, this book has been used as an introductory text for demography courses in our M.A. programme in Population and Development.

It is now six years since the first edition of this book was published. In this second edition sections of the book remain unaltered as many of the basic techniques have not changed. However, a number of chapters have been revised to include some of the more recent demographic techniques and slight changes have been made in emphasis and presentation in certain chapters, based on our experience in using this book as a basic text. Selected demographic and statistical data have also been updated. Since the object of the book is to explain clearly and briefly the basic techniques rather than to place emphasis on the actual numerical results, some data (e.g. life table) remain unchanged. Students are encouraged to repeat all examples and exercises using the most recent data available for their own country.

Finally, we have included a few exercises at the end of each chapter because we have found it most desirable for students to search through the usual data sources and attempt practical problems. In response to many requests, this edition includes the answers to selected exercises.

A H POLLARD
FARHAT YUSUF
G N POLLARD

1

Sources of demographic statistics

1.1 What is demography?

In the 1930s the population growth rates of a number of Western countries dropped to such low levels that there was considerable concern over future prospects for these countries. In the post-war period the growth rates of the developing countries have reached such high levels that the available resources cannot fully support the growing numbers of people, causing hardship, misery and starvation. On the other hand, the population growth rates in the developed countries, after experiencing the effects of a post-war 'baby boom', have again declined to very low levels and the problems of the developed countries now include excessive urbanization, pollution and general environmental deterioration and ageing of the population. In all countries the need for adequate demographic analysis and population planning remains essential for the future of mankind.

Literally translated from the Greek the term 'demography' means 'description of the people'. According to the United Nations Multilingual Demographic Dictionary, 'Demography is the scientific study of human populations, primarily with respect to their size, their structure and their development'. Demography is therefore concerned with the current size and characteristics of human populations, how they were attained and how they are changing.

It should be obvious that there are only three ways in which the number of people in a given area can change: a birth may occur, a death may take place, or a migrant may enter or leave. These three factors – fertility, mortality and migration – which continuously operate on a population and determine its size and growth form the major subject matter of demography and are referred to as 'components of population growth'. However, the demographer also studies other factors such as marriage, divorce, social mobility (change in social status and condition), etc., which do not affect the total size of the population but do determine the structure or composition of the population. Demography is concerned with the collection and analysis of data relating to all these factors and the interpretation of these data against their social, biological, economic, political, geographical, ecological and historical background.

Government and private enterprise need to consider anticipated changes in population size, structure and composition in making their short term and long term plans. Is the population growing larger, smaller or remaining stationary? What are the ages and sexes of the population and how are the relative numbers of each age-sex group changing? What proportion are single, married, widowed or divorced and what are the current trends in marital status? Are people continuing to move from the rural areas to the cities or can this be arrested? Will immigration remain at current levels and what changes can be expected in the nationality of migrants? Are we having fewer or more children and what effect will this have on educational facilities in the future? What are the causes of deaths and how do these vary with age and sex? Will we need more homes for the aged, more doctors (and what kinds of doctors?) and where will they be needed? Some countries have introduced programmes designed to change the rate of population growth and a demographer is needed to evaluate the effectiveness of these programmes. Will monetary incentives have any real effect on the rate at which babies are born? Can we expect further improvement in the number of years a person expects to live? These, and more, are the questions a demographer endeavours to answer. In short, he is concerned with the careful, objective and systematic study of the population.

1.2 The beginning of demography

The study of the numerical size, growth and characteristics of human populations has a long history. Ancient Chinese, Greek and Arab philosophers such as Confucius, Plato, Aristotle and Khaldun concerned themselves with the various population issues of their days. The ancient statesmen and thinkers held opinions based on political, military, social and economic considerations about such issues as the most desirable number of people or the need to stimulate or retard population growth.

Confucius and other ancient Chinese philosophers noted that excessive population growth may reduce output per worker, depress levels of living for the masses and engender strife. Mention was also made of the concept of optimum population and some of the factors affecting population growth. Plato, Aristotle and other Greek writers discussed the question of optimum population with respect to the Greek city state and the ideal conditions for the full development of man's potential. The Romans viewed population questions in the perspective of a great empire and the advantages for military purposes and this is reflected, for example, in the laws of Augustus. The Hebrew sacred books also placed much emphasis on procreation and multiplication. Early and medieval Christian writers considered population questions almost entirely from a moral and ethical standpoint, but again favoured population growth. The views of Moslem authors on population resemble those of the Hebrew and Christian authors.

However it was the publication in 1662 of John Graunt's *Observations Upon the Bills of Mortality* that really marks the beginning of demography. Some (e.g. Sutherland, 1963) claim that Graunt was the founder of statistics as well. Early in the sixteenth century weekly bulletins on death from the plague were first published for each London parish. Gradually they became a more regular series and from early in the seventeenth century all causes of death were considered and the weekly totals of christenings were added. From this very limited data Graunt discovered what is now known as the principle of statistical regularity, obtained a constant sex ratio at birth of 14 males to every 13 females, estimated the crude death rate, and recognized seasonal and annual variations. He showed that the urban death rate was higher than the rural one and demonstrated that the population of London was maintained by migration from the country and was not as large as was popularly believed. Graunt's investigation of mortality by cause of death makes interesting reading but his greatest achievement undoubtedly was the first life table. These and other 'observations' were the result of a systematic and thorough critical analysis of the most unpromising material which still serves as an example to all workers in the field of demography. After this beginning it was left to Graunt's friend, Sir William Petty, to convert his work into the beginnings of 'political arithmetic' which gradually became known as demography.

If Graunt is considered to be the father of demography, then the Reverend Thomas Robert Malthus (1766–1834) is generally considered to be the father of substantive demography, and is certainly the better known. He achieved this position not because what he said was all new, not because what he said was all true, but because he initiated tremendous controversy and debate over the relationship between food and population – debate which has continued from his lifetime to the present day and is as relevant today as it was when first proposed. His essay was first published in 1798 as *An Essay on the Principle of Population*. It was revised and substantially expanded as a second edition in 1803 and further revised in 1806, 1807, 1817 and 1826, with a final posthumous seventh edition in 1872.

Basically Malthus' principle of population was that human populations tended to increase at a more rapid rate than the food supply needed to sustain them. To balance the two, checks would be imposed on population growth and these were all resolvable into vice and misery and (added in the second edition) moral restraint. The only moral restraint recognised by Malthus was the postponement of marriage with no extramarital sex during the postponed period. Moral restraint was to be the saviour of mankind.

The checks on population growth noted by Malthus were described as 'preventive' and 'positive' checks or, as they are now called, factors affecting fertility and mortality respectively. Positive checks were identified as causes which shorten human life, e.g. diseases, epidemics, famine, plague, etc. (all forms of misery) and wars, excesses of all kinds, etc. (forms of misery brought about by vice). Preventive checks were the kind which reduced fertility and – apart from moral restraint – included promiscuity, homo-sexuality, adultery, abortion and birth control (all vices). Malthus recognised that pre-ventive and positive checks varied inversely, i.e. fertility and mortality must be either both high or both low. Finally, it should be noted that Malthus' great hope, 'moral restraint' or delayed marriage, did not encompass abstinence or any birth control* after marriage, partly because of their immorality and partly because of their tendency to remove a necessary stimulus to industry. The fear of having a large number of children causes man to work much harder than he would if the family size could be knowingly controlled.

From the technical methods of Graunt and the substantive arguments of Malthus the subject of demography has developed to a major field of study in the social sciences. In this book we consider the basic demographic techniques required by students special-izing in population studies as well as those specializing in such fields as economics, sociology and human geography. Population questions cannot be examined seriously

*Proponents of birth control, who otherwise support the Malthusian argument, became known as neo-Malthusians.

without at least a basic grounding in the precise statistical analysis of population data. The biological, historical and social contexts in which population changes take place cannot be overlooked in any interpretation of the data, but the emphasis given here is clearly on the technical aspects.

1.3 Demographic data

Almost all basic demographic data come from censuses or surveys (to determine size and composition) or from the vital registration system (to determine change).

The statistical distributions of the individuals in a population according to such characteristics as age, sex, marital status, education, occupation, etc., are referred to broadly as the 'population composition'. Changes in the size and composition of a population are brought about through the occurrence of what are called 'vital events'. Some of these events, such as births, deaths and migration, alter the population size. Others, for example marriages and divorces which transfer people from one marital status category to another, merely affect the population composition.

A population is thus subject to constant change as a result of these vital events. Consequently, statistics about population composition and size always refer to the position at a particular date, for example a census conducted on 30 June 1976.

On the other hand, since vital events do not all occur at once, statistics relating to them are expressed as the number of events which occurred during a specific period of time, for example during the period 1 January 1980 to 31 December 1980.

Information about the size and composition of a population is usually obtained from censuses or demographic surveys, while statistics about vital events are usually collected through what is known as the vital registration system. These are the three major sources of demographic data. In some countries where the registration system is not in operation or is ineffective, attempts have been made to collect statistics about vital events through demographic surveys. Some Scandinavian and other countries maintain a continuous registration of their population in the form of population registers, in which all vital events and population movements are recorded. There are many other minor sources such as social security records or family planning records from which some limited information can be obtained.

1.4 The population census

History
The practice of census-taking, in some form or another, is almost as old as civilization itself. There are records of statistical enumerations in Babylonia (4,000 B.C.), China (3,000 B.C.) and Egypt (2,500 B.C.). References to census type operations in Palestine and Rome and eventually the whole Roman Empire are found in the Bible. Most of these population counts, like the English Domesday inquest of 1086, were partial in coverage because of the rather limited use to which these data were to be put. Generally they were limited to landholders or heads of households or males of military age or taxpayers, and were for military, labour or tax purposes. Few results survive. Among the first censuses in the modern sense were those of Quebec (1666), Italy and Sicily (seventeenth century), Sardinia, Parma, Tuscany, Prussia, Iceland, Denmark and Sweden (eighteenth century), The U.S.A. commenced census-taking in 1790 and the U.K. and France in 1801. Up to

the beginning of the twentieth century less than 20 per cent of the world's population had been counted by population censuses. Today only eleven countries (six in Africa and five in Asia), out of 200 countries with populations exceeding 5,000 persons, still have never taken a census. With the assistance of the United Nations-sponsored World Population Census Programme, the majority of countries took censuses during the period 1965–74 and have repeated or will repeat the performance during 1975–84.

Definition

The modern population census may be defined as the process of collecting, compiling, evaluating, analyzing and publishing demographic, social and economic data about the entire population of a well defined territory at a specified time. It is a massive, complex and costly statistical operation and thus is usually carried out by the government, which has the necessary legal authority to ensure completeness of coverage. The census usually requires some years of careful planning so that often plans for the next census are well advanced before the complete results of the previous census are known. The actual field-work does not take more than a couple of weeks, but even with the help of modern electronic data-processing equipment, the compilation and publication of census data takes years to complete. Censuses are usually taken at regular intervals (say five or ten years) to ensure that comparable information is collected in a fixed sequence.

Planning and execution of the census

During the planning stage of a population census the persons responsible have to:

(i) decide on the system of enumeration to be used;
(ii) fix the date of the census and set out the pre-census programme;
(iii) decide on the type and content of the questionnaire;
(iv) test all forms and procedures including final pre-test;
(v) prepare detailed maps and list all dwellings;
(vi) recruit and train the field staff;
(vii) plan the programme for processing of the data;
(viii) inform the public and obtain their co-operation.

Some of these points require further discussion to appreciate the alternatives available, the expected problems and how they are overcome.

Populations are usually enumerated either on a *de facto* or a *de jure* basis. Under the de facto system a person is counted wherever that person is found at the time of census enumeration. Under the de jure system, people are enumerated at their *place of usual residence*, irrespective of where they were at the time of the census. Both systems have their particular advantages and disadvantages. The main advantage of the de jure method is that it gives a picture of the permanent population. The main advantage of the de facto method is that it offers less chance of double counting or omission of persons. The de facto system is the more commonly used and is recommended by the United Nations Population Commission. Theoretically speaking both de facto and de jure systems should yield the same population total, provided there is no migration in and out of the country. However, significantly different population figures at sub-national level could result if different systems of enumeration are used.

As regards the timing of a census, it is clearly better for it to be conducted at a time when population movement is at a minimum. The height of the holiday season, for example, would not be a good time to conduct a census. Also, when a series of censuses is conducted in respect of a particular territory the censuses should, if possible, be conducted on the same day of the year.

There are two basic types of census questionnaires – the 'individual' type and the 'household' type. The former is required to be filled in separately in respect of each individual, while the latter asks for information in respect of all members of the household. The household questionnaire which, except in countries with low literacy levels where interviewers or canvassers are required, is usually completed by the head of the household, is being increasingly used in both developed and developing countries. A census questionnaire usually asks for the age, sex, marital status, place of birth, nationality, relationship to head of household, ethnic origin, educational level, occupation, religion, etc. of each member of the household. In countries where information about vital events is lacking or inadequate, questions on fertility and sometimes on mortality are also asked in the censuses. If the questionnaire is of the individual type, what is called a housing census is often conducted either concurrently or before the population census in order to obtain information about the type of house, the form of ownership and other related questions. With the household type questionnaire this information is usually asked for on the population census questionnaire.

It is most important to have the questionnaire thoroughly pre-tested in the field in order to ensure that it will yield the required information. This pre-tests both the questionnaire and the field operations.

Before starting the actual census enumeration, the whole country has to be divided into census blocks of a size which can be handled by one interviewer. The size of a block varies according to the density of population, geographic characteristics of the area, means of transport and communication, etc. If a housing census precedes the population census, the job of specifying the boundaries of census blocks (which includes preparing lists of dwellings) is done as a part of the housing census. Otherwise it has to be done as a separate operation prior to the actual population census.

Recruitment of qualified and conscientious field staff and their proper training is an extremely important aspect of the planning of a population census. In some of the developing countries certain government officials are required to carry out the enumeration in addition to their normal duties. This is a rather risky practice, as the quality of census data depends to a great extent on the proper training of the field staff and on their efficiency, conscientiousness and motivation.

With the use of modern high-speed electronic data-processing equipment it is hoped that the time lag between the collection of census data and their publication will be shortened substantially. However, it must be recognized that one of the most time-consuming operations is the coding and preparation of the census input data for computer use. Once the data are in a computer-acceptable form, programmes can be written to edit the data for internal consistency and the occurrence of errors. Tabulating the census data is a fairly routine and standard operation.

Informing the public that the census is to be taken and requesting their co-operation is an important stage in both developing and developed countries. In developing countries the presence of interviewers requesting personal information is likely to be viewed with some suspicion unless the population is adequately warned. In developed countries invasion of privacy may be a problem affecting completeness of coverage, and confidentiality, together with the national importance of the census, should be stressed.

The voluminous information collected in a census may be tabulated separately for each item of information appearing on the questionnaire, or in cross-classifications using two, three or more of the items. *Table 1.1* shows the distribution of West Malaysia's population by age, sex and ethnic origin, as reported in the 1970 census. If we consider only columns (1) and (12) of this table we have the age distribution for the population of West Malaysia. This is a one-way table. If we consider columns (1), (10) and (11) we have a two-way table giving the age-sex distribution of the population of West Malaysia. If we consider columns (1) to (9) inclusive we have a three-way table giving a cross-classification by age, sex and ethnic origin.

Table 1.1

Population (in thousands) of West Malaysia by age, sex and ethnic origin

Age	Malay		Chinese		Indians		Others		All ethnic origins		
	M	F	M	F	M	F	M	F	M	F	Total
(1)	(2)	(3)	(4)	(5)	(6)	(7)	(8)	(9)	(10)	(11)	(12)
0–14	1,069	1,054	685	642	213	204	13	12	1,980	1,912	3,892
15–44	914	962	652	654	193	182	17	15	1,776	1,813	3,589
45–64	259	261	172	183	74	43	5	4	510	491	1,001
65 and over	66	62	64	65	14	6	1	1	145	134	279
Unknown	13	12	8	8	3	2	1	0	25	22	47
Total	2,321	2,351	1,581	1,552	497	437	37	32	4,436	4,372	8,808

(*Source:* 1970 census of West Malaysia)

It should be pointed out that certain items of information collected in the census are tabulated for the country as a whole, others may be tabulated for various states or provinces and still others may be tabulated for local government areas.

The range of questions asked at a census has gradually extended over the years. However, quite recently, in many countries, there have been campaigns to protect the rights of individuals and to prevent the invasion of privacy. With the advent of computer-stored data banks, fears have been expressed that the guarantees of confidentiality, which apply to most government-collected data and particularly the census data, may not be strictly enforced. The questions asked in a census can, and in some cases have, become a political issue and some authorities have expressed the opinion that it may become necessary to eliminate some of the more personal questions or even to change from a compulsory census to a voluntary one.

1.5 The registration of vital events

History

The modern civil system for the compulsory registration of births, deaths and marriages is the end result of an evolutionary process that began with the recording of christenings, burials and weddings by the clergy in parish registers. In the early sixteenth century as a result of the plague epidemic, weekly statements of deaths from plague called the 'Bills of Mortality' were required to be compiled by each parish priest in London. Gradually other causes of deaths were included, as well as christenings and weddings, and extended to cover all English parishes. However it was not until the 1837 Births, Marriages and Deaths Registration Act that registration became a civil event and a central records office was established. Perhaps the longest continuous series of national vital registration statistics is that of Sweden, for which the data are available since 1748, although compulsory civil registration was enacted in the various Scandinavian countries in the seventeenth century. Vital registration systems have since been established in most developed countries and are gradually being introduced in developing countries. In Australia, provisions for the registration of births, deaths and marriages have been in force since the middle of the nineteenth century.

Definition and collection procedure

Information about vital events is usually collected by means of the compulsory registration of such events within a short time after their occurrence. The registration method is defined as 'the continuous and permanent, compulsory recording of the occurrence and the characteristics of vital events primarily for their value as legal documents as provided by law and secondarily for their usefulness as a source of statistics'. In almost all developed countries such registration of births, deaths, marriages and divorces is compulsory, and must be made by lodging a standard form giving certain essential information. Certificates issued by the official legally responsible for administering the registration system (called the Registrar) are used for purposes of identification and for legal contracts, life assurance policies and so on, where proof of such characteristics as age, marital status, etc., is required. The appropriate certificates are also required before payment of social welfare benefits, settlement of estates and inheritances, etc. In many countries, particularly in developing countries, the registration system does not work very efficiently. This is at least in part due to lack of interest by the general public who do not find in their daily activities much use for the certification of vital events. The data collected, when incomplete, are of little use in estimating birth and death rates and other methods (see Chapter 12) must be used. The dual function (legal and statistical) of the registration of vital events must be stressed as this affects the questions asked and the data collected.

Vital statistics data collected

The birth registration form usually includes characteristics of the event or child such as date of occurrence, date of registration, name, sex, type of birth (live or still, single or multipe), legitimacy and place of occurrence, and characteristics of the parents such as date of birth (or age), name, date of marriage, occupation, usual residence and names and ages of the previous children born to the mother. The form also usually includes the names of medical personnel who attended the birth of the child. This form usually has to be completed in respect of a still birth, that is a baby born dead, as well as in respect of a live birth.

The death registration form usually records the name, age, sex, marital status, occupation, place of birth, date and cause of death of the deceased.

The marriage registration form includes dates of birth (or ages), occupations, religions, birth-places, places of usual residence, previous marital status of both the bride and bridegroom, together with the date and place of the marriage. Divorce data collected includes date of divorce, dates of birth (or ages) of both partners, date of marriage, number of children, occupation and place of usual residence.

Migration data

Information about international arrivals and departures is collected by immigration officials at all ports of embarkation and disembarkation. Information is therefore collected on the day of the event by immigration officials rather than there being a legal responsibility for individuals to report vital events to the Registrar of Births, Deaths and Marriages. For this reason migration data are not always included in the definition of the vital registration system, although the demographic importance of migration as a vital event must be recognized.

All international passengers (or, where the volume of traffic is very large, a sample of passengers) have to complete an embarkation card (for departures) or a disembarkation card (for arrivals). These cards seek information such as age, sex, marital status, occupation and nationality of the passenger, as well as the purpose of visit to the country and the expected length of stay in the case of arriving passengers, and the reason for leaving and expected length of stay overseas for departing passengers.

Processing the data

Information collected through the registration system is usually passed to the official central statistical agency for compilation and preparation of tables. Elaborate tabulations are usually published. The more important of these are, in the case of births, listings by duration of marriage, number of previous children, ages of parents and various cross-classifications of these; in the case of deaths, listings for each sex by age and cause of death; and in the case of marriages, listings by age and birth-place of bride and of bridegroom. For arrivals and departures, tables are prepared separately for long-term and short-term population movements, giving details such as age, sex, marital status, occupation, nationality, and expected length of stay.

1.6 Sample surveys

Another major source of demographic data is the sample survey. Some examples of its use are:

(i)   To collect vital statistics where the official registration system is inadequate or non-existent, as is the case in most developing countries.

(ii) To collect supplementary demographic and other data where it is not feasible to collect the same from the population census (e.g. public opinion polls; surveys on topics such as labour force and invalidity; and surveys on the knowledge, attitude and practice of family planning methods called KAP surveys).

(iii) To test the accuracy of the traditional sources of demographic data (e.g. census pre-testing of questionnaire and census post-enumeration quality check in a sample of census blocks).

(iv) To conduct a sample census (e.g. collecting data for only 10 per cent of the population; collecting age and sex data for the whole population but socio-economic data for only a sample of the population; processing only a part of the information collected to save time and money and present a wider range of tabulations).

The quality of the statistics from this source depends heavily on the size of the sample, the design of the sample and the way the survey is carried out. The subject of sample surveys and sampling theory is considered in Chapter 9.

1.7 Population registers

In those countries which possess a system of continuous registration it is possible to maintain a separate card for each individual from the time of his birth (or immigration) to his death (or emigration) and to continually update the record by recording such additional registration data as marriage, divorce, birth of children, etc. These are called population registers and are maintained in the Netherlands, Belgium, Finland, Sweden, Norway, Denmark, Iceland, Italy, Gibraltar, West Germany, Belgium, Israel, Japan, Taiwan, the U.S.S.R., Bulgaria and Czechoslovakia. A regular census then provides an accurate check of the data as all census returns can be matched against the population register.

The advantages of the system include the completeness of coverage, accuracy, contact with individuals if required and the possibility of drawing specific samples of the population. Disadvantages are the high cost to set up and maintain, the need for a high cultural and educational level and the fact that the existence of such records is regarded by many as an invasion of civil liberties. In many cases population registers were established primarily for purposes of identification, for population control and for police purposes and little demographic use has been made of them for demographic purposes.

Partial registers are established for specific administrative purposes and cover only those persons directly affected by the particular programme. These are considered under other miscellaneous sources of data.

1.8 Other sources

Apart from the population census, the registration of vital events and demographic sample surveys, there are many other sources of demographic data of somewhat lesser importance. These are usually records held by various government and semi-government departments which are useful in demographic analysis. In some cases the information is not available in published form and may have to be obtained from the departmental records. Some examples are the data on registrations for military service, employment statistics, social service records about pensions and child endowments, primary vaccination statistics, the records of hospitals and educational institutions, electoral rolls, taxation records, etc. In many developing countries which have official family planning programmes the family planning records can also provide some useful demographic information.

1.9 The balancing equation

The most basic method of analysis in demography is the decomposition of population change ($P_t - P_0$) into its components (B, D, I, E) which may be expressed by the fundamental balancing equation

$$P_t - P_0 = B - D + I - E$$

where P_t = population at end of period

P_0 = population at beginning of period

B = births during period

D = deaths during period

I = immigrants during period

E = emigrants during period

With de jure populations only immigrants and emigrants should be used, travellers being ignored. With de facto populations total arrivals and departures should be used. The formula is sometimes written

$$P_t = P_0 + B - D + I - E \qquad \text{(for population estimates)}$$

or $\qquad M = I - E = (P_t - P_0) - (B - D) \quad$ (for estimating net migration)

To be exactly true it must be applied to a fixed territory and must contain no measurement error. Consider Australia 1954–61.

$P_0 = 8,986,530 \qquad$ at 30 June 1954 (census)

$B = 1,544,240$

$D = 600,551$

during period
1 July 1954 to 30 June 1961

$I = 1,766,858$

$E = 1,182,104$

giving $\qquad P_t = 10,514,973 \qquad$ at 30 June 1961 (estimate)

The actual census population on 30 June 1961 was 10,508,186, giving an error of 6,787. Expressed as a percentage of the later census population, this error, called the error of closure, is -0.06%. The error arises because of incomplete coverage of the population in the 1954 and 1961 censuses and incomplete registration of births, deaths, immigrants and emigrants. The subject of errors in demographic data is treated in Chapter 11, but it is interesting to note that the 1976 Australian census population was adjusted by 2.71% for underenumeration, being inflated from a count of 13,548,472 to a population of 13,915,500. The 1971 census was adjusted for 1.3% net underenumeration. If the 1954 and 1961 census populations were inflated for the same net underenumeration as found for the 1971 census the revised census populations become 9,103,000 and 10,645,000 respectively and the error of closure becomes $+0.13\%$. Usually an error of this magnitude is considered reasonable.

1.10 Publications containing demographic data

The most important publications containing demographic data for a country are the various census volumes and the annual compilations of vital events based on the official vital registration records. Some countries publish a yearbook which includes the most important tabulations of demographic data from various sources as well as a brief description of those sources. At the international level, the United Nations publishes an annual Demographic Year Book which contains demographic statistics for member countries. The various specialized agencies of the United Nations, such as the International Labour Office (ILO), the World Health Organization (WHO), the United Nations Educational Scientific and Cultural Organization (UNESCO), also publish international statistics which are very useful for demographic analysis.

For further reading

1. Benjamin, B., *The Population Census*, Heinemann, 1970.
2. United Nations, *Demographic Year Book*, annual.
3. United Nations, *Determinants and Consequences of Population Trends*, 1974.
4. United Nations, Handbook of Household Surveys, *Studies in Methods*, Series F, No. 10, 1964.
5. United Nations, Handbook of Population Census Methods, *Studies in Methods*, Series F. No. 5, 1954.
6. United Nations, Handbook of Vital Statistics Methods, *Studies in Methods*, Series F, No. 7, 1955.
7. United Nations, *Principles and Recommendations for the 1970 Population Censuses*. Statistical Papers, Series M, No. 44, 1967.
8. *Year Book of the Commonwealth of Australia*, for any year (or equivalent publication for other countries).

Exercises

1.1 Select a particular country and write an essay on
   (i)   the methodology of its latest population census, and
   (ii) the method of recording vital events.

1.2 Answer the following questions by using the United Nations Demographic Year Book for any recent year.
   (i)   Name the 5 largest cities in each of England, India, Japan and U.S.A.
   (ii) Which are the 10 most populous countries in the world?
   (iii) Rank the following major areas and regions of the world according to their population and then according to their land area:
          Africa, America, Asia, Europe, Oceania and the U.S.S.R.
   (iv) In which of the countries listed below does the total number of males exceed the total number of females?
          Algeria, Australia, Canada, France, Ghana, India, Indonesia, Japan, Mexico, New Caledonia, Singapore, Sri Lanka, U.S.A., U.S.S.R., Venezuela and West Germany.
   (v)   For the following countries, obtain the number of males and females aged 15–49 who were single and those who were married:
          Australia, Canada, India, Japan, and U.S.A.
          Comment on any abnormal features.

1.3 Select a particular country and endeavor to reconcile two successive census population counts with the registration of births, deaths, immigration (or arrivals) and emigration (or departures) in the intervening period.

2
Some basic demographic measures

2.1 Absolute and relative numbers

Most sources of demographic data publish the information in terms of absolute numbers. For example, according to the 1977 United Nations Demographic Year Book, the number of live births during 1976 was 3,165,000 in the United States, 1,934,958 in Japan and 227,645 in Australia. For some purposes these absolute numbers are of interest. Generally, however, when we are making international comparisons, our aim is for example, to compare the incidence of births in different populations. The absolute number of births has therefore to be related in some way to the size of the population producing those births. By relating the absolute number of births to the absolute number of persons in the population, we obtain what we might term the 'relative' number of births. These relative numbers can be used for comparing the incidence of births in the above-mentioned three countries. Comparisons are usually made by means of ratios, proportions, percentages and rates. We shall now give demographic examples of the use of such relative numbers.

2.2 Ratios

According to the 1970 census of the Republic of South Africa, the total population, expressed in millions, was 21.45 consisting of Africans 15.06, whites 3.75, coloureds 2.02 and Asians 0.62. The ratio of Africans to whites was therefore 15.06/3.75 or 4.01. This may be expressed as 4 Africans per one white or 401 Africans per 100 whites. If we wished to describe the population of various racial groups relative to the number of whites in South Africa, we could say that for every 100 whites there were 401 Africans, 54 coloureds and 17 Asians.

2.3 Proportions and percentages

If we wish to express the number in a particular group relative to the total number, then this is often set out as a proportion. For example, the proportion of the population of South Africa which is African is about 7 out of 10. The distribution of the population by racial groups can best be expressed in the form of percentages or numbers per 1,000 as shown on the following page.

	Percentage	*per 1,000*	*Proportion*
African	70.2	702	.702
Whites	17.5	175	.175
Coloureds	9.4	94	.094
Asians	2.9	29	.029
Total	100.0	1,000	1.000

2.4 Rates

In sections 2.2 and 2.3, the comparisons have been made between the numbers for two items at the same point of time. However, when we are studying the relative incidence of births, deaths, marriages, migration and other vital events, it is apparent that the number of these events depends on the interval of time chosen. This interval is usually one year. A common method of comparing the incidence of births in several countries is to calculate for each country the number of births during one year per 1,000 persons in the population of that country at the middle of the year. The result is called a rate, in this case a rate per 1,000 per annum. If we convert the absolute number of births given in section 2.1 to rates by dividing by the mid-1976 population of the relevant country, we obtain the following rates:

United States	14.7 births per 1,000 population per year
Japan	16.3 births per 1,000 population per year
Australia	16.4 births per 1,000 population per year.

Similar rates can be calculated for other vital events also.

2.5 Frequency distributions

Demographers are frequently required to present a profile of the population according to such characteristics as the age, sex, religion, occupation, etc. of its members, or to indicate for example, the relative frequencies of large and small families. These characteristics are known as variables. If we wish to describe the population according to only one of these characteristics, it may be done by means of a frequency distribution. Thus the number of marriages in Australia during 1978 according to the age of the bride could be set out as in *Table 2.1* by actual numbers, by proportions or by percentages.

It should be noted that the demographer is studying the characteristics of a group, then he can study the characteristics one at a time by means of a number of univariate distributions similar to that in *Table 2.1*, or he can study two or more variables concurrently. Thus, if he wants to study the interrelation between the age of bride and the age of bridegroom, to see for example to what extent brides marry bridegrooms of about the same age, then he would need a bivariate frequency distribution as shown in *Table 2.2*.

It should be noted that the marginal totals in *Table 2.2*, namely the bottom line and the extreme right hand column are the two univariate frequency distributions. It is, however, much easier to obtain some idea of the ages of the husbands which, say, brides under 20 or brides 30–34 marry, if the table is expressed in the form of percentages as shown in *Table 2.3*.

Table 2.1
Marriages in Australia by age of bride: 1978

Age of bride	Number	Proportion	Percentage
Under 20	22,290	.216	21.6
20–24	44,094	.428	42.8
25–29	16,114	.157	15.7
30–34	7,810	.076	7.6
35 and over	12,650	.123	12.3
All ages	102,958	1.000	100.0

(*Source: Marriages 1978*. Australian Bureau of Statistics)

Table 2.2
Marriages in Australia by ages of bride and bridegroom: 1978

Age of bride	Age of bridegroom					
	Under 20	20–24	25–29	30–34	35 and over	All ages
Under 20	3,588	15,282	2,768	502	150	22,290
20–24	907	25,672	13,480	3,051	984	44,094
25–29	77	2,520	7,031	4,106	2,380	16,114
30–34	13	414	1,609	2,452	3,322	7,810
35 and over	7	123	449	1,118	10,953	12,650
All ages	4,592	44,011	25,337	11,229	17,789	102,958

(*Source: Marriages 1978*. Australian Bureau of Statistics)

Table 2.3
Percentage distribution of marriages by bridegroom's age for various ages of bride:
Australia, 1978

Age of bride	Age of bridegroom					
	Under 20	20–24	25–29	30–34	35 and over	All ages
Under 20	16.1	68.6	12.4	2.2	0.7	100.0
20–24	2.1	58.2	30.6	6.9	2.2	100.0
25–29	0.5	15.6	43.6	25.5	14.8	100.0
30–34	0.2	5.3	20.6	31.4	42.5	100.0
35 and over	0.1	1.0	3.5	8.8	86.6	100.0
All ages	4.5	42.7	24.6	10.9	17.3	100.0

(*Source: Marriages 1978*. Australian Bureau of Statistics)

If the object of the investigation is to study how ages of bride vary for a given age of bridegroom then exactly the same basic data are most usefully presented in the percentage distribution illustrated in *Table 2.4*.

The same basic data are presented in yet a third form of percentage distribution in *Table 2.5*. This table shows the percentage of marriages in which the bride's and the bridegroom's ages lie within certain limits. For example, the figure in the top left hand corner of the table indicates that in 3.5 per cent of the marriages both bride and bridegroom were under 20. The marginal distributions, namely the figures in the bottom line and the extreme right hand column, are the two univariate percentage distributions by bridegroom's age and bride's age respectively in the form of *Table 2.1*.

Table 2.4

Percentage distribution of marriages by bride's age for various ages of bridegroom: Australia 1978

Age of bride	Age of bridegroom					
	Under 20	20–24	25–29	30–34	35 and over	All ages
Under 20	78.1	34.7	10.9	4.5	0.8	21.6
20–24	19.7	58.3	53.2	27.2	5.5	42.8
25–29	1.7	5.7	27.7	36.6	13.4	15.7
30–34	0.3	1.0	6.4	21.8	18.7	7.6
35 and over	0.2	0.3	1.8	9.9	61.6	12.3
All ages	100.0	100.0	100.0	100.0	100.0	100.0

(*Source: Marriages 1978.* Australian Bureau of Statistics)

Table 2.5

Percentage distribution of marriages by ages of bride and bridegroom: Australia, 1978

Age of bride	Age of bridegroom					
	Under 20	20–24	25–29	30–34	35 and over	All ages
Under 20	3.5	14.8	2.7	0.5	0.1	21.6
20–24	0.9	24.9	13.1	2.9	1.0	42.8
25–29	0.1	2.5	6.8	4.0	2.3	15.7
30–34	0.0*	0.4	1.6	2.4	3.2	7.6
35 and over	0.0*	0.1	0.4	1.1	10.7	12.3
All ages	4.5	42.7	24.6	10.9	17.3	100.0

(*Source: Marriages 1978.* Australian Bureau of Statistics)

* Percentages less than 0.1 per cent

2.6 Population pyramids

The age-sex distribution of a population can be most clearly presented in a graphical form known as a 'population pyramid'. *Figure 2.1* shows the population pyramid for Australia drawn on the basis of the 1977 estimated age-sex distribution. It is apparent from this figure that ages are marked off on the Y-axis with age 0 at the origin. Male population totals for various age groups are shown on the negative side and the corresponding female population totals on the positive side of the X-axis. The population pyramid itself consists of 18 horizontal bars on the male and female sides. The height of each bar represents the age group and the length shows the population in that age group. Usually the population pyramids are drawn by taking age data in 5-year age groups, but they could be drawn for age data given in any other age interval or in single years of age.

When comparing the pyramids for two or more populations, it is essential to use the percentage distributions by age and sex. These percentages are calculated by expressing each age-sex category as a percentage of the total population. *Figure 2.2* shows the population pyramid for Australia (1961 census) superimposed on the pyramid for West Malaysia (1957 census). It is apparent from this figure that the West Malaysian pyramid is more broadly based than that for Australia. That is, up to the age group 25–29 the West Malaysian pyramid is wider than the Australian, while above this age group the Australian pyramid envelopes the West Malaysian pyramid. These differences in the percentage age-sex distribution for the two countries can be explained by the fact that the fertility and mortality levels prevalent in West Malaysia are much higher than those in Australia. The effect of fertility and mortality levels on the age-sex distribution will be studied in more detail in Chapter 7.

Figure 2.3 shows the population pyramid for West Germany (1972), with an explanation of some of the variations from the smooth sided pyramid shape.

2.7 Sex ratio

The sex ratio is usually calculated by taking the number of males in a population and dividing it by the number of females in the same population. The sex ratio is usually expressed as the number of males per 100 females. According to the 1976 censuses of Australia and Japan, the sex ratios in these countries were 100.6 and 96.9 males per 100 females respectively. The sex ratio of a population depends largely on the relative mortality of males and females and, where there is substantial migration, on the age-sex distribution of the migrant intake or outflow. Major wars generally lower the sex ratio due to the substantially higher male mortality. Similarly, populations which receive a higher intake of male migrants tend to have higher sex ratios.

The sex ratios may be calculated separately for various ages or age groups. These are called age specific sex ratios. The sex ratio at birth is fairly constant for most countries of the world at around 105 male births per 100 female births. In the absence of significant migration, the usually lighter female mortality causes the sex ratio to fall steadily with increasing age. The effect of major wars on the sex ratio of the generation affected can be seen for many decades thereafter. For example, in West Germany the sex ratio for the age group 20–39 years was 63 males per 100 females at the 1946 census. Clearly the sex ratio for this generation will continue to be low in subsequent censuses. The sex ratio is also high in areas such as the Northern Territory of Australia because of the continued

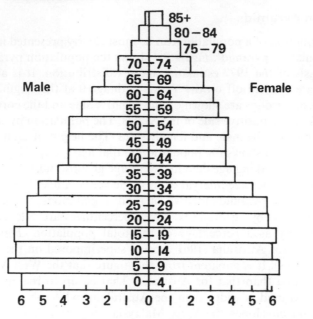

Figure 2.1: Population pyramid for Australia June 1977

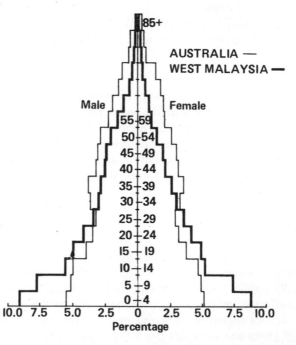

Figure 2.2: Population pyramid for Australia (1961 Census) and West Malaysia
(1957 Census)

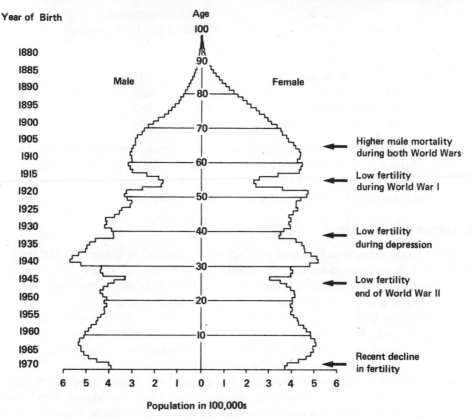

Figure 2.3: Population pyramid for West Germany (1972)

large male immigration. The sex ratio for age group 20–39 years for the Northern Territory was found in the 1976 census to be 123 males per 100 females.

2.8 Child-woman ratio

The child-woman ratio is usually calculated by taking the number of children in the age group 0–4 (both sexes combined) and dividing it by the number of women at the reproductive ages, usually taken as the ages 15 to 44 years. In countries where the birth registration system is inadequate, one can use child-woman ratios as a rough measure of fertility. The number of children and the number of women are obtained from a population census or a demographic survey. When comparing the fertility of two or more countries by means of child-woman ratios it should be remembered that children in the age group 0–4 are the survivors of the past five years' births and if infant and childhood mortality have been particularly high in one country, the child-woman ratio will provide an underestimate of the fertility levels prevalent in that country.

For illustrative purposes the child-woman ratios have been computed from the age-sex distributions of the following countries, as reported in the United Nations Demographic Year Book for 1975.

	Child-woman ratio
Country	*(Children per 1,000 women)*
Australia (1973)	406
United States (1974)	312
England & Wales (1973)	342
Mexico (1974)	836
Indonesia (1971)	667
West Malaysia (1973)	629

These figures suggest that the fertility levels in developing countries (Mexico, Indonesia and West Malaysia) were much higher than in the developed countries. The difference would, in fact, have been greater had the infant and childhood mortality rates in developing countries been about the same as in the developed countries.

2.9 Dependency ratio

The dependency ratio, which is useful in economic studies, is defined as the number of persons in a population who are *not* economically active for every 100 economically active persons in that population. When precise information about the economic activity of individuals in a population is not known, it is usual to use as a rough guide the ratio of the population in the age groups 0–14 and 65 and over, to the population in the age group 15–64 years. This estimate of the dependency ratio can thus be calculated from the age distribution of the population. Some recent estimates of dependency ratios for selected countries are shown in *Table 2.6*.

It is evident from the above table that the dependency ratios were much higher in developing countries than in developed countries. The table also shows that the higher incidence of fertility and mortality in the developing countries results in a higher proportion of the population in the 0–14 age group and a lower proportion in the 65 and over age

Table 2.6

The percentage of population aged 0–14, 15–64 and 65 and over in selected countries and the resulting dependency ratios

Country	Percentage of population aged			Dependency ratio (per 100)
	0–14	15–64	65 and over	
Australia (1976)	27.1	64.0	8.9	56.2
United States (1976)	24.4	64.9	10.7	54.1
England (1975)	23.4	62.6	14.0	59.7
Japan (1976)	24.2	67.4	8.4	48.4
India (1974)	40.1	56.7	3.2	76.4
Indonesia (1971)	44.0	53.5	2.5	86.9

(*Source: United Nations' Demographic Year Book, 1977*)

group. Thus, the dependency ratios calculated by the above procedure are significantly affected by the fertility and mortality levels prevalent in the population.

2.10 Population growth rate

For most of the developed countries an estimate of the total population is available each year. In such cases it is a fairly simple procedure to calculate the annual population growth rate since it is obtained by dividing the increase in population during the year by the population at the beginning of that year. For many countries however, accurate figures for births, deaths and migration are not available and the total population is only known accurately at census dates. We need to be able to estimate the annual population growth rate from these census figures. If we let the unknown growth rate be $100r$ per cent per annum, the initial population be P_0 and the population after n years be P_n, then

$$P_n = P_0(1 + r)^n \qquad \dots\dots\dots\dots\dots(1)$$

In the case of India, censuses were taken in 1961 and 1971. The ratio of enumerated population in 1971 to that in 1961 was 1.2457. Thus, the annual growth rate r is given by

$$(1 + r)^{10} = 1.2457$$

hence $\qquad 10 \log (1 + r) = 0.0954$

giving $\qquad \log (1 + r) = 0.00954$

therefore $\qquad (1 + r) = 1.022$

and $\qquad r = .022$

Thus, the average growth rate of the population of India was 2.2 per cent per annum during the intercensal decade 1961–1971. This result could alternatively have been obtained by the use of compound interest tables.

In calculating the value of r between two population counts, care must be taken to ensure that the geographic area covered in both counts is identical, otherwise some adjustments will have to be made. For example, in the 1961 census of Indonesia the population of West Irian was not enumerated as it was then part of Dutch New Guinea. Therefore when calculating the population growth rate for Indonesia during the intercensal decade 1961–1971, one should either exclude the population of West Irian from the 1971 census or include some estimate of the 1961 population of that territory with the 1961 census population of Indonesia.

It is also important to note the actual day and month of the year when each population count was taken. The time interval should be calculated at least to the nearest month but preferably to the nearest day.

2.11 Inter-censal and post-censal population estimates

Given the total population at two census dates, and having calculated the average annual growth rate between the two census dates (by the procedure outlined in section 2.10), estimates of the population at any time between these two dates can be made by substituting the relevant value of n in formula (1) of section 2.10. This assumes that this same growth rate applied throughout the inter-censal period. In the same way post-censal estimates can be made. Thus, if it is reasonable to assume that the population growth rate in India since 1971 continued at 2.2 per cent per annum, then, since the census population on 1 April 1971 was 546.956 million, we could estimate the population on 1 April 1980 as $546.956 \, (1.022)^9$ or 665 million. The subject of population estimates and projections is dealt with in greater detail in Chapter 8.

2.12 Crude rates

Crude rates are usually calculated by dividing the number of vital events which occurred in a population in one calendar year by the size of the population at the middle of that year. The mid-year population is taken as an estimate of the average population during the whole calendar year. The most frequently used crude rates are the crude birth rate and the crude death rate.

In Australia 224,181 live babies were born and 108,425 persons died during the period 1 January to 31 December 1978. The estimated total population was 14,248,600 persons as on 30 June 1978. Thus, during the year 1978, the crude birth rate in Australia was 15.7 births per 1,000 population per year and the crude death rate was 7.6 deaths per 1,000 population per year. Because of the incomplete registration of vital events in a large number of developing countries, it is difficult to calculate directly their crude birth and death rates. However, some recent statistics show that in most of the developing countries crude birth rates vary between 30 and 50 births per 1,000 population per year, and crude death rates between 10 and 20 deaths per 1,000 population per year.

The difference between the crude birth rate and the crude death rate is called the crude rate of natural increase. This is obviously different from the population growth rate which is the result of the interaction of all the four components of population growth.

Other crude rates such as the crude immigration rate, crude emigration rate, crude marriage rate, crude divorce rate can also be calculated by dividing the number of the particular vital event in a calendar year by the mid-year population, and multiplying by 1,000.

2.13 Specific rates

The chances of having a baby, of dying, or of marrying are not the same for all members of the population. These chances depend on a number of factors, the most important of which is age. Crude rates take no account of these relevant factors but simply produce an average for all the population. In studying fertility or mortality, for example, a more accurate analysis is required and it is therefore necessary to calculate separate rates taking these relevant factors into account. As mortality varies with age it is important to relate the deaths at each age to the number of persons in the population at that age and so obtain death rates for each age. The word 'specific' is used to indicate that these rates are specified according to age and they are called age specific death rates. Further, as males experience somewhat different mortality from females, usually age specific death rates are calculated for each sex separately. These are called age-sex specific mortality rates. Similar terms are used when other vital events are being studied. The specific rates may be calculated by specifying one, two or more factors. It may be noted that in calculating specific rates, whether they be fertility rates, mortality rates, or marriage or other rates, we use the best available estimate of the population which is 'exposed to the risk' of that particular event.

2.14 Age specific fertility rates

Fertility, which is the term used by demographers to refer to the actual number of children born, varies with a number of factors such as age, duration of marriage and number of previous children. For the present we shall refer only to age specific fertility rates and discuss other aspects of fertility in Chapter 6.

A schedule of age specific fertility rates is usually calculated only for females, although rates for males can also be computed. The age specific fertility rate for women of a given age (or age group) x is the number of babies born to women of that age (or age group) per 1,000 women of that age (or age group) in the population in the middle of that year. The symbol f_x is usually used to represent the age specific fertility rate for women aged x. The method of calculation of age specific fertility rates is illustrated in *Table 2.7*.

It may be pointed out that in column (3), both nuptial and ex-nuptial births have been included. If the number of women in column (2) were divided into those who were then married and those who were not (including single women), and the number of babies born were divided into nuptial and ex-nuptial births, one could calculate age specific marital fertility rates and age specific illegitimacy rates by using the same procedure as that outlined in *Table 2.7*.

Table 2.7

Calculation of age specific fertility rates for Australian women in 1978

Age	Number of women (mid-1978)	Babies born (during 1978)*	Age specific fertility rate per 1,000 women per year $\frac{(3)}{(2)} \times 1,000$
(1)	(2)	(3)	(4)
15–19	629,200	19,115	30.4
20–24	591,700	69,145	116.9
25–29	577,500	84,277	145.9
30–34	536,200	39,797	74.2
35–39	425,000	10,043	23.6
40–44	378,500	1,792	4.7

Note: Births to women under 15 were included in the 15–19 age group and to women 45 and over in the 40–44 age group.

(*Source: Births 1978.* Australian Bureau of Statistics)

2.15 Age specific mortality rates

The age specific mortality rate for persons of a given age (or age group) x is the number of persons who died aged x in a certain year divided by the population aged x in the middle of that year. These rates are usually expressed as per 1,000 persons per year and are calculated separately for males and females. The age specific mortality rates derived in the above manner are also called 'central death rates' and are denoted by the symbol m_x. Table 2.8 illustrates the calculation of age specific mortality rates for selected age groups of Australian males and females in 1978.

Table 2.8

Calculation of age-sex specific mortality rates for selected age groups in Australia, 1978

Age	Population (mid-1978)		Deaths (during 1978)		Age specific death rate, per 1,000 persons per year	
	Male	Female	Male	Female	Male $\dfrac{(4)}{(2)}$	Female $\dfrac{(5)}{(3)}$
(1)	(2)	(3)	(4)	(5)	(6)	(7)
15–24	1,267,400	1,220,900	2,084	647	1.6	0.5
25–34	1,149,700	1,113,700	1,560	656	1.4	0.6
35–44	849,100	803,500	2,041	1,110	2.4	1.4
45–54	788,600	746,200	5,315	2,798	6.7	3.7
55–64	622,200	649,600	11,048	5,819	17.8	9.0
65–74	386,600	461,400	16,617	10,066	43.0	21.8

(*Source: Deaths 1978.* Australian Bureau of Statistics)

By averaging three years' deaths, namely the deaths at age $x - 1$ during the year prior to the census, the deaths aged x during the census year and the deaths aged $x + 1$ during the year after the census, an average number of deaths at age x is determined. This is done to smooth out the irregularities from year to year in the number of deaths by age. Despite having taken a three year average of deaths some irregularities may still remain and it is therefore frequently desirable to apply a further smoothing process to the rates obtained. This process, called 'graduation', is dealt with fully in a number of actuarial texts.* Age specific mortality rates are usually calculated for single years of age, but may be calculated for age groups particularly when the number of deaths is small and causes wide fluctuations in rates for single years of age.

*See for example Benjamin, B. and Pollard, J. H., *The Analysis of Mortality and Other Actuarial Statistics*, Heinemann, 1980.

2.16 Age specific marriage and remarriage rates

These rates are also usually calculated for both sexes separately. In the case of females, the age specific marriage rates are obtained by dividing the number of marriages of spinsters of a given age by the number of spinsters of that age at the middle of that year. Age specific remarriage rates for females are calculated by dividing the number of marriages of widows and divorced women of a given age during a year by the number of widows and divorced women of that age in the population at the middle of that particular year. Rates for males are calculated in a similar manner. The calculation of age specific marriage and remarriage rates for Australian women during 1976 is set out in *Table 2.9*. As the number of single, married, widowed and divorced persons is only available at the date of a census it is usually only for census years that these rates are calculated. Therefore, for most countries the published data concerning marriage is usually limited to the total number of marriages and the crude marriage rate which is calculated by dividing the number of marriages in one year by the total mid-year population.

The analysis of marriage patterns is a much more difficult problem than the analysis of other vital events and requires a different approach. This arises because the number of females of a given age who *can* marry depends on the number of available 'eligible' males. If these number 20 per cent below the number of marriageable females, then female

Table 2.9

Calculation of marriage and remarriage rates for Australian women, 1976

Age	Mid-1976 population of		1976 marriages among		Marriage rates $\frac{(4)}{(2)}$	Remarriage rates $\frac{(5)}{(3)}$
	Spinsters	Widows and divorced women*	Spinsters	Widows and divorced women*		
(1)	(2)	(3)	(4)	(5)	(6)	(7)
15–19	550,573	265	28,029	34	.0509	.1283
20–24	221,026	6,554	43,787	2,104	.1981	.3210
25–29	73,150	17,721	10,560	5,195	.1444	.2932
30–34	32,184	19,049	2,834	4,032	.0881	.2117
35–39	20,396	20,061	1,029	2,863	.0505	.1427
40–44	15,826	22,291	427	2,214	.0270	.0993
45–49	16,759	31,562	271	2,085	.0162	.0661
50–54	17,600	44,549	210	1,512	.0119	.0339
55–59	16,964	56,239	140	975	.0083	.0173
60+	86,260	447,525	147	1,525	.0017	.0034

* Excludes women who were reported as married but permanently separated.

(*Source:* Census of Australia, 1976 and *Marriages 1976*. Australian Bureau of Statistics)

marriage rates will tend to be low and male rates high. Such large differences do in fact occur in many countries. For example, for ages 15 to 54 in 1921, the number of marriageable women per 100 marriageable men was 87 in New Zealand and 119 in England and Wales.*

The number of marriages each year tends to fluctuate with changes in the level of economic activity. For this reason and because of the difficulty mentioned earlier of obtaining the necessary data to calculate age specific marriage rates, a common method of indicating marriage patterns in a population is to specify, for each sex, the proportion of population at each age which is reported as married.

2.17 Labour force participation rates

The labour force participation rate for males at a given age is the proportion of the male population of that age who are classified as being members of the labour force. The definition of labour force is not uniform for all countries and has varied from time to time even within the one country. This fact must be kept in mind when making comparisons between countries or within the same country at different times. Despite the inconsistencies and the difficulty of definition it is a useful concept in dealing with the economic aspects of human populations. Labour force participation rates are usually calculated separately for males and females, particularly because of the tradition in many societies for women to concentrate on household and other domestic duties. Female rates are usually calculated specific for marital status as well because the participation rates for married females are substantially different to those for unmarried females. *Table 2.10* illustrates the calculation of age-sex specific labour force participation rates for Australia for 1971.

2.18 Density of population

Density of population is usually calculated on a national basis. It is obtained by dividing the total population by the land area and is expressed as the number of persons per square mile or per square kilometre. It is a rather misleading indicator of the population distribution, since countries are not uniformly inhabited. For example, in Indonesia 64.2 per cent of the total population (according to 1971 census) resides on the islands of Java and Madura which constitute only 6.9 per cent of the land area. Thus, the density of population on these islands was 575 persons per square kilometre, while on the other hand, the outer islands such as Kalimantan, Sumatra and West Irian had very low population densities. In countries such as Australia, where the density of population (according to the 1976 census) was 1.8 persons per square kilometre, 61.0 per cent of the population lived in the 5 major cities which are quite densely populated.

2.19 Probability of dying

Consider a closed population (i.e. one which is free from migration) and in which there were 112 persons aged exactly 18 years on 1 January 1972. Assume that on 1 January 1973, when they would be aged exactly 19 years, only 100 of the original 112 had survived.

---

*Pollard, A. H.: Measurement of the Intensity of Marriage With Allowance for the Relative Numbers and Age Distributions of the Sexes, *Journal of the Institute of Actuaries Students' Society*, Vol. XI, Part 1, 1953.

Table 2.10

Calculation of the age-sex specific labour force participation rates for Australia, 1971

Age	Population (mid-1971)		In the labour force		Labour force participation rate (%)	
	Male	Female	Male	Female	Male $\frac{(4)}{(2)} \times 100$	Female $\frac{(5)}{(3)} \times 100$
(1)	(2)	(3)	(4)	(5)	(6)	(7)
15–19	567,960	542,236	316,624	282,297	55.7	52.1
20–24	558,166	538,779	497,515	315,597	89.1	58.6
25–34	893,224	841,436	846,380	326,981	94.8	38.9
35–44	788,487	738,864	748,135	328,172	94.9	44.4
45–54	732,252	712,208	681,081	284,909	93.0	40.0
55–59	301,464	303,971	266,417	86,045	88.4	28.3
60–64	243,740	257,804	184,302	41,125	75.6	16.0
65 and over	446,861	618,134	99,185	25,723	22.2	4.2

(*Source:* Census of Australia 1971)

Note: At the 1971 census the following questions were asked and anyone reporting 'yes' to any one of these questions was classified 'in the labour force':

(i)   Did this person have a full- or part-time job, or business or farm of any kind last week?

(ii)   Did this person do any work at all last week for payment or profit?

(iii)   Was this person temporarily laid off by his employer without pay for the whole of last week?

(iv)   Did this person look for work last week?

For each of the original 112 persons who started the year 1972 the probability of dying during that year was 12/112. If the 12 deaths had occurred uniformly over the year then the mid-year population of this group or cohort would be 106 and the age specific death rate then would be 12/106.

In more general terms, if P_x is the population aged x at the middle of the year and D_x the number of deaths aged x during the year, then if we write m_x and q_x for the age specific death rate and probability of dying at age x we have

$$m_x = \frac{D_x}{P_x}$$

and

$$q_x = \frac{D_x}{P_x + \frac{1}{2}D_x}$$

Dividing the numerator and the denominator by P_x we have

$$q_x = \frac{D_x/P_x}{1 + \frac{1}{2}D_x/P_x}$$

$$= \frac{m_x}{1 + \frac{1}{2}m_x}$$

$$= \frac{2m_x}{2 + m_x}$$

The above formula is the standard approximation used for deriving values of q_x from the values of m_x which are obtained from official data. It is described as an approximate formula, for it is no more than that, despite what appears to be a 'proof' above. The deaths aged x during the year are not all aged x exactly at the beginning of the year and so the deaths D_x and the population P_x do not belong to the same cohort. The formula is however quite useful in preparing life tables. q_x is usually referred to as the rate of mortality.

For further reading

1. Barclay, G. W., *Techniques of Population Analysis*, Wiley, 1962.
2. Cox, P. R., *Demography*, Oxford University Press, 1970.
3. Shryock, H. S. and Siegel, J. S., *The Methods and Materials of Demography*, U.S. Government Printing Office, 1973.
4. Spiegelman, M., *Introduction to Demography*, Harvard, 1968.

Exercises

2.1 Please read the following paragraph carefully:
'Australia has a land area of 2,941,526 square miles. In mid-1961 it had a population of 10,508,186 persons which increased to 11,550,462 persons by the middle of 1966. About 22.65 per cent of the 1961–1966 increase was due to net migration. Between 1 January and 31 December 1966, a total of 222,626 babies were born, of whom 50.98 per cent were male babies. Around 6.74 per cent of the 1966 population consisted of females in the age range 20 to 29 years who had borne 61.58 per cent of the babies born during 1966. In the same year 102,703 persons died of whom 2,394 died due to road accidents'.

Now estimate the following for Australia:
(i)   the crude birth rate in 1966
(ii)   the crude death rate in 1966
(iii)   the density of population in 1966
(iv)   the sex ratio at birth in 1966
(v)   the increase in population between 1961 and 1966 due to the net overseas migration
(vi)   the proportion of deaths which occurred in 1966 which were due to road accidents
(vii)   the age specific birth rate for women aged 20–29 years in 1966
(viii) the average annual intercensal population growth rate, 1961–1966.

2.2 Indonesia consists of more than 3,000 islands and covers an area about 1,100 miles from north to south and 2,800 miles from east to west, the total land area being 735,269 square miles (including West Irian). In mid-1961 the population of Indonesia was 97 million, of which 15.46 per cent were less than 5 years of age and 30.93 per cent were females in the age group 15–44 years. In 1963 West Irian with an estimated mid-1961 population of 700,000 became part of Indonesia. There are marked regional variations in population density in Indonesia. In mid-1971 the islands of Java, Madura and Bali had two-thirds of Indonesia's population, while these islands cover only 7 per cent of the land area. In 1961, 4.85 million babies were born in Indonesia, 51.22 per cent being male, and only 2,111,545 of these male babies survived the first year of life. It has been estimated that in mid-1971 the population of Indonesia was 120 million.

On the basis of the above information calculate the following:
(i)   the density of population for the islands of Java, Madura and Bali, in 1971
(ii)   the sex ratio at birth in Indonesia, in 1961
(iii) the crude birth rate in Indonesia, in 1961
(iv)   the male infant mortality rate for Indonesia, in 1961
(v)   the average annual intercensal rate of population growth in Indonesia between mid-1961 and mid-1971
(vi)   the expected population of Indonesia on 31st December 1977, under the assumption that the average annual rate of population growth estimated above will prevail from mid-1971 to the end of 1977
(vii) the child-woman ratio for Indonesia, in 1961.

2.3 The following values of $(1 + r)^n$ have been taken directly from compound interest tables.

Value of r	.0025	.005	.0075	.010	.0125	.015	.02	.025	.03
$n = 50$	1.133	1.283	1.453	1.645	1.861	2.105	2.692	3.437	4.384
$n = 10$	1.025	1.051	1.078	1.105	1.132	1.161	1.219	1.280	1.344

Plot the above data and use the graphs to determine from the following figures the average annual growth rate of world population between the years shown

Year	1750	1800	1850	1900	1920	1930	1940	1950	1960	1970
World population (in millions)	791	978	1,262	1,650	1,860	2,069	2,295	2,515	2,998	3,632

Does an estimate of 6,130 m. for the world's population in the year 2000 look reasonable in the light of the above figures? What future annual rate of growth does this assume? What further information would you ask for to obtain a better estimate?

2.4 Estimates of the population (in millions) of the continents at various times are as follows:

	1750	1800	1850	1900	1950	2000
Asia	498	630	801	925	1,381	3,458
Europe	125	152	208	296	392	527
U.S.S.R.	42	56	76	134	180	353
North America	2	7	26	82	166	354
Latin America	16	24	38	74	162	638
Africa	106	107	111	133	222	768
Oceania	2	2	2	6	13	32
World	791	978	1,262	1,650	2,515	6,130

Analyze the above data using (i) graphs, (ii) rates of growth, (iii) distribution of population, and comment on your results.

3
The life table

3.1 Introduction

In many of the problems which the demographer is asked to tackle, he needs to be able
to estimate the number of persons likely to be alive five or ten years later (say) out of an
initial group of people. The number of survivors will, of course, depend on the age of these
people. Let us assume that the group initially numbered 100,000 and were all of exactly
the same age 20, i.e. had all just attained their 20th birthday. If we had set out in a table
the numbers likely to survive to age 21, 22, 23, etc., then this survivorship table would
enable us to tackle a number of demographic problems. Such a survivorship table is in
fact merely one of the columns of what is known as a life table or a mortality table which
is without doubt the most versatile and most useful of the demographer's tools. The life
table is a mathematical model that portrays mortality conditions at a particular time
among a population and provides a basis for measuring longevity. With a current life
table one can determine such factors as:
(i)   the probability of dying within one year of persons at each age;
(ii) the average number of years a newborn infant can expect to live;
(iii) the average number of years of life remaining to a person of any age;
(iv) the probability of surviving from any given age to any other given age;
(v)   the probability of surviving for any given number of years, for persons at any age;
(vi) the number of persons at a particular age, above or below a particular age or between
      any two ages under conditions of a stationary population.
The life table is based on age specific mortality rates observed for a population for a
particular year or other short period of time. In the Australian life tables the Bureau of
Statistics uses the Census population (say 30 June 1976) and the average deaths over the
three years 1975–77.

3.2 Constructing a life table

With short-lived animal populations the number of survivors after various intervals of
time can be observed experimentally and from this survivorship table a full life table
can be constructed. Such an approach is not possible with human lives. Here the only

information which is usually available to us about mortality at any age is the central death rate m_x. From this we are able to derive the proportion of people of a given age who die within one year, i.e. the rate of mortality q_x as explained in section 2.19. However, we need know only the rate of mortality at each age to be able to construct the complete life table.

We shall now show how this is done assuming that we are given the following values of q_x:

Age(x)	q_x
0	.02239
1	.00181
2	.00120
3	.00090
4	.00066
5	.00058

It is customary to commence the survivorship column of a life table at a selected age with a selected (round figure) number of persons at that age. The selected number of persons at the first age in the table is called the *radix* of the table. The selected age is usually 0 since generally we want to consider the population for the whole of life from birth to death, but some other age may be selected if we are only interested in certain ages. For example, in life assurance tables age 11 is sometimes used, as death cover may only be granted legally from age 11 onwards.

We shall commence at birth with a radix of 100,000. By definition, the rate of mortality q_x is the proportion of persons now aged exactly x who, on the average, may be expected to die before age $x + 1$. Hence, if we have 100,000 persons aged exactly 0 (i.e. just born) and $q_0 = .02239$, this means that on the average 2,239 out of every 100,000 may be expected to die before age 1. Hence, if we trace 100,000 persons aged exactly 0 through the following year, 2,239 may be expected to die and $100,000 - 2,239$ or 97,761 may be expected to reach age 1. Since $q_1 = .00181$, 181 out of every 100,000 aged 1 may be expected to die before age 2. But out of our original group of 100,000 births only 97,761 reached age 1 and hence we may expect $\frac{181}{100,000} \times 97,761$ or 177 to die before age 2 and therefore 97,584 to reach age 2. Proceeding in this way until all the original 100,000 who started at age 0 have died we obtain d_x the number of persons who, on the average, die at age x last birthday (i.e. between x and $x + 1$ exactly), and l_x the number of persons who, on the average, attain exact age x (out of the original cohort of l_0 persons).

The arithmetical process explained above is summarized in the equations

$$d_x = l_x \times q_x \qquad \qquad \text{......................(1)}$$

and $$l_{x+1} = l_x - d_x \qquad \qquad \text{......................(2)}$$

It is convenient to include in a life table not only the proportion of persons aged x who, on the average, may be expected to die within a year (q_x) but also p_x the proportion of persons now aged exactly x who, on the average, may be expected to survive one year (to age $x + 1$ exactly). Since a person must either die or survive, the probability of dying at age x plus the probability of surviving to age $x + 1$ equals unity, or

$$p_x = 1 - q_x \qquad \qquad \text{......................(3)}$$

and hence the values of p_x may be obtained.

We record below the values of these four life table functions for ages 0 to 5. We repeat that these values are all based on the mortality as expressed by the values of q_x given earlier. These values of q_x are the only data needed to enable a life table for these ages to be constructed.

Age(x)	l_x	d_x	p_x	q_x	Age(x)
0	100,000	2.239	.97761	.02239	0
1	97,761	177	.99819	.00181	1
2	97,584	117	.99880	.00120	2
3	97,467	88	.99910	.00090	3
4	97,379	64	.99934	.00066	4
5	97,315	56	.99942	.00058	5
.	.	.	.	.	.
.	.	.	.	.	.
.	.	.	.	.	.

The student should be warned, and will no doubt learn from experience, that one error in the d_x or l_x column will result in all the subsequent parts of the life table being incorrect.

The values of q_x which we have used are those for Australian males 1960–62 and the values for all ages and the resultant full life table are given in the Appendix. This life table is called the A^{M61} table and the corresponding life table for females (also given in the Appendix) is called the A^{F61} table. These life tables are included for demonstration purposes only and all students are encouraged to repeat all examples and solve all problems using the most recent life table calculated for their own country.

It is most important to note that this life table is not limited in its use to dealing with problems concerning only persons aged 0. It can also give the subsequent history of and solve problems concerning persons of any higher age. If we were to draw a horizontal line in the A^{M61} table between ages 29 and 30 then we have below that line the full subsequent history of 94,726 lives aged 30. This constitutes a life table with radix l_{30} equal to 94,726. This subsidiary life table depends only on values of q_x from age 30 onwards and that part between ages 30 and 35 is reproduced below:

Age(x)	l_x	d_x	p_x	q_x	Age(x)
30	94,726	149	.99843	.00157	30
31	94,577	152	.99839	.00161	31
32	94,425	158	.99833	.00167	32
33	94,267	164	.99826	.00174	33
34	94,103	172	.99817	.00183	34
35	93,931	182	.99806	.00194	35
.	.	.	.	.	.
.	.	.	.	.	.
.	.	.	.	.	.

We shall see the importance of this principle in the solutions of problems later in this chapter. For each question considered it is not necessary to reconstruct the life table over the age range desired beginning with a radix 100,000. The ratios obtained in life table problems are independent of the radix selected.

3.3 Graphs of l_x, q_x, d_x

The graphs of l_x, q_x and d_x for human populations follow a fairly standard pattern irrespective of sex or of the country to which they refer. In *Figure 3.1* we set out solely to illustrate their general shape, the graphs of these three functions in the case of the A^{M61} life table.

The graph of the survivorship function l_x must, of course, be continually decreasing. It falls fairly rapidly at the first few ages of life because infant mortality for all human populations is comparatively high. The rate of fall slows down over the middle of the life span where mortality is lighter. The curve then falls fairly steeply at higher ages where mortality for all human populations is again comparatively high.

The graph of the rate of mortality q_x commences at a high figure (infant mortality), falls rapidly to a minimum at about age 10, climbs to a temporary maximum at about age 19 (due to accident mortality), falls to a temporary minimum around age 26 (as the higher accident period passes) and then increases more and more steeply through life.

The graph of the number of deaths at each age (d_x) commences at a very high figure (infant mortality), falls rapidly to a minimum at about age 10, climbs to a temporary

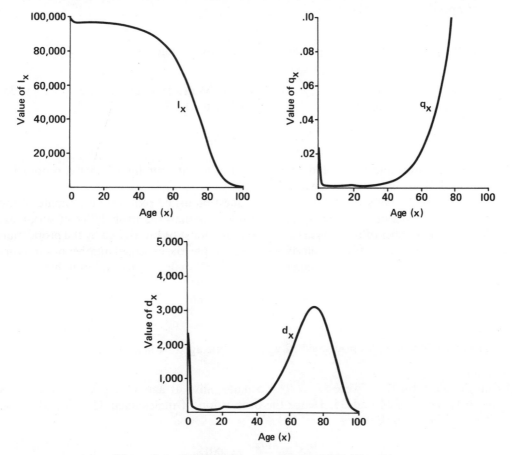

Figure 3.1: Graphs of l_x, q_x, d_x from A^{M61} life table

maximum at about age 19 (accident mortality), falls to a temporary minimum around age 26, increases to its greatest maximum at about age 75 and then decreases again since, although the death rate continues to increase, fewer people are still alive and exposed to the risk of death.

To fully appreciate the shape of these curves and the differences between male and female curves, and also those for developed and developing countries, students should draw each of these curves for a developed and a developing country separately for males and females.

3.4 Use of l_x and d_x columns

We shall now see how the l_x and d_x columns can be used to answer questions on the proportion of persons surviving from one age to a higher age, the proportion dying before a particular age or at a particular age, the proportion dying between two ages and other questions involving proportions and numbers of persons living or dying. Unless otherwise specified the life tables used in the following problems are the A^{M61} and A^{F61} tables given in the Appendix.

Problem 1
What is the proportion of men aged 31 expected to live to age 35?

Solution
Out of l_{31} or 94,577 men alive at age 31, l_{35} or 93,931 are expected to be alive at age 35. Hence the proportion of men surviving from age 31 to age 35 is

$$\frac{l_{35}}{l_{31}} = \frac{93,931}{94,577} = .99317$$

Note that this same question could be asked in a different way, namely 'what proportion of men aged 31 are expected to die after age 35?'

It should also be noted that sometimes the question asked requires an estimate of the number of survivors out of a group of persons rather than the probability of surviving. In this case the number of persons in the initial group must be multiplied by the proportion surviving to obtain the number of survivors. For example, the expected number of survivors from age 31 to age 35 out of an original group of 2,000 males all aged 31 exactly is

$$2,000 \times \frac{93,931}{94,577} = 1,986.$$

Problem 2
What proportion of males now aged 32 will die while aged 34 last birthday?

Solution
From the life table there were $l_{32} = 94,425$ males alive at age 32 and $d_{34} = 172$ males dying between ages 34 and 35. Hence the proportion of males aged 32 expected to die whilst aged 34 last birthday is

$$\frac{d_{34}}{l_{32}} = \frac{172}{94,425} = .00182$$

Problem 3
What is the average number of males who might be expected to die between ages 31 and 35 out of 3,000 males now aged 30?

Solution
From the life table there were $l_{30} = 94,726$ males alive at age 30, $l_{31} = 94,577$ alive at age 31 and $l_{35} = 93,931$ alive at age 35. The number dying between ages 31 and 35 is $d_{31} + d_{32} + d_{33} + d_{34} = 152 + 158 + 164 + 172 = 646$. This can be obtained more simply from $l_{31} - l_{35} = 94,577 - 93,931 = 646$. If there were 94,726 males alive aged 30, then 646 would be expected to die between ages 31 and 35. But in this problem there were 3000 males aged 30, so the number expected to die between ages 31 and 35 is

$$3000 \times \frac{l_{31} - l_{35}}{l_{30}} = 3000 \times \frac{646}{94,726} = 20.46 \doteqdot 20.$$

Problem 4
What is the chance that a female aged 31 and a male aged 33 will both die within 20 years?

Solution
The chance that the female aged 31 will die within 20 years is $\frac{l_{31} - l_{51}}{l_{31}}$, the values being taken from the A^{F61} table.

The chance that the male aged 33 will die within 20 years is $\frac{l_{33} - l_{53}}{l_{33}}$, the values being taken from the A^{M61} table.

The chance that both will die within 20 years is

$$\frac{l_{31} - l_{51}}{l_{31}} \times \frac{l_{33} - l_{53}}{l_{33}} = \frac{96,570 - 92,283}{96,570} \times \frac{94,267 - 86,119}{94,267} = .00384$$

$$\text{or about 1 in 260.}$$

Problem 5
What is the chance that a male child just born to a mother aged 31 and a father aged 33 will be alive 20 years later but orphaned by both of his parents?

Solution
The chance that the baby will survive 20 years

$$= \frac{l_{20}}{l_0} = 0.96215$$

The chance that both parents will die within 20 years

$$= .00384 \text{ (from the previous problem).}$$

Hence the chance that the baby will be alive in 20 years but orphaned by both parents

$$= 0.96215 \times 0.00384$$
$$= 0.00369$$

$$\text{or about 1 in 271.}$$

Problem 6

A company has entered into an arrangement with 1,000 males aged 31 to pay the next of kin of each one who dies before age 35 $100 for each year or fraction of a year that he lives (in the future). How much would the company expect to pay out?

Solution

Out of l_{31} or 94,577 males aged exactly 31

$$\text{\$}$$

d_{31} or 152 die between ages 31 and 32 and receive $152 \times 100 =$ 15,200

d_{32} or 158 die between ages 32 and 33 and receive $158 \times 200 =$ 31,600

d_{33} or 164 die between ages 33 and 34 and receive $164 \times 300 =$ 49,200

d_{34} or 172 die between ages 34 and 35 and receive $172 \times 400 =$ 68,800

(The others reach age 35)   Total   164,800

Hence if there were 94,577 males the company would pay out $164,800. Therefore with 1,000 males the expected payout is

$$\frac{1,000}{94,577} \times 164,800 = \$1,742.$$

Problem 7

Set out the l_x, q_x, d_x and p_x columns of a life table from age 40 to 45 given the following information:

The probability at birth of living to age 40 = .86

$$l_0 \quad = 100,000$$
$$q_{40} = \quad .003$$
$$q_{41} = \quad .003$$
$$q_{42} = \quad .004$$
$$q_{43} = \quad .004$$
$$q_{44} = \quad .005$$
$$q_{45} = \quad .005$$

Solution

We are given that 86% of people aged 0 live to age 40 and that $l_0 = 100,000$. Hence l_{40} must equal 86,000. The section of the life table from age 40 to age 45 is therefore as follows:

Age(x)	l_x	d_x	p_x	q_x
40	86,000	258	.997	.003
41	85,742	257	.997	.003
42	85,485	342	.996	.004
43	85,143	341	.996	.004
44	84,802	424	.995	.005
45	84,378	422	.995	.005

3.5 The functions L_x and T_x

The life table functions which we have introduced so far are used for solving problems which involve probabilities of living or of dying. The demographer is, however, often concerned with problems of quite a different type, which need for their solution other functions, which are therefore included in most life tables.

A hypothetical population which throughout the past has had no migration, has experienced constant age specific mortality, has been increased by a constant number of births each year and decreased by the same constant number of deaths each year is obviously of constant size and is known as a stationary or life table population. The demographer frequently needs to know the relative number of persons in various age groups in such a stationary population. Problems are also frequently encountered where we require to know the average future lifetime of a group of people, or the total number of years likely to be lived in the future by a group of people.

These two types of problem, although quite different in concept, can both be solved by adding two new functions L_x and T_x to the life table so far constructed. The values for both of these new functions can be quite simply determined from the values of l_x.

Let us consider the population which would result at the present time from a constant number of births l_0 per annum occurring uniformly over every year in the past.

Of the births which occurred *exactly* three years ago the fraction now alive would be $\dfrac{l_3}{l_0}$ and they would be exactly 3 years of age.

Of the births which occurred *exactly* four years ago the fraction now alive would be $\dfrac{l_4}{l_0}$ and they would be exactly 4 years of age.

The number of persons now alive and aged between 3 exactly and 4 exactly (which we shall call L_3) would be the survivors out of the births which occurred between three and four years ago. If births and deaths were uniformly spread over the year the fraction surviving to the present time would be the average of $\dfrac{l_3}{l_0}$ and $\dfrac{l_4}{l_0}$.

Hence, the number now alive and aged between 3 and 4 would be:

$$l_0 \times \tfrac{1}{2} \times \left[\frac{l_3}{l_0} + \frac{l_4}{l_0} \right] = \frac{l_3 + l_4}{2}.$$

$$\text{Thus } L_3 = \tfrac{1}{2}(l_3 + l_4)$$

$$\text{and in the general case } L_x = \tfrac{1}{2}(l_x + l_{x+1}). \qquad \dots\dots\dots\dots(4)$$

The values of L_x for all ages in the life table can therefore be filled in by taking the averages of adjacent values of l_x. Thus we can define the L_x column as the number of persons between exact age x and exact age $x + 1$ in the stationary population which results from l_0 births per annum, uniformly spread over the year for all years in the past.

For the mathematically inclined, a simpler proof of the above formula is to note that L_x is the area under the l_x curve between ages x and $x + 1$, i.e.

$$L_x = \int_0^1 l_{x+t}\, dt \doteq \tfrac{1}{2}(l_x + l_{x+1})$$

It should be noted in passing that, at young ages, deaths are *not* uniformly distributed over the year and it is a common practice to modify the formula for L_0 and L_1 to allow for this.

Although more accurate methods are often used approximations such as

$$L_0 = .3l_0 + .7l_1 \qquad\qquad \dots\dots\dots\dots (4A)$$

$$L_1 = .4l_1 + .6l_2 \qquad\qquad \dots\dots\dots\dots (4B)$$

are found to be quite suitable.

Sometimes it is necessary to calculate the proportion of persons surviving to some fractional age such as $x + \frac{1}{2}$. For numerical values in such cases it is customary to use linear interpolation. Thus $l_{x+1/2} = \frac{1}{2}(l_x + l_{x+1})$ which equals L_x. Another useful approximation is $L_{x-1/2} = l_x$.

T_x is the number of persons aged x and over in the stationary population which results from l_0 births per annum spread uniformly over the year for all years in the past. Clearly

$$T_x = L_x + L_{x+1} + L_{x+2} + \dots\dots \qquad\qquad \dots\dots\dots\dots (5)$$

and hence $T_x = \sum\limits_{t=0}^{\omega} L_{x+t}$, where ω is the highest age achieved. Values of T_x are so often required that they are also set out in the life table. The T_x column can be calculated simply by adding up the L_x column progressively from the bottom since obviously

$$T_x = T_{x+1} + L_x$$

The number of persons between (say) ages 30 and 50 in a life table population can be obtained by adding all the values of L_x from L_{30} to L_{49}. However since T_{30} is the number aged 30 and above, and T_{50} is the number aged 50 and above, the number between ages 30 and 50 must be $T_{30} - T_{50}$. It is because the subtraction of two values of T_x is so much simpler than adding many values of L_x that the T_x column is introduced into the life table.

The total life table population is obviously T_0. As it remains constant with l_0 births per annum, there must also be l_0 deaths per annum and hence both the crude birth rate and the crude death rate in the stationary or life table population are l_0/T_0.

3.6 Use of L_x and T_x columns – stationary populations

If we are able to assume that the population under consideration is in a stationary condition we can use the L_x and T_x columns of the life table to answer questions involving the proportion or number of persons in that stationary population who are of a particular age or in a particular age group.

Problem 8
A population which is in a stationary condition experiences A^{M61} mortality. It is expected that 5% of males aged 18, 10% of males aged 19, 9% of males aged 20, 8% of males aged 21, 6% of males aged 22, 3% of males aged 23 and .05% of males aged 24 and over will eventually be enrolled at a new university. Calculate the expected age distribution of the student male population of this university.

Solution
In a stationary population the number of people aged 18 is L_{18}; the number aged 19 is L_{19}; etc. The population aged 24 and over is T_{24}. Each of these is then multiplied by the

proportion of the population who are students to give the student population from which we obtain the age distribution.

Age	Stationary population		Proportion students	Student population	Age distribution (%)
18	$L_{18} =$	96,463	.05	4,823	11.6
19	$L_{19} =$	96,299	.10	9,630	23.1
20	$L_{20} =$	96,132	.09	8,652	20.8
21	$L_{21} =$	95,968	.08	7,677	18.4
22	$L_{22} =$	95,807	.06	5,748	13.8
23	$L_{23} =$	95,652	.03	2,870	6.9
24	$T_{24} = 4,465,972$		.0005	2,233	5.4
			Total	41,633	100.0

Problem 9

In a stationary population experiencing A^{M61} mortality, what percentages of the total population are aged:

(a)   0 to 15 years
(b)   15 to 65 years
(c)   65 years and over?

Solution

The total population is T_0 and the numbers in the three age groups are respectively $T_0 - T_{15}$, $T_{15} - T_{65}$ and T_{65}. Hence the required fractions are

$$\frac{6,791,451 - 5,332,388}{6,791,451}, \quad \frac{5,332,388 - 844,586}{6,791,451}, \quad \frac{844,586}{6,791,451}$$

or 21.5%, 66.1%, 12.4% which total 100% as they should.

Problem 10

A stationary population is supported by 8,000 births per annum and experiences A^{M61} mortality.

(a) If 30% of persons aged from 17 to 22 are medically unfit for military service, estimate the number aged 17 to 22 in the population who are unfit for military service.

(b) If 20% of persons aged 60 to 65 are retired estimate the number of retired persons in this age group in this population.

Solution

The life table population is supported by l_0 births per annum. Hence the stationary population we are considering is $\frac{8,000}{l_0}$ times the size of the life table population. This fraction is called the reduction factor and in this case equals $\frac{8,000}{100,000}$ or 0.08.

Hence the required answers are:

(a) $0.08 \times 0.3 \times (T_{17} - T_{22}) = 0.08 \times 0.3 \times (5,138,893 - 4,657,431)$
$= 11,555$ persons.

(b) $0.08 \times 0.2 \times (T_{60} - T_{65}) = 0.08 \times 0.2 \times (1,208,805 - 844,586)$
$= 5,828$ persons.

Problem 11

The population of an isolated community not subject to migration has been constant at 160,000 for a very long period of time. Estimate the number of persons in it aged over 65 assuming it experiences A^{M61} mortality.

Solution

The life table population totals T_0 and hence the reduction factor is $\frac{160,000}{T_0}$ or .023559

Hence the estimated number of persons over 65 is

$$.023559 \times T_{65} \text{ or } 19,898.$$

Problem 12

A stationary population is supported by 10,000 births per annum and experiences A^{M61} mortality. If we consider the working population to be all persons aged 20 to 65:

(a) What is the number of persons of working age?
(b) How many deaths occur each year of persons of working age?
(c) What is the average death rate for this particular age group?

Solution

The reduction factor is $\frac{10,000}{l_0}$ or 0.1

(a) The number aged 20–65 is therefore

$$0.1 \times (T_{20} - T_{65}) = 0.1 \times (4,849,531 - 844,586)$$
$$= 400,495.$$

(b) A stationary population supported by l_0 births per year will experience each year d_{20} deaths aged 20 last birthday, d_{21} deaths aged 21 last birthday, etc. Hence the total deaths aged 20–65 will be

$$d_{20} + d_{21} + \,.......... + d_{64}$$

which equals $l_{20} - l_{65}$.

Hence, when there are 10,000 births yearly supporting a stationary population the annual deaths aged 20–65 must be

$$0.1 \times (l_{20} - l_{65}) = 0.1 \times (96,215 - 67,699)$$
$$= 2,851.6 = 2,852.$$

(c) The number of persons aged 20–65 in this particular population is 400,495 from (a) and the annual number of deaths aged 20–65 is 2,852 from (b) and hence the average death rate per 1,000 for this particular age group is

$$\frac{2,852}{400,495} \times 1,000 = 7.12 \text{ per } 1,000.$$

Problem 13

If a population is built up by births uniformly increasing at the rate of 1% per annum, how would the number of persons aged 35 compare with the number aged 20?

Solution

If the population were built up from constant births the ratio would be

$$\frac{L_{35}}{L_{20}} = \frac{93,840}{96,132}.$$

But the 35-year-olds were born 15 years before the 20-year-olds. Hence, with the increasing number of births, the younger group started with a cohort $(1.01)^{15}$ times the number in the cohort which started the older group.

$$\text{Hence the ratio} \qquad = \frac{93,840}{96,132} \times \frac{1}{(1.01)^{15}}$$

$$= .8408.$$

Problem 14

A population which has 600 males aged 60–64 and 1,200 males aged 65 and over experiences 1,000 male live births spread evenly over the following 5 years. Estimate the number of male infants aged 0–4 and the number of males aged 65 and over at the end of the 5 year period.

Solution

The proportion of l_0 live births spread evenly over the year that will be alive x years later is given by $\frac{L_x}{l_0}$.

The number of the 1,000 male live births spread evenly over 5 years that will be alive at the end of the 5 year period is given by $1,000 \times \dfrac{L_0 + L_1 + L_2 + L_3 + L_4}{l_0 + l_0 + l_0 + l_0 + l_0}$

$$= 1,000 \times \frac{T_0 - T_5}{5 l_0} = 1,000 \times \frac{488,383}{500,000} = 977$$

The number of the 600 males aged 60–64 still alive at the end of 5 years

$$= 600 \times \frac{T_{65} - T_{70}}{T_{60} - T_{65}} = 600 \times \frac{307,642}{364,219} = 507$$

The number of the 1,200 males aged 65 and over still alive at the end of 5 years

$$= 1,200 \times \frac{T_{70}}{T_{65}} = 1,200 \times \frac{536,944}{844,586} = 763$$

Hence the total number of males aged 65 and over at the end of 5 years is $507 + 763 = 1,270$.

3.7 The number of years expected to be lived in the future

The T_x column is useful in another way. Assume we have l_{18} persons who at the present time are aged 18 exactly. How many years in the future will all these l_{18} persons be expected to live between them?

Let us assume that deaths between two ages occur uniformly over the year. Then, out of the l_{18} persons, l_{19} will reach their 19th birthday and by then will have lived one year. Those who die between age 18 and age 19, namely d_{18}, will on the average live half a year. Hence the number of years lived by the l_{18} persons between ages 18 and 19

$$= l_{19} + \tfrac{1}{2}d_{18}$$
$$= l_{19} + \tfrac{1}{2}(l_{18} - l_{19})$$
$$= \tfrac{1}{2}(l_{18} + l_{19})$$
$$= L_{18}.$$

The total number of years which these l_{18} persons will live between them throughout the future equals

$$L_{18} + L_{19} + L_{20} + \ldots\ldots\ldots = T_{18}.$$

Thus T_x not only equals the number of persons over age x in a stationary population supported by l_0 births per annum but it also equals the total number of years expected to be lived in the future by a group of l_x persons now aged x. It follows that the average future lifetime of persons aged $x = T_x \div l_x$. This is known as the complete expectation of life and is written $\mathring{e}_x$.

Hence $\qquad\qquad\qquad\qquad \mathring{e}_x = \dfrac{T_x}{l_x}.$ $\qquad\qquad \ldots\ldots\ldots\ldots(6)$

Again, for the mathematically inclined, l_{x+t} persons survive to age $x + t$ and live dt years between $x + t$ and $x + t + dt$. Hence, if we define

L_x the number of person years lived between x and $x + 1$ by l_x persons alive at age x
T_x the number of person years lived after age x by l_x persons alive at age x
$\mathring{e}_x$ the average number of years lived after age x by persons now aged x exactly (expectation of life at age x)

$$L_x = \int_0^1 l_{x+t}\,dt \doteq \tfrac{1}{2}(l_x + l_{x+1})$$

$$T_x = \int_0^{\omega} l_{x+t}\,dt = \sum_{t=0}^{\omega} L_{x+t}$$

$$\mathring{e}_x = \frac{1}{l_x}\int_0^{\omega} l_{x+t}\,dt = \frac{T_x}{l_x}$$

The dual use of the L_x and T_x columns should be carefully noted.

The full A^{M61} and A^{F61} life tables showing these various functions are given in the Appendix.

3.8 Use of L_x, T_x, $\mathring{e}_x$ columns – expected years lived

We shall now see how the L_x, T_x and $\mathring{e}_x$ columns are used to answer questions on the total number of years which a group of persons between them may be expected to live either during their lifetime or between two specific ages, and questions on the expectation of life, the average age at death, etc.

Problem 15
What are the expected ages at death, assuming A^{M61} mortality, of three groups of persons now aged 20, 40 and 60 respectively?

Solution

Persons now aged 20 on the average are expected to live a further $\mathring{e}_{20}$ years and hence their average age at death is

$$20 + \mathring{e}_{20} = 20 + 50.4 = 70.4 \text{ years.}$$

For persons now aged 40 and 60 respectively the average ages at death are

$$40 + \mathring{e}_{40} = 40 + 31.8 = 71.8 \text{ years}$$

$$60 + \mathring{e}_{60} = 60 + 15.6 = 75.6 \text{ years.}$$

Problem 16

A student noted that the average age at death of judges was higher than that of the average population and concluded that the mortality of judges was lighter than that of the average person in the population. Is his logic correct?

Solution

No. It can be seen from the answer to the previous problem that the average age at death increases as the age of the group we are studying increases. Judges are not appointed until middle age whereas when we are considering the average population we are considering a population from birth; hence even if both groups experienced the same age specific mortality we would expect the average age at death of judges to be the higher.

Problem 17

What will be the average age at death of those persons now exactly 40 who will die between ages 40 and 60?

Solution

The l_{40} persons aged 40 (i.e. 92,859) live $T_{40} - T_{60}$ (i.e. 2,956,204 − 1,208,805) years between age 40 and 60. But of these years, $l_{60} \times 20$ (i.e. 20 × 77,456) are lived by those who reach age 60. Hence the years lived by those who die between ages 40 and 60

$$= (2,956,204 - 1,208,805) - 1,549,120$$
$$= 198,279 \text{ years.}$$

The number of the l_{40} persons who die before age 60

$$= l_{40} - l_{60} = 92,859 - 77,456 = 15,403$$

Hence the average number of years lived after age 40 by those who die between 40 and 60

$$= \frac{198,279}{15,403} = 12.87 \text{ years.}$$

Hence the average age at death of those persons now 40 who die between 40 and 60 = 40 + 12.87 = 52.87 years.

3.9 Abridged life tables

It will be noted that the A^{M61} life table occupies two full pages of this book. It takes up this space because the unit of time used is one year and the human life span may extend to 100 years. If we are comparing life tables for a number of countries it is likely that a smaller life table may be desirable. For some countries data are only available in 5 or even 10 year age groups. In such cases what is called an abridged life table is constructed. The principles are just the same as for the complete life table but the unit of time, instead of being a year, may be for example a decade.

If deaths and population had only been available for 10 year age groups then instead of q_x we would have obtained the probability that a person aged x dies within 10 years, which we shall write $_{10}q_x$.

An abridged life table for Australian males (1960–62) could be built up in the same way as our complete life table was built (see *Table 3.1*).

The survivorship column l_x contains every tenth value shown in the l_x column of a complete life table. Each entry in the $_{10}d_x$ column is the sum of the corresponding ten values of d_x in the complete life table i.e. $d_x + d_{x+1} + \ldots\ldots + d_{x+9}$. The values of $_{10}q_x$ and $_{10}p_x$ are respectively the probabilities of dying within ten years and of surviving ten years.

The number living between ages 0 and 10 in a stationary population, written $_{10}L_0$, may be obtained from the average of l_0 and l_{10} as before, but we need to multiply by 10 to account for the persons at each of the ten yearly ages. Thus

$$_{10}L_0 = 10 \times \frac{100{,}000 + 97{,}062}{2} = 985{,}310.$$

The other values of $_{10}L_x$ may be obtained in a similar way. The T_x column is obtained by adding the $_{10}L_x$ column successively from the bottom of the table. Values of $\mathring{e}_x$ are again obtained by dividing T_x by l_x. Proceeding in this way we obtain the abridged life table given in *Table 3.1*.

Table 3.1

Abridged life table for Australian males 1960–62

Age (x)	l_x	$_{10}d_x$	$_{10}q_x$	$_{10}p_x$	$_{10}L_x$	T_x	$\mathring{e}_x$	Age (x)
0	100,000	2,938	0.02938	0.97062	985,310	6,802,840	68.03	0
10	97,062	847	0.00873	0.99127	966,385	5,817,530	59.94	10
20	96,215	1,489	0.01548	0.98452	954,705	4,851,145	50.42	20
30	94,726	1,867	0.01971	0.98029	937,925	3,896,440	41.13	30
40	92,859	4,386	0.04723	0.95277	906,660	2,958,515	31.86	40
50	88,473	11,017	0.12452	0.87548	829,645	2,051,855	23.19	50
60	77,456	22,512	0.29064	0.70936	662,000	1,222,210	15.78	60
70	54,944	30,275	0.55102	0.44898	398,065	560,210	10.20	70
80	24,669	20,869	0.84596	0.15404	142,345	162,145	6.57	80
90	3,800	3,720	0.97895	0.02105	19,400	19,800	5.21	90
100	80	80	1.00000	0.00000	400	400	5.00	100
110	0	0	1.00000	0.00000	0	0	0	110

It will be noted that the values of $_{10}L_x$ in this table are not the sum of the corresponding ten values in the complete life table and the values of T_x in the abridged life table are not identical with the values of T_x in the complete life table. This arises because in using the formula

$$_nL_x = \frac{n}{2}(l_x + l_{x+n})$$ . . . . (7)

we are in effect assuming that the deaths $_{10}d_x$ are uniformly spread over the 10 year age group. This is of course far from being correct in the higher age groups and produces absurd results for $\mathring{e}_x$ at the higher ages in the table. Allowance could easily be made for the fact that deaths are not uniformly spread over the age group by using a more complicated formula to obtain $_{10}L_x$. If however, we are only concerned with values in the table away from the higher ages the error is generally negligible. A much more accurate result would have been obtained had we used quinquennial age groups because the assumption of uniformity of deaths is more nearly satisfied with quinquennial groups. It is not necessary to use equal age intervals and it is common to see abridged life tables published for ages 0, 1, 5, 10, 15, 20, ..., in which case you will need the additional column showing the various values of $n = 1, 4, 5, 5, 5,..........$ and will need to alter the column headings to $_nd_x$, $_nq_x$, etc.

For further reading

1. Barclay, G. W. *Techniques of Population Analysis*, Wiley, 1962.
2. Dublin, L. I., Lotka, A. J. and Spiegelman, M. *Length of Life*, 1949.
3. Shryock, H. S. and Siegel, J. S., *The Methods and Materials of Demography*, U.S. Government Printing Office, 1973.

Exercises

Values of $_5q_x$ recently quoted for females in Pakistan, a country with comparatively heavy mortality, and in Norway, a country with light mortality follow. This is the basic information required for Exercises 3.1 to 3.10.

Age (x)	Pakistan	Norway
0	.25004	.01888
5	.02994	.00143
10	.02382	.00089
15	.03183	.00153
20	.04009	.00167
25	.04512	.00214
30	.05100	.00342
35	.05651	.00478
40	.06191	.00796
45	.06941	.01118
50	.09111	.01821
55	.11850	.02908
60	.17188	.05114
65	.23456	.09119
70	.33517	.15671
75	.45991	.27304
80	.62371	.43975
85	1.00000	1.00000

3.1   Construct abridged life tables with radix 100,000 and with values of l_x taken to the nearest unit for females in Pakistan and females in Norway based on the above values of $_5q_x$. The tables should include l_x, $_5d_x$, $_5q_x$, $_5p_x$, $_5L_x$, T_x and $\overset{\circ}{e}_x$ columns.

3.2   Draw graphs of l_x, $_5d_x$, $_5q_x$, $_5p_x$, and $\overset{\circ}{e}_x$ for the two countries and comment on the differences.

3.3   Determine from the life tables calculated in Exercise 3.1 the following probabilites for each country:
(i)   that a female aged 0 will live to age 5
(ii)   that a female aged 5 will live to age 25
(iii)   that a female aged 10 will die after 30
(iv)   that a female aged 15 will die before 35
(v)   that a female aged 10 will die between 20 and 30
(vi)   that two females aged 15 will both die within 10 years.

3.4   Out of 900 females now aged 15 exactly how many might be expected to die between their 25th and 30th birthdays? (Obtain an answer for both countries).

3.5   A certain town in Pakistan in one normal year recorded the following number of deaths of females under age 20:

Age	Number of deaths recorded
0 – under 5	2,500
5 – under 10	350
10 – under 15	300
15 – under 20	400

(i)   Using the relevant abridged life table estimate the female population under age 20 in this Pakistani town.
(ii)   If a town in Norway had this same under 20 population how many under 20 female deaths would you expect it to experience in a year?

3.6   The approximate number of female graduates from a certain institution at the end of last year were:

Assumed exact age at graduation	Number
19	300
20	400
21	500
22	200

Use values of $_5p_x$ in the life tables for Pakistan and Norway to estimate the total number of these graduates who will be alive 10 years after graduation. Make the calculation for both countries and compare the results.

(*Note:* Values of $_5p_x$ are not available for individual values of x; they can however be estimated by graphical or other means from the values which are available.)

3.7   How many years in total would you expect 2,000 females now aged 30 to live between age 30 and age 60 if 1,000 of the females are in Pakistan and 1,000 in Norway?

3.8   Compare the average ages at death in Pakistan and Norway for females now aged

(i) 0   (ii) 20   (iii) 40   (iv) 60.

3.9   Compare the average ages at death in Pakistan and Norway of those females now exactly 40 who will die between ages 40 and 60.

3.10   Assuming that the number of births in Pakistan has been increasing at 3% per annum and in Norway at 1% per annum estimate and compare the age distributions of the two populations.

3.11 A certain Australian industry recruits a constant number of new employees each year all at age 20, and they all retire at age 60. Assuming there are no resignations
(i) How many years service does the industry obtain on the average from each employee?
(ii) What is the ratio of retirements each year to new recruits?
(iii) What is the ratio of staff over 50 to total staff?
(iv) What is the ratio of retired persons to active staff?
(v) What is the ratio of deaths each year of retired persons to deaths of persons on active service?

3.12 Write down formulae (i.e. in terms of symbols) for the following:
(i) the probability that a male aged exactly 20 lives to 60
(ii) the probability that a male aged exactly 20 dies aged 45 last birthday
(iii) the probability that a male aged exactly 30 dies between his 40th and his 60th birthdays
(iv) the probability that a male aged exactly 20 dies after age 70
(v) the value of the product $p_{20}\, p_{21}\, p_{22}\, p_{23}\, p_{24}\, p_{25}\, p_{26}\, p_{27}\, p_{28}\, p_{29}$
(vi) the value of the product $p_{30}\, p_{31}\, p_{32}\, p_{33}\, p_{34}\, q_{35}$

(vii) the value of $\displaystyle\sum_{x=20}^{\infty} d_x$

(viii) the value of $\displaystyle\sum_{x=20}^{50} d_x$

(ix) the value of $\displaystyle l_{20} - \sum_{x=20}^{40} d_x$

(x) the number of drivers' licences to be issued each year at age 18 exactly to maintain the number of licenced drivers in a community at 50,000 (assume that a licence once granted is never withdrawn)
(xi) the number of these drivers who would be over 80
(xii) the average number of years for which a person would hold a licence
(xiii) the number of drivers' licences to be issued each year at age 18 exactly to maintain the number of licenced drivers in a community at 50,000 if licences are automatically withdrawn at age 80
(xiv) the average number of years for which the drivers in (xiii) would hold a licence
(xv) the number of licences which would be withdrawn each year under (xiii)
(xvi) the proportion of licenced drivers in (xiii) who are retired, if retirement takes place compulsorily at and only at age 65.

3.13 Using the A^{M61} table compare the average death rate of the 10–20 age group with that of the 60–70 age group.

3.14 Using the A^{M61} and A^{F61} tables, calculate the chance that a son just born to a mother aged 25 and a father aged 30 will be alive in 15 years time but
(i) orphaned only by his father,
(ii) orphaned by at least one of his parents?

4
Applications of stationary population models

4.1 Introduction

We described the life table technique in Chapter 3 as being a very versatile tool and in that chapter we used it to solve some demographic problems. It is obviously a technique which can be applied whenever we have problems involving the number of 'survivors' out of an original group of people. In some problems we are concerned merely with survival curves, in others with stationary populations where exits have to be replaced by new entrants. The life table approach has been used for the study of animal, bird and fish populations, the staffing of companies, survival following major operations or following the onset of disease, the wearing out and replacement of equipment, replacement of stocks and many other similar problems.

This chapter does not in fact introduce any new theory. Its purpose is to show the wide range of problems for which the life table technique is useful. It does this by presenting the solutions to a number of varied problems. These problems are somewhat more complex and probably more difficult than those dealt with in Chapter 3 but the student is advised to master them as he should be rewarded by obtaining a better understanding of the life table technique.

4.2 Stationary population models in manpower planning

Stationary population models have been used to provide a framework for management decisions. Many of these studies are only concerned with the number of persons remaining in the service of the employer, and hence the rate of discontinuance of employment used in building a survivorship table includes losses from all causes including death, resignation, dismissal and retirement often called a wastage rate. If one is studying the stability of employment then a useful measure of stability might be the expectation of service analogous to the expectation of life. The use of these models is most appropriate when all persons enter the service at about the same age since mortality is largely a function of age, and resignation largely a function of length of service. In some industries the wastage rate is so high that age may be ignored and rates are based on years of service only. A stationary population requires a constant intake of new employees each year. This assumption is roughly satisfied in special situations in practice, but even where it is not, models based on this assumption can serve as a guide to management. The long-term effect of alternative manpower policies which might be adopted can usually be estimated by using hypothetical populations. Some rather hypothetical problems follow to give further practice in using life tables. Where mortality data are required in these problems the A^{M61} table is used.

Problem 1
The wastage rates in two large factories have been found to be as follows:

Year	Factory A	Factory B
0	0.50	0.667
1	0.50	0.500
2	0.50	0.300
3	0.50	0.250
4	0.50	0.200
5	0.50	0.067
6	0.50	1.000
7	0.50	
8	0.50	
9	0.50	

Calculate, in each case, the average length of service of an employee and the annual intake required to maintain the staff at 1,500 persons.

Solution
From these wastage rates the l_x or survivorship column can be obtained in the usual way and on the assumption that withdrawals are uniformly spread over the year the L_x and T_x columns may be calculated. The result of these calculations follows.

Year	Factory A l_x	Factory A L_x	Factory A T_x	Factory B l_x	Factory B L_x	Factory B T_x
0	1,000	750	1,498	1,000	667	1,339
1	500	375	748	333	250	672
2	250	188	373	166	141	422
3	125	94	185	116	102	281
4	62	46	91	87	78	179
5	31	23	45	70	68	101
6	16	12	22	65	33	33
7	8	6	10	0	0	0
8	4	3	4			
9	2	1	1			
10	1	0	0			

Average length of service $= \dfrac{T_0}{l_0}$. Hence the average length of service for employees of Company A and Company B are 1.498 and 1.339 years respectively or roughly $1\frac{1}{2}$ and $1\frac{1}{3}$ years.

A steady intake of l_0 or 1,000 new employees would produce a total staff of T_0 or 1,498 for Company A and 1,339 for Company B. Hence if the total staff in each case is to be maintained at 1,500 the annual intake should be:

$$\text{for Company A} \qquad 1,000 \times \frac{1,500}{1,498} = 1,001 \text{ persons}$$

$$\text{for Company B} \qquad 1,000 \times \frac{1,500}{1,339} = 1,120 \text{ persons}$$

Problem 2

The staff of a firm which recruits 400 employees each year uniformly over the year has reached a stationary condition. The new employees all join at age 18 exactly.
(a) How many persons would be on staff aged between 50 and 65?
(b) If the staff retire on their 65th birthday, how many retire each year?
(c) What would the firm's total active staff be?
(d) How many pensioners would it have on its books?
(e) What would the answers to (a) to (d) be if 10% of the staff resign at age 21?

Solution

(a) If l_{18} were to be recruited each year, the number on staff aged 50–65 would be $T_{50} - T_{65}$. Hence the answer is

$$\frac{400}{l_{18}}(T_{50} - T_{65}) = \frac{400}{96,541}(2,046,228 - 844,586) = 4,979.$$

(b) If l_{18} were recruited each year on their 18th birthday, l_{65} would retire each year on their 65th birthday. Hence the answer is

$$\frac{400}{l_{18}} \times l_{65} = \frac{400}{96,541} \times 67,699 = 280.$$

(c) l_{18} recruits each year would produce at any moment of time a total staff aged 18–65 of $T_{18} - T_{65}$. Hence, in this case, the total active staff is

$$\frac{400}{l_{18}}(T_{18} - T_{65}) = \frac{400}{96,541}(5,042,293 - 844,586) = 17,392.$$

(d) In the same way we can show that the number of pensioners would be

$$\frac{400}{l_{18}} \times T_{65} = \frac{400}{96,541} \times 844,586 = 3,499.$$

(e) In this case only 90% of those aged over 21 remain with the firm. Hence, the respective answers are:
(i)   Staff 50–65 $= .9 \times 4,979 = 4,481$
(ii) Number retiring each year $= .9 \times 280 = 252$
(iii) Total staff $= \dfrac{400}{l_{18}} \times \left[(T_{18} - T_{21}) + .9(T_{21} - T_{65})\right]$
         $= 15,773$
(iv) Number of pensioners $= .9 \times 3,499 = 3,149.$

Problem 3

The staff of a firm which recruits 300 employees each year uniformly over the year has reached a stationary condition. New employees all join at age 18 exactly; 15% resign at age 21, 10% resign at age 25, 5% retire at age 55, a further 5% retire at age 60 and 100% retire at age 65. What is the total number on staff?

Solution

The reduction factor is $\dfrac{300}{l_{18}}$ to bring the life table figures to the scale of this particular problem.

Age group	Number in life table	Fraction remaining in the age group after allowing for resignations and retirement
18–21	$T_{18} - T_{21}$	1
21–25	$T_{21} - T_{25}$	.85
25–55	$T_{25} - T_{55}$	.85 × .9
55–60	$T_{55} - T_{60}$	.85 × .9 × .95
60–65	$T_{60} - T_{65}$	.85 × .9 × .95 × .95

The answer, which could have been written down immediately, is therefore

$$\frac{300}{l_{18}}\left[(T_{18} - T_{21}) + .85(T_{21} - T_{25}) + .85 \times .9(T_{25} - T_{55}) + .85 \times .9 \times .95(T_{55} - T_{60})\right.$$

$$\left. + .85 \times .9 \times .95 \times .95(T_{60} - T_{65})\right] = 10{,}158.$$

Problem 4

A company's staff, consisting of 1,000 men who all entered at age 20, has reached a stationary condition.

   Assuming that

(1) 15% of those attaining age 21 resign at that age, 10% resign at age 22 and 5% at age 23, after which there are no resignations; and

(2) 10% of those attaining age 55 retire at that age, 40% retire at age 60 and 100% at age 65,

   determine

(a) the number resigning each year, and

(b) the number of pensioners on the books at any time.

Solution

If there were l_{20} entrants each year the staff would be

$$L_{20} + .85L_{21} + .85 \times .9L_{22} + .85 \times .9 \times .95(T_{23} - T_{55}) + .85 \times .9 \times .95$$

$$\times\left[.9(T_{55} - T_{60}) + .9 \times .6(T_{60} - T_{65})\right]$$

$$= L_{20} + .85L_{21} + .765L_{22} + .72675(T_{23} - .1T_{55} - .36T_{60} - .54T_{65})$$

$$= 2{,}801{,}155$$

But the staff is actually 1,000. Hence the numbers obtained from the life table for (a) and

(b) must be reduced in the ratio

$$\frac{1,000}{2,801,155}$$

(a) The number resigning each year will be

$$\frac{1,000}{2,801,155}(.15\,l_{21} + .1 \times .85\,l_{22} + .05 \times .9 \times .85\,l_{23})$$

$$= \frac{1,000}{2,801,155} \times 26,219 = 9.4 = 9$$

(b) The number of pensioners on the books at any time will be

$$\frac{1,000}{2,801,155} \times .85 \times .9 \times .95(.1\,T_{55} + .4 \times .9\,T_{60} + .6 \times .9\,T_{65})$$

$$= \frac{1,000}{2,801,155} \times .72675 \times 1,052,635$$

$$= 273.$$

4.3 Stationary population models in replacement theory

A standard management problem is to determine the steady rate at which items which wear out or are used up have to be replaced by new items. Examples are the replacement of stock which is being sold, the maintenance of a stock of machine components held in case of machine breakdown due to component failure, the replacement of machines which wear out and the replacement of hospital in-patients who depart. These are all cases of stationary populations for which the life table technique may be used. Some problems of this type follow.

Problem 5
A maternity hospital delivers 10 new-born babies per week, 30% of them leave hospital within a week, 10% of the remaining 1 week old babies leave before they are 2 weeks old, 20% of the remainder leave before they are 3 weeks old, 40% of the remainder before they are 4 weeks old, 70% of the remainder before they are 5 weeks old and all the remainder leave before they are 6 weeks old. How many cots are needed?

Solution
A life table may be constructed in the usual way and the result is as follows:

x	l_x	d_x	q_x	L_x	T_x
0	100	30	.3	85.0	272.7
1	70	7	.1	66.5	187.7
2	63	12.6	.2	56.7	121.2
3	50.4	20.2	.4	40.3	64.5
4	30.2	21.1	.7	19.6	24.2
5	9.1	9.1	1.0	4.6	4.6
6	0				

If there are 10 new-born babies admitted each week then the stationary population resulting will be

$$\frac{10}{l_0} \times T_0 = \frac{10}{100} \times 272.7 = 27.27 = 27$$

Problem 6
A tobacconist takes in a stock of 100 packets of a new brand of cigarettes. In the first week he sells 20% of them, in the second week 45% of the remaining, in the third week 50% of the remaining and in the fourth week 65% of the remaining. In the fifth week he sells all he has left.
(a) Draw up a weekly 'life' table for the 100 packets of cigarettes.
(b) What is the chance that one of the original 100 packets
    (i)   is sold in the first week?
    (ii) is sold in the second week?
    (iii) is unsold by the fourth week?
(c) (i)   Suppose that over the ensuing year he finds that he sells 500 packets of these cigarettes each week which are replaced continuously by a salesman throughout the week. If the retail price of the cigarettes is \$1.00 per packet, what is the retail value of his stock at any time?
    (ii) If he lowers the price of the 3 week old packets to 90c and of the 4 week old packets to 80c each, what would be his weekly income from his stock?
    (iii) Assuming that sales may take place at any time of the day and on any day of the week how long on the average would a packet of cigarettes lie on the shelves before being sold?

Solution
(a) The life table is as follows:

Week	x^*	l_x	d_x	q_x	L_x	T_x
1	0	100	20	.20	90.0	203.7
2	1	80	36	.45	62.0	113.7
3	2	44	22	.50	33.0	51.7
4	3	22	14.3	.65	14.9	18.7
5	4	7.7	7.7	1.00	3.8	3.8
6	5	0				

*Note: It is usual in a life table to specify the age or duration x as at the beginning of each interval.

(b) (i) 0.20   (ii) $\frac{36}{100} = 0.36$ (iii) $\frac{22}{100} = 0.22$

(c) (i) If his intake of stock is 500 packets per week his scale of operations is $\frac{500}{l_0}$ or five times the size of the life table. His stock therefore numbers $5 \times 203.7 = 1,018.5$

packets.

∴ Retail value of stock $= 1.0 \times 1,018.5 = \$1,018.50$.

(ii) If he sold all the packets for \$1.00 his weekly income would be $500 \times 1.0 = \$500$. However he sells 5×7.7 or 38.5 packets of 4 week old stock and 5×14.3 or 71.5 packets of 3 week old stock. Because of the discounts his weekly income is therefore reduced by $71.5 \times .10 + 38.5 \times .20 = \$14.85$.

∴ Weekly income $= 500 - 14.85 = \$485.15$.

(iii) Average length of life on shelves $= \dfrac{T_0}{l_0}$

$$= \frac{203.7}{100} = 2.037 \text{ weeks.}$$

4.4 Stationary population models in measuring contraceptive effectiveness

There are two types of problem under this heading for which life table techniques may be used. The first is to measure the effectiveness of a particular method of contraception by considering the numbers using the method who subsequently become pregnant. The 'survivors' here are those who do not become pregnant. The second type of problem is to measure the extent to which females who use the intra-uterine contraceptive device are able to retain that device. A problem which illustrates the use of the life table technique in this situation follows.

Problem 7

The intra uterine device (IUD) is becoming quite a popular method of contraception in many developing countries of Asia, Africa and Latin America. Large scale field trials have found this method to be safe, cheap and reliable. Despite all its good points this method does not suit some women. Their IUD has to be taken out because of complaints such as excessive bleeding, irregular menstruation and pains. To study the effectiveness of this method of contraception, IUD retention surveys have been conducted in various developing countries. One such survey was conducted in February 1972. In this survey 2,479 women were interviewed who had an IUD insertion during the month of January 1970. They were asked whether they had retained their IUD until the 24th month, during which month it was the practice to arrange a special medical check-up and remove the IUD. The reasons for losing their IUD and the duration of use were determined. The results of the survey indicated that 180 women lost their IUD during the first month after insertion and 162 during the second month after insertion. The corresponding figures for the third to the twenty-third month were 90, 85, 76, 180, 162, 90, 85, 76, 63, 51, 72, 85, 87, 72, 78, 70, 65, 90, 92, 89, 88.

(a) Calculate the probability that

    (i)   a woman who retained an IUD for the first six months will still have it by the end of the 20th month

    (ii) a woman who retained an IUD up to the beginning of the 10th month will lose it after the 18th month

    (iii) Mrs. X who has retained her IUD until now, the beginning of the 11th month, and Mrs. Y who has also retained her IUD until now, the beginning of the 13th month, will both lose their IUD's within the next six months.

(b) A family planning clinic performs 100 IUD insertions every month. The women lose their IUD following the same loss pattern as noted above.
Calculate
(i) the number of women called up per month for the special terminal medical check-up
(ii) the number of women clients of the clinic who at any time are wearing IUD's
(iii) the average number of months a woman who has just had an IUD insertion is expected to retain her IUD.

Solution

Month	x	l_x	d_x	L_x	T_x
1	0	2,479	180	2,389	29,120
2	1	2,299	162	2,218	26,731
3	2	2,137	90	2,092	24,513
4	3	2,047	85	2,004	22,421
5	4	1,962	76	1,924	20,417
6	5	1,886	180	1,796	18,493
7	6	1,706	162	1,625	16,697
8	7	1,544	90	1,499	15,072
9	8	1,454	85	1,412	13,573
10	9	1,369	76	1,331	12,161
11	10	1,293	63	1,261	10,830
12	11	1,230	51	1,205	9,569
13	12	1,179	72	1,143	8,364
14	13	1,107	85	1,064	7,221
15	14	1,022	87	979	6,157
16	15	935	72	899	5,178
17	16	863	78	824	4,279
18	17	785	70	750	3,455
19	18	715	65	682	2,705
20	19	650	90	605	2,023
21	20	560	92	514	1,418
22	21	468	89	424	904
23	22	379	88	335	480
24	23	291	291	145	145
25	24	0			

(a) (i) Probability $= \dfrac{l_{20}}{l_6} = \dfrac{560}{1,706} = 0.33$

(ii) Probability $= \dfrac{l_{18}}{l_9} = \dfrac{715}{1,369} = 0.52$

(iii) Probability $= \dfrac{l_{10} - l_{16}}{l_{10}} \times \dfrac{l_{12} - l_{18}}{l_{12}}$

$= \dfrac{1,293 - 863}{1,293} \times \dfrac{1,179 - 715}{1,179} = 0.13$

(b) The reduction factor to reduce the life table to the scale of operation of the clinic

$$= \frac{100}{l_0} = \frac{100}{2,479} = .04034$$

  (i) These are the removals in the 24th month.
       Number $= .04034 \times 291 = 11.7$ or 12 (say)
  (ii) Number $= .04034 \times T_0 = 1175$
  (iii) Expected life $= \frac{T_0}{l_0} = \frac{29,120}{2,479} = 11.75$ months.

4.5 Stationary population models in social planning

It was mentioned in the fourth paragraph of Chapter 1 that demographic data are now collected largely to enable effective economic and social planning to take place. The determination of electoral boundaries, calculating the chance that a slight swing in voting will cause a change of government, estimating the costs of social security programmes, determining the number and location of new schools and universities, etc. are all largely demographic problems. We now pose a simple hypothetical problem which gives a rough idea of how the life table can be used for such problems when the population being considered is approximately stationary.

Problem 8
The population of a certain country is in a stationary condition and is subject to A^{M61} mortality. In this country
1. voting is compulsory for all citizens over age 21
2. school education is compulsory for all children between ages 5 and 15 years
3. there is a social security scheme which provides the following benefits:
    (i) an annual allowance of $1,000 for each child under the minimum school leaving age
    (ii) a housing grant of $2,000 in cash to each couple on their first marriage
    (iii) a cash grant of $200 is paid for every death under age 10, and of $400 for every death over age 10
    (iv) an old age pension of $4,000 per annum to each person over age 65.
Assuming there are 1,000 births each year in the country, and no migration
(a) What is the total population of the country?
(b) If there are two political parties, and 60% of voters under age 45, and 40% of voters over age 45 support party A, and the remainder support party B
    (i) Which party has majority support?
    (ii) What percentage of voters would have to change allegiance to deny the majority party its advantage?
    (iii) How would your answers to (b) (i) and (b) (ii) change if the voting age were lowered to 18 years?
(c) Assuming elections are held every five years, what percentage of voters vote for the first time at each election?
(d) If all citizens marry for the first time at age 25, what is the annual number of marriages?
(e) What is the total number of children under minimum school leaving age?

(f) What is the annual number of deaths?
  (i)   under age 10?
  (ii) age 10 and over?
(g) What is the total number of pensioners?
(h) (i)   What is the annual outgo of the social security scheme?
  (ii) Which benefit of the scheme is the most expensive?
  (iii) What would be the additional annual cost of the child allowance, if the minimum school leaving age were raised to 16 years?
(i) If three-quarters of the population between ages 15 and 25, and one-half of the population between ages 25 and 65 years are employed in the labour force, what annual tax will each have to pay to support the social security scheme entirely out of direct taxation?

Solution

The reduction factor $= \dfrac{1,000}{l_0} = .01$

(a) Population $= .01 \times T_0$ $= 67,915$

(b) (i) Total voters $= .01\, T_{21}$ $= 47,534$

   Voters for A $= .01 \left[.6(T_{21} - T_{45}) + .4\, T_{45} \right] = 23,529$

   $\therefore$ Voters for B $= 24,005$
      $\therefore$ B has the majority support.

  (ii) If $\frac{1}{2}(24,005 - 23,529)$ or 238 voters change allegiance B would lose its majority.
   Hence the answer is $\dfrac{238}{47,534} \times 100 = 0.5\%$

  (iii) Total voters $= .01\, T_{18}$ $= 50,423$

   Voters for A $= .01 \left[.6(T_{18} - T_{45}) + .4\, T_{45} \right] = 25,262$

   Voters for B $= 25,161$

   Hence A would then have majority support. To give B majority support $\frac{1}{2}(25,262 - 25,161)$ or 51 voters would have to change allegiance. This is 0.1% of voters.

(c) All voters under age 26 would vote for the first time. Hence the percentage is

$$\frac{T_{21} - T_{26}}{T_{21}} \times 100 = 10.06\%.$$

(d) Annual number of marriages $= .01 \times l_{25} \times \frac{1}{2}$

$$= 477$$

(e) Number of children under minimum school leaving age

$$= .01(T_0 - T_{15})$$

$$= 14,591$$

(f) (i)   Annual number of deaths under age 10

$$= .01(l_0 - l_{10})$$

$$= 29.38 \text{ or } 29 \text{ (say)}$$

(ii)   Annual number of deaths age 10 and over

$$= .01 \, l_{10}$$

$$= 970.62 \text{ or } 971 \text{ (say)}$$

(N.B. These total 1,000 as they should)

(g)   Number of pensioners $= .01 \, T_{65}$

$$= 8,446$$

(h) (i)   Annual outgo for $

child allowance $= .01 \times 1,000(T_0 - T_{15})$ $\quad = 14,590,630$

housing grant $= .01 \times 2,000 \, l_{25} \times \frac{1}{2}$ $\quad = \quad 954,320$

death grant $= .01\left[200(l_0 - l_{10}) + 400 \, l_{10}\right] = \quad 394,124$

old age pension $= .01 \times 4,000 \times T_{65}$ $\quad = 33,783,440$

Total annual outgo $= \overline{49,722,514}$

(ii)   The old age pension. See (h) (i).

(iii)   Additional cost if minimum age were raised to 16

$$= .01 \times 1,000 \times L_{15} = \$967,890$$

(i)   If the required tax is t then the tax revenue

$$= t \times .01\left[.75(T_{15} - T_{25}) + .5(T_{25} - T_{65})\right]$$

$$= 24,843.81 \times t$$

For tax revenue to equal the cost of the social security scheme

$$t = \frac{49,722,514}{24,843.81} = \$2,001 \text{ per person employed.}$$

Exercises

4.1   Write down the formulae (i.e. in terms of symbols only) for the following:
  (i)   the total amount likely to be paid out by a company which undertakes to pay $100 to each of 1,000 people now aged exactly 20 provided they die before reaching age 50
  (ii)   the total number on the staff of a company which recruits 100 men per year uniformly over the year all at exact age 18 and retires everyone at age 60
  (iii)   the number of pensioners which would be on its books
  (iv)   the number on its staff between ages 40 and 60
  (v)   the number who retire each year
  (vi)   the number who die each year whilst still on staff
  (vii)   the number of pensioners who die each year

(viii) the number of pensioners aged 70–80 who die each year

(ix) if $100 is paid as a gift when each employee celebrates 25 years of service, the amount paid each year for this purpose

(x) if 10% of the staff in (ii) resign on their 21st birthday and 5% on their 25th birthday, the total number on staff

(xi) the average number of years likely to be lived after age 60 by a person now aged exactly 40

(xii) the number of years likely to be lived between ages 50 and 70 by 1,000 persons now aged exactly 30

(xiii) the number of persons which a company needs to recruit each year on their 18th birthday to maintain a staff of 3,000 employees if they all retire at 60.

4.2 A company staff in a stationary condition is maintained by 1,000 entrants each year (uniformly over the year) all at exact age 20. The withdrawals from the staff are so distributed over the first few years after entry that it may be assumed that 10% of those who reach age 23 withdraw at that age and that 5% of those who reach age 26 withdraw at that age, 40% of those who reach age 60 retire at that age and all who reach 65 retire at that age. Write down formulae (i.e. in terms of the usual life table symbols) for the following:

(a) the total number on the staff

(b) the total number of pensioners

(c) the number of pensioners aged between 60 and 65

(d) the number on the staff aged between 25 and 40

(e) the number who retire each year

(f) the number who die each year while still on the staff

(g) the average number of years likely to be worked with the company by a new recruit at age 20

(h) the average number of years likely to be worked with the company after age 40 by a member now aged 25

(i) the probability that a member of the staff now aged 25 exactly will still be on the staff at age 63.

4.3 An aviary of birds which has a constant intake of 1,500 new-born birds per year experiences the following mortality rates:

Age (x)	q_x
0	.3
1	.1
2	.2
3	.4
4	.7
5	1.0

(i) What is the total number of birds in the aviary at any time?

(ii) What is the number living between ages 1 and 4?

(iii) If the owner wanted the population to be a steady 5,000 how many extra new-born birds would he have to add each year?

4.4 A company operates a fleet of 100 trucks of the same kind on a 24 hour a day service. New trucks cost $50,000. For various reasons 5% of the trucks are replaced in their first year of service (second hand value = $40,000), 10% of those remaining are replaced in their second year of service (second hand value = $35,000), 20% of those remaining are replaced in their third year of service (second hand value = $30,000), 50% of those remaining are replaced in their fourth year of service (second hand value = $25,000), 90% of those remaining are replaced in their fifth year of service (second hand value = $20,000) and all those remaining are replaced in their sixth year of service (second hand value = $15,000). What is the cost per annum to the company to maintain its fleet at 100 trucks?

4.5 The hypothetical replacement rates per annum of electric light poles (i.e. the probability at the beginning of the year that a pole will, in the next 12 months, be in such a state that it must be replaced) are

Year	Replacement rate
0	0.1
1	0.2
2	0.3
3	0.4
4	0.5
5	0.6
6	0.7
7	0.8
8	0.9
9	1.0

(a) One thousand new poles have just been 'planted'. Draw up a table to show
    (i)   how many of these 'original' poles will be standing in 1, 2, 3, ... 10 years' time
    (ii) the number of these 'original' poles which will need to be replaced during the first, second, third, etc. years
(b) (i)   What is the probability that a pole just 'planted' will be standing in 5 years' time?
    (ii) What is the probability that a pole 'planted' 3 years ago will last more than 3 more years?
    (iii) What is the probability that a pole 'planted' exactly a year ago will be replaced in from 3 to 5 years' time?
(c) If the electricity authority in an old settled area where no new connections are possible has, for some decades, 'planted' uniformly over the year 1,000 poles per annum (i.e. replacements), draw up a table to show
    (i)   the total number of poles now standing
    (ii) the number of poles standing, by age of pole
(d) (i)   How many poles are aged between 2 and 5 years?
    (ii) If it is the policy of the authority to paint poles as soon as they have been standing for 5 years, how much would it cost them a year at $10 a pole to get a contractor to do the job?
(e) (i)   What is the average life of a pole?
    (ii) What is the average future life of poles 3 years old?
(f) (i)   A firm which supplies 400 poles per year is thinking of guaranteeing its poles for 2 years. If the cost of replacement to it is $500 per pole, what is the expected cost per annum of the guarantee?
    (ii) A paint firm has submitted a quotation in which it undertakes in the future to apply to new poles on 'planting' and to poles exactly 4 years old two coats of paint, and one coat to poles exactly 2 years, 6 years and 8 years after planting. What would their quotation be on an annual basis at $10 a pole per coat?

4.6 A *stationary* male population supports a regular army of 300,000. Recruits enter at age 20 exactly at a commencing salary of $9,000 per annum with annual increments of $600 per annum and serve for 5 years in the regular army. On their 25th birthday two options only are open to them namely
    (i)   to resign from the regular army but serve in the reserves for a further 7 years at no salary
    (ii) to make the army their career and continue as members of the regular army. In this case their salary jumps immediately to $15,000 per annum with annual increments of $300 per annum to a maximum of $21,000 per annum, and thereafter their salary remains constant. Retirement from the regular army is optional at age 55 and compulsory at age 60. A pension of $15,000 per annum is payable from the time of retirement (irrespective of whether they retire at 55 or 60) until death.
On their 25th birthday 95% resign from the regular army and 5% remain as members. Of the members of the regular army 40% exercise their option to retire at age 55.
   Give expressions in terms of the usual life table functions in the simplest form for
(i)   the number of recruits per annum
(ii) the number of reserves

APPLICATIONS OF STATIONARY POPULATION MODELS 61

(iii) the total sum payable each year in pensions
(iv) the total sum payable each year in salaries
(v) the probability of a recruit age 20 exactly retiring at age 60.

4.7 A bank employs 300 clerks; they enter at age 18 at a salary of $6,900 per annum which is increased $300 a year to a maximum of $15,000; at age 60 they retire on a pension. Assuming that 10% leave the bank after exactly five years' service and that after 20 years' service 5% are promoted from the clerical staff to higher positions, find the ultimate state of the clerical staff in the following particulars:
(i)   total annual sum payable in salaries
(ii) number superannuated each year
(iii) number of pensioners on the books.

5
Mortality

5.1 Introduction

The most striking demographic event in the past three centuries has been the unprecedented increase in population, primarily due to the remarkable fall in mortality rates. This improvement in mortality has however not been shared equally by all groups of people in the world.

In Australia from 1905 to 1978 the expectation of life for males increased by 15 years from 55 to 70 and for females by 18 years from 59 to 77.* Most of the improvement has occurred at ages under 45 and has been more marked for women than for men. Over the same period the expectation of life at age 60 for males has increased by two years from 14.4 to 16.7 years but for females has increased by 5 years from 16.2 to 21.4 years. Similar trends to these apply in most developed countries.

In the developing countries the most significant improvement in mortality has taken place since 1940. For example in Mauritius from 1942–46 to 1961–63 the life expectancy increased from 32 to 59 years for males and from 34 to 62 years for females. Although females generally have lower overall mortality, in some countries this does not apply at all ages. In a number of the developing countries female mortality is higher than male at ages 1–4 and in the peak childbearing ages.

Facts such as these are of interest for their own sake. But what is more important, they point to signs of change in particular populations. They indicate trends, differences or uniformities which assist in the long-term aim of extending the length of human life in all countries. They enable the areas of greatest concern to be more quickly pinpointed for further medical and scientific research, and better provision of public health facilities. There are many other reasons for the accurate measurement of mortality. For example, actuaries need death rates for the determination of premiums for life assurance and demographers require suitable mortality rates to carry out population projections.

---

* *Year Book*, *Australia*, No. 63, 1979, Australian Bureau of Statistics.
  Australian Demographic Statistics Quarterly, December 1979 and March 1980, Australian Bureau of Statistics.
  Deaths, *Australia*, 1978, Australian Bureau of Statistics.

5.2 Cause of death studies

One of the most important tabulations and one which is presented by most countries which publish death statistics, is the tabulation for each age-sex group of deaths by cause of death. The cause of death used for statistical purposes is of necessity a statistical concept since the death certificate from which the information is obtained is required to state the primary, secondary and even other causes of death, but only one is usually used for statistical purposes. Most countries use a standard international set of rules by means of which one cause of death is selected even though death may have resulted from a combination of causes. The aim is to encourage uniformity and assist in making international comparisons. To assist further in this aim the World Health Organization publishes a *Manual of the International Statistical Classification of Diseases, Injuries, and Causes of Death*, commonly known as the ICD. For simplicity and brevity the complete list is often abbreviated to a list of 50 major groups of causes of death. These lists are revised regularly, the ninth and most recent revision was published in 1977.

Care must be exercised in making comparisons of death rates between countries and particularly comparisons of death rates at different times. Changes in the trend of death rates from a particular cause may have been brought about by a change in the rules for obtaining the single cause of death required for statistical purposes. Changes in the trend may also be due to improvements in diagnostic aids and in increases in medical knowledge. For example, the development of radiology has facilitated the detection of gastric and duodenal ulcers and much of the increased mortality from this cause is probably merely the result of better diagnosis. Differences also occur between countries and over time in certification procedures and medical customs and in the quality and accuracy of the basic data and these too may have affected the death rates being studied.

5.3 Death rates and ratios specific for cause

If the total deaths during a particular period are subdivided by cause, then the proportions of the total deaths which are due to specific causes are called cause specific death ratios. For example, in Australia in 1973 there were 110,822 deaths in total and of these 2,616 were classified as being due to pneumonia. The cause specific death ratio for pneumonia therefore was 2,616/110,822 = .024. These ratios thus give an indication of the relative incidence of a specific cause of death in a particular country. Despite the qualifications given in section 5.2 the cause specific death ratios for different countries in the early 1970's presented in *Table 5.1* give some indication of the existence of different disease patterns.

It is the more common practice however to calculate cause specific death rates. Here the number of deaths from the particular cause during the year is divided by the total population at the middle of the year and the rate so obtained is generally expressed per 100,000 population. For example, in Australia in 1973 there were 2,616 deaths from penumonia and the estimated mid-year population was 13,131,600 giving a cause specific death rate for pneumonia of 2,616/13,131,600 = .000199 or 19.9 deaths per 100,000 population. The denominator used for these rates is of necessity the total population and not merely the population of persons suffering from the particular disease. This latter figure might be regarded as a more reasonable estimate of the exposed to risk population but it is not available. Cause specific death rates per 100,000 population for selected countries in selected years are given in *Table 5.2*. Significant differences do exist but again care should be taken in interpreting the figures.

An analysis of cause specific death rates and cause specific death ratios shows clearly that falls in mortality have been basically due to decreases in the number and proportion of deaths from infectious and parasitic diseases. The proportion of deaths due to cancer and to circulatory and other degenerative diseases has consequently increased.

It should be noted in passing that the cause specific death rate and cause specific death ratio usually do not take age and/or sex into consideration. Thus male and female deaths are combined as are deaths of young adults and deaths of old persons. Although two

Table 5.1

Cause specific death ratios for selected countries

Country	Cause of death				
	Accidents	Heart disease	Neoplasms	Pneumonia	Tuberculosis
Australia (1973)	.061	.359	.177	.024	.001
U.S.A. (1974)	.054	.385	.189	.027	.002
England and Wales (1973)	.028	.333	.206	.080	.002
Singapore (1974)	.047	.172	.171	.083	.040
Angola (1972)	.096	.037	.033	.103	.023
Mexico (1973)	.049	.093	.046	.131	.019

(*Source: United Nations' Demographic Year Book,* 1975)

Table 5.2

Cause specific death rates for selected countries

Country	Cause of death					
	Accidents	Heart disease	Neoplasms	Pneumonia	Tuberculosis	All causes
Australia (1973)	51.9	302.6	149.3	19.9	1.0	843.9
U.S.A. (1974)	49.5	352.4	172.9	24.9	1.7	915.1
England and Wales (1973)	33.9	397.7	246.7	95.1	2.7	1194.7
Singapore (1974)	25.0	90.8	90.2	43.7	21.3	526.8
Angola (1972)	25.0	9.5	8.5	26.7	6.0	260.1
Mexico (1973)	40.4	76.3	37.4	107.4	15.8	817.1

(*Source: United Nations' Demographic Year Book,* 1975)

cause specific death rates may be equal, from an economic point of view one may be much more important than the other because the former affects mainly young lives. The effect of ignoring the age-sex distribution of the population can be seen by comparing, in *Table 5.2*, the death rates from all causes for Singapore (527 per 100,000) and England and Wales (1,195 per 100,000). On an age specific basis death rates in Singapore are the higher but because of its younger population it has a lower rate if age is ignored.

5.4 Death rates by age and sex

Specific causes of death do not strike both males and females and all age groups with the same intensity. Extreme examples are congenital malformations which seriously affect mortality rates in only the very youngest age groups, heart disease which has little effect in the younger ages but is a major cause of death in the older age groups and complications of pregnancy and childbirth to which, obviously, only women are exposed. Sufficient differences do exist to make it desirable to calculate both cause specific death rates and 'all causes' death rates specific for age and sex.

For all causes combined, female mortality in infancy and throughout life in most countries is lower than male mortality, and the difference is becoming more marked. The exception is in certain developing countries such as Bangladesh, India, Pakistan and Sri Lanka where there is still very high female mortality around the childbearing ages. With respect to age, mortality rates start at a high level at birth, fall rapidly to a minimum at about age 10 and thereafter increase throughout life, except in the case of developed countries where a short peak occurs around age 19 due to high accident mortality, and in the case of some developing nations where a short peak occurs in the female mortality curve around the peak childbearing ages due to high mortality at childbirth.

The magnitude of these differences makes it essential to calculate death rates separately by sex and by age groups. These rates are called age-sex specific death rates. By thus separating the population into sex and age groups a table of rates is obtained for each sex and age which is unaffected by the age-sex distribution of the population. This problem is considered in more detail in section 5.9. The age-sex specific mortality rates for Australia (1975) and West Malaysia (1975) are shown on an arithmetic scale in *Figure 5.1(a)* and on a logarithmic scale in *Figure 5.1(b)*.

5.5 Other factors affecting mortality

Mortality varies quite substantially with age and sex making it essential to obtain death rates specific for age and sex. It may, however, be desirable to obtain rates specific for other factors as well because of the considerable differences in mortality which appear to result from them. Race and occupation are two such factors.

Generally death rates for white races are lower than for black races, while the rates for yellow races are intermediate. These differences apply whether between countries or between different races in the same country. However this probably reflects social, economic and environmental factors rather than biological or genetic differences.

In the 19th century significant differences in mortality existed between occupations. In general mortality was lowest for the professional classes and highest for unskilled labourers. In today's improved industrial environment these differences have been virtually elimi-

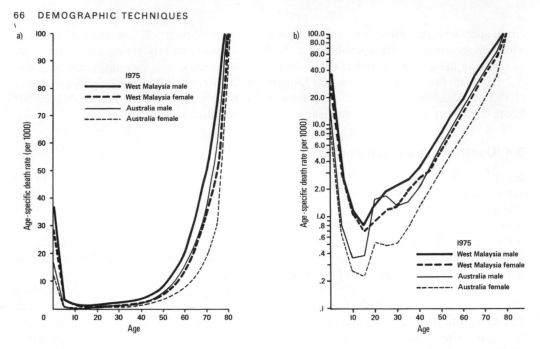

Figure 5.1: Age and sex specific death rates for Australia (1975) and West Malaysia (1975).

nated. Nevertheless, there are still certain occupations with higher death risks, e.g. dogmen, miners, car racers, pilots and professional boxers.

The analysis of occupational mortality is complicated by the difficulty in relating deaths to the correct exposed to risk population. Transfers to other occupations frequently take place after serious illness or impairment but before death. For this reason wicker basket workers are reported to be a group with about the highest mortality. This is due to the fact that this is an occupation frequently given to persons during rehabilitation from serious illness (e.g. strokes or injury).

Also, what appear to be occupational mortality differences are often the result of different living conditions rather than the direct effect of the occupation. This is usually established by considering the mortality of wives. If the latter is also high then we assume the extra mortality is due to poorer living conditions. If the latter is near to 'normal' then we assume the higher male mortality is due to the special occupational risk.

Mortality differences do occur with other factors but these are generally of minor significance compared with age, sex and possibly race. Included in this category are marital status, place of residence, manner of living and genetic differences. A full discussion of the effect of these factors on mortality is not appropriate in a textbook on demographic techniques but a brief reference needs to be made to them as such knowledge may be necessary for a critical analysis of demographic data or for planning a mortality study.*

*For further reference see, for example, United Nations, *The Determinants and Consequences of Population Trends*, 1974.

Some brief notes follow:

(i) *Marital status*

Married persons generally have lower mortality than unmarried persons, the difference being greater for men than for women. This is partly due to the fact that there is selection in favour of healthy persons at marriage and partly due to differences in habits and living conditions.

(ii) *Place of residence*

Rural mortality has generally been less than urban, but the differences are now small. Some diseases thrive in hot climates others in cold so that climatic variations may be expected. For this reason also, with the same place of residence, seasonal fluctuations in mortality occur.

(iii) *Manner of living*

In general the healthier the social conditions, as measured by quality of housing, sanitation, medical facilities, etc., the lower the death rate. The general habits of life, including smoking, eating and drinking also affect mortality.

(iv) *Genetic factors*

A few diseases do have a genetic mode of transmission from one generation to another and so there is some justification for expecting longevity to run in families. However, the number of these diseases is small and their effect on mortality uncertain so that heredity differences are now considered to be comparatively unimportant.

5.6 Infant mortality

Infant mortality could be measured by dividing the number of deaths under age 1 during the year by the estimated mid-year population aged under 1. However the mid-year population is only available in a census year and in other years has to be estimated from the number of births which have occurred. It is customary therefore to relate the number of deaths of persons under age 1 during a year to the number of live births which occurred during the year as this latter figure is readily available and is a reasonable estimate of the exposed to risk population.

Thus the infant mortality rate is defined as the number of deaths of infants under 1 year of age registered in a given year per 1,000 live births registered in the same year. It should be pointed out that this definition is adopted although the correct exposed to risk population includes some births in this year and some from the preceding year. The infant mortality rate deserves special consideration because it is in this rate that the greatest improvement in mortality has taken place, mainly through public health measures and medical discoveries. John Graunt in 1662 observed that the infant mortality rate in Great Britain was of the order of 300 deaths per 1,000 live births. By 1901 this rate had been reduced to 151 deaths per 1,000 live births. In 1971 there were 18 deaths per 1,000 live births. In Australia the infant mortality rate dropped from 104 in 1901 to 12 deaths per 1,000 live births in 1978. The range in current levels of infant mortality in the world is quite large and varies from about 8 per 1,000 live births in Sweden to over 100 in many of the developing countries.

The causes of infant deaths can generally be separated into two broad groups. Endogenous deaths or deaths due to the circumstances of the confinement or to pre-natal conditions resulting in disabilities existing at birth such as congenital malformations, birth injuries and prematurity, generally bring about death within the first four weeks of life. The term neonatal mortality is used to describe mortality in this period. Exogenous causes such as infections and accidents then take over as the major causes of death. To describe mortality after four weeks but within the first year of life the term post-neonatal mortality is used. Australian figures for 1977 are given in *Table 5.3*. Each rate is calculated by dividing the number of deaths at each age in 1977 by the number of births during 1977 and multiplying by 1,000. The tremendous drop in infant mortality rates during this century has generally been due to reductions in post-neonatal mortality rather than in neonatal mortality. This has been brought about largely by the provision of better maternal and child health services, and consequently the infant mortality rate has been used as a fairly reliable index of social and public health conditions. It is now customary to consider also the early neonatal mortality rate, which is the number of deaths in the first week of life per 1,000 live births. Neonatal deaths combined with stillbirths (late foetal deaths of 28 or more weeks' gestation) constitute perinatal mortality. Mortality from all foetal deaths, miscarriages, and abortions and from stillbirths is also studied but the statistics are most unreliable.

Table 5.3

Infant mortality per 1,000 live births by sex, age and cause: Australia 1977

Causes of death	Sex	Age						Total infant mortality
		Neonatal			Post neonatal			
		under 1 day	1 day to under 1 week	1 week to under 4 weeks	4 weeks to under 3 months	3 to 6 months	6 months to 1 year	
Endogenous	M	5.43	2.41	.90	.56	.29	.25	9.84
	F	4.25	1.82	.93	.41	.28	.23	7.92
Exogenous	M	.20	.20	.50	1.18	1.27	.79	4.14
	F	.21	.22	.26	.64	.87	.75	2.94
Total	M	5.63	2.61	1.40	1.74	1.56	1.56	13.98
	F	4.46	2.04	1.18	1.05	1.05	1.16	10.86

(*Source:* Causes of Death, 1977. Commonwealth Bureau of Census and Statistics)

5.7 Maternal mortality

It is possible to obtain an age-cause specific rate of mortality where the cause of death is childbirth and complications of pregnancy. The exposed to risk population used in calculating such a rate would be the total number of women in the population at the given age. It is, however, possible to obtain an accurate figure for those exposed to risk for this is clearly the number of women having confinements during the year. This in turn is almost equal to the number of births. Hence maternal mortality is usually measured by means of the maternal mortality rate defined as the number of deaths of women during a given period due to childbirth and complications of pregnancy for every 100,000 births during that period. With improvements in the standard of ante-natal care and obstetrical skill and other advances in medical science, maternal mortality has fallen markedly particularly in the developed countries. In New Zealand, for example, in the 20 years following 1942, the maternal mortality rate fell from 253 per 100,000 births to 17 per 100,000. In the U.S.A. in 1968 the rate for non-white mothers was 64 per 100,000 births compared with 17 per 100,000 for white mothers. The maternal mortality rate has the advantage over the usual death rate from puerperal causes in that the former is related to the number of births and hence automatically makes adjustment for the lower risk when fertility falls.

5.8 Expected number of deaths

On many occasions it is necessary to compare the actual mortality experience of a particular population with that expected under some hypothesis. For example, a life insurance company may wish to compare the number of deaths of policyholders during a year with the number expected according to its premium formula. In another usual case the actual number of deaths in one section of the total population is compared with the number of deaths expected in that section if the mortality rates of the total population were to apply. This method is used to determine, for example, whether the mortality of one occupation is above or below the population average. If the age and sex distribution of the section being considered is similar to that of the whole population, crude death rates could be used to obtain the expected deaths. For example in the state of N.S.W. there were 41,803 deaths in 1968. The estimated N.S.W. population in mid-1968 was 4,381,416 and the crude death rate for Australia was 9.10 deaths per 1,000 population. On the basis of the Australian crude death rate N.S.W. would have expected 39,871 deaths. This is slightly less than the number which occurred, indicating that on this basis N.S.W. mortality was slightly higher than Australian mortality. However, the assumption of a similar age and sex distribution is only rarely satisfied and the above difference between the actual and 'expected' number of deaths could have been due to differences in the age-sex distributions of N.S.W. and Australia.

The Maori population in New Zealand has a considerably younger age distribution than the New Zealand population. Consequently in calculating the expected number of deaths in the Maori population on the assumption that the New Zealand death rates apply it is essential to apply these age specific death rates to the Maori population by age. The calculations are as follows:

Age	1966 New Zealand age specific death rates (per 1,000)	1966 Maori population	1966 Expected Maori deaths
0– 4	4.37	39,539	173
5–14	0.45	61,728	28
15–24	1.02	34,725	35
25–44	1.76	43,686	77
45–64	10.44	17,626	184
65 +	68.74	3,855	265
Total		201,159	762

Thus if the Maori population were to have experienced New Zealand age specific death rates the number of deaths during 1966 would have been 762. The actual number of deaths was 1,291 indicating that Maori mortality in 1966 was much higher than that of the total New Zealand population. The importance of taking the age distribution into account is illustrated by the fact that if age had been ignored and the crude death rate used a Maori mortality of 72% of that of the total New Zealand population would have been indicated.

The population of male Members of Parliament is another population whose age distribution is so different from that of the general population that it is essential to use age specific death rates to calculate the expected number of deaths. In this case the population size is so small that it may be desirable to consider the performance over a number of years. The population at risk must therefore be converted to person-years at risk at each age before applying the age specific death rates. The calculation, using data for Great Britain,* proceeds as follows:

Age at death	Total person-years at risk 1945–67	Age specific death rates (per 1,000)	Expected deaths
25–34	636	1.53	1.0
35–44	3,473	2.74	9.5
45–54	5,626	7.71	43.4
55–64	5,265	22.05	116.1
65–74	2,731	54.12	147.8
75–84	963	122.95	118.4
85 +	124	250.81	31.1
Total	18,818		467.3

Thus if Members of Parliament were to experience the age specific death rates of Great Britain, the expected number of deaths during the period 1945–67 would have been 467. The actual number of deaths was 296 indicating that the mortality of Members of Parliament was only about 63% of that of the British population.

5.9 Direct standardization

It is possible to compare the mortality of two populations by calculating for each population the death rates for each sex by age and comparing the corresponding rates. It is difficult to make a comparison between such a mass of figures and usually in practice it is therefore desirable to have a single figure to express the relative mortalities. We obtained a single figure and made a quite straightforward statement about the mortality of male Members of Parliament in Great Britain in the last paragraph. We shall now consider such single figure measures of mortality.

The crude death rate introduced in Chapter 2 is the simplest single figure which may be used. This rate is really the weighted mean of the death rates at each age, the weights

*Pincherle, G., Mortality of Members of Parliament, *British Journal of Preventive and Social Medicine*, Vol. 23, 1969.

used being the numbers at each age in the population being studied. If two populations of quite different age distributions are being compared the weights used are quite different and this method could give very misleading results. For example in 1966 the crude death rate for Maoris was 6.37 per 1,000 persons while for non-Maoris it was 9.07 deaths per 1,000 persons. However, it can be seen from *Table 5.4* that although the crude death rate for Maoris was lower than for non-Maoris the age specific rates for Maoris were *higher* at all ages. The explanation for the anomaly is the considerably greater proportion of the Maori population at younger ages where death rates are low. It is clear that where the age structure of populations differs widely, the crude death rate is a most unreliable indicator of mortality differences. This same point was noted at the end of section 5.3.

In many mortality comparisons the age distribution of the population is similar and the above-mentioned defect is not serious. The crude death rate is widely used under such circumstances because of its ease of calculation. Quite often the population structure and the age specific death rates are not known, only the total population and total deaths being available, and in such cases there is no alternative to the use of the crude death rate. However if age specific death rates are known it seems more reasonable to use weights which are constant than weights which vary from one population to another. If the weights used are the numbers at each age or in each age group in some standard population the

Table 5.4

Direct standardization of death rates for age

Age	Standard population (N.Z. population 1966)	Maori		Non-Maori	
		Age specific death rates 1966	Expected deaths cols (2) × (3)	Age specific death rates 1966	Expected deaths cols (2) × (5)
(1)	(2)	(3)	(4)	(5)	(6)
0– 4	306,643	7.45	2,284	3.92	1,202
5–14	565,756	.91	515	.39	221
15–24	436,019	1.53	667	.98	427
25–44	640,711	3.52	2,255	1.63	1,044
45–64	504,697	20.92	10,558	10.04	5,067
65+	223,093	93.52	20,864	68.50	15,282
Total	2,676,919		37,143		23,243
Standardized death rate			13.88		8.68
Crude death rate (for comparison)			6.37		9.07

(*Source: New Zealand Year Book,* 1971)

resulting average rate is called the standardized death rate. It may be defined as the overall death rate that would have prevailed in a standard population if it had experienced at each age the death rates of the population being studied.

There is no uniquely correct standard population and each investigator is free to use his judgement in choosing an appropriate standard. The choice made may affect the results obtained but generally not significantly. The investigator is usually more concerned with the direction and approximate size of differences in mortality between different population groups than with an exact figure and these can be satisfactorily determined with any reasonable standard population. Thus for example in comparing mortality between urban and rural N.S.W. in 1950 a reasonable standard might be the population of N.S.W. in 1950, or at the nearest census or the corresponding figures for Australia. However it would be quite unreasonable to use (say) the population of Ethiopia in 1891 which is very far removed from the population under consideration both geographically and in time.

Consider again the death rates in *Table 5.4* of the Maori and non-Maori populations of New Zealand. The total New Zealand population can be taken as the standard population and when the death rates of the Maori and the non-Maori populations are applied to this standard population we obtain the number of deaths expected in the standard population if Maori and if non-Maori death rates prevailed. Thus if the 306,643 persons aged 0–4 in the standard population (column 2) experienced the Maori age specific death rate for this age group of 7.45 deaths per 1,000 persons (column 3), then we would expect 306,643 × .00745 or 2,284 deaths to occur (column 4). Similarly, if the 565,756 persons aged 5–14 in the standard population experienced a death rate of .91 deaths per 1,000 persons, then we would expect 515 deaths to occur. Repeating for all age groups and then adding, we see that 37,143 deaths would be expected to occur in the standard population if it experienced the same death rates as the Maori population. On the other hand if we repeat the process with the non-Maori death rates (column 5) we see that 23,243 deaths (column 6) would be expected to occur in the standard population.

When the expected number of deaths is divided by the total population in the standard population and multiplied by 1,000, standardized death rates are obtained. Thus the standardized death rates for Maoris and non-Maoris are respectively 13.88 and 8.68 deaths per 1,000 persons. These compare with crude death rates of respectively 6.37 and 9.07 deaths per 1,000 persons. At all ages the age specific death rates are higher for Maoris than for non-Maoris so that clearly the standardized death rates give a much more reliable indication of the difference in mortality between the two populations than do the crude death rates.

Since populations can vary in the sex ratio at each age it is desirable to standardize for sex as well. The procedure is exactly the same. In this case the standard population is given by age and sex and the death rates specific for age and sex also. The expected deaths for each sex and age group are calculated by multiplying the population of that sex and age group by the corresponding age and sex specific death rate. The total expected deaths is the sum of the expected deaths for all ages and both sexes. The standardized death rate is then the total expected deaths divided by the total standard population and multiplied by 1,000. This process extends to enable standardization to be carried out simultaneously for several variables. The only requirement is that there be available a standard population and the death rates of the population being studied both specific for each of the variables considered.

5.10 Indirect standardization

Whereas direct standardization consists essentially of applying different age specific rates to a standard population structure, an alternative is to apply a standard set of age specific rates to the populations being studied, comparing the actual number of deaths with the number expected on the assumption that these standard death rates applied. This is called indirect standardization. The calculation of the expected number of deaths is identical with the procedure described in section 5.8. It is particularly applicable when the age specific death rates for the population being studied are not known, but when the total number of deaths is known.

For example, consider again the comparison between Maori and non-Maori mortality. Assume that we do not know the age specific death rates for each population so that direct standardization is not possible. From the 1966 census we have the age distribution of the Maori and non-Maori population but all that is known about mortality is the total deaths for each population and it is desired to standardize for age effects. Take the New Zealand population as standard and assume that the age specific death rates for New Zealand are known.

The method of calculation of the indirect standardized death rate is given in *Table 5.5.*

Table 5.5

Indirect standardization of death rates for age

Age	Standard death rates (N.Z. death rates 1966)	Maori		Non-Maori	
		Population 1966	Expected deaths (2) × (3)	Population 1966	Expected deaths (2) × (5)
(1)	(2)	(3)	(4)	(5)	(6)
0– 4	4.37	39,539	173	267,104	1,167
5–14	0.45	61,728	28	504,028	227
15–24	1.02	34,725	35	401,294	409
25–44	1.76	43,686	77	597,025	1,051
45–64	10.44	17,626	184	487,071	5,085
65+	68.74	3,855	265	219,238	15,070
Total	(8.86)*	201,159	762	2,475,760	23,009
Total deaths actually registered		1,291			22,487
Standardized mortality ratio (SMR):					
$\dfrac{\text{Actual deaths}}{\text{Expected deaths}}$		1.694			.977
Indirect standardized death rate (SMR × CDR)		15.01			8.66

*Crude death rate (CDR)

(*Source: New Zealand Year Book,* 1971)

First the expected number of deaths in the Maori population are calculated assuming the death rates of the standard (New Zealand) population apply. These calculations are identical with those in section 5.8. The process is then repeated for the non-Maori population. It can be seen that in the Maori population on our assumption 762 deaths were expected but 1,291 actually occurred. In the non-Maori population 23,009 deaths were expected but in fact 22,487 occurred. Thus Maori mortality was above expectation and non-Maori mortality was below expectation. This is evident by calculating the standardized mortality ratio – the ratio of actual deaths to expected deaths – which is .977 for the non-Maoris and 1.694 for Maoris. When this ratio is multiplied by the crude death rate in the standard population the indirect standardized death rate for each population is obtained. These rates show fairly close agreement with the direct standardized death rates and both are a much better single figure index of the mortality of each population than the crude death rate.

5.11 Component analysis

A form of standardization which is becoming increasingly popular is the 'component analysis', first proposed by Kitagawa.* The procedure involves splitting the difference between two crude rates into components due to differences in age specific rates and due to differences in age composition. For illustrative purposes, let us decompose the difference between two crude death rates, M_1 and M_2, which may refer to two different populations or to one population at two points of time. Assuming that we are dealing with the same population at two points of time,

$$M_1 = \frac{\sum_{i=0}^{\omega} (r_{i1} \cdot n_{i1})}{\sum_{i=0}^{\omega} n_{i1}} \quad \text{and}$$

$$M_2 = \frac{\sum_{i=0}^{\omega} (r_{i2} \cdot n_{i2})}{\sum_{i=0}^{\omega} n_{i2}}$$

where n_{i1} and r_{i1} are respectively the number and death rate for persons aged i at time 1 and n_{i2} and r_{i2} are similarly defined for time 2. Let p_{i1} and p_{i2} be the proportions of the population aged i at times 1 and 2 respectively.

The difference $M_2 - M_1$ can be decomposed into the following:

(a) Component due to the effects of differences in age composition of the population during the time period 1 to 2

$$= \sum_{i=0}^{w} r_{i2}(p_{i1} - p_{i2})$$

*Kitagawa, E., Components of Difference Between Two Rates, *Journal of the American Statistical Association*, Vol. 50, 1955.

(b) Component due to the effect of differences in age specific death rates during the time period 1 to 2

$$= \sum_{i=0}^{\omega} p_{i2}(r_{i1} - r_{i2})$$

(c) Interaction/residual

$$= \sum_{i=0}^{\omega} (r_{i1} - r_{i2})(p_{i1} - p_{i2})$$

Similar expressions could be algebraically derived for decomposing the differences between other demographic parameters such as general fertility rates, total fertility rates, crude marriage rates, etc.

5.12 Generation mortality

Age specific mortality rates are usually calculated each year by dividing the deaths at each age during that calendar year by the estimated mid-year population at that age. In census years the population enumerated at the census is used and the derived values of q_x are the basis of the life tables which are constructed. In this way the most recent age specific mortality rates are obtained. However, each rate is based on the experience of a different group of people. The mortality now of persons aged 70 may be affected by diseases and environmental factors which were important many years ago but which will have little bearing on the mortality at age 70 of persons now aged 20. Yet in using life tables based on the values of q_x for a particular calendar year we are in effect assuming that each person will experience, as he passes through each age, the mortality experienced by the different groups of people during this particular calendar year. This method of studying mortality based on the results of many different groups of people in the one calendar year may produce misleading results if conditions are changing or if the particular year is abnormal. It may, therefore, be desirable to study a particular generation and to trace its mortality year by year from its year of birth to the present time. This is a true survivorship approach and is called the generation or cohort method and is very useful in studying mortality trends. Such studies are also called longitudinal studies.

A good example of the misleading conclusions which can result from the use of the calendar year method is the measurement of age specific mortality from tuberculosis. A glance at age specific death rates in the 1940's produces the unexpected result that the peak mortality rate is at ages over 60. In *Table 5.6* mortality rates are given for deaths from tuberculosis for various calendar years. In 1880 the peak was in the 20–29 age group and in subsequent years the peak occurred at higher and higher ages until in 1940 the peak was in the 60–69 age group. If, however, the age specific mortality is studied by reading the table diagonally downwards from left to right it can be seen that the peak in all cohorts is still in the 20–29 age group. The generation rates are given in *Table 5.6* by the diagonals parallel to the one marked for the generation aged 0–9 in 1880. The mortality from tuberculosis has fallen markedly in every year and in every age group and in this situation the calendar year approach has lead to the misleading conclusion that the peak mortality has moved to higher ages whereas in fact it has remained in the 20–29 age group.

Table 5.6

Age specific death rates per 100,000 from tuberculosis; males, Massachusetts, 1880–1940

Age	Year						
	1880	1890	1900	1910	1920	1930	1940
0– 9	803	627	340	230	132	52	13
10–19	126	115	90	63	49	21	4
20–29	444	361	288	207	149	81	35
30–39	378	368	296	253	164	115	51
40–49	364	256	253	253	175	118	86
50–59	366	325	267	252	171	127	92
60–69	475	346	304	246	172	95	109
70+	672	396	343	163	127	95	79

(*Source:* Merrell, M. Time-specific life tables contrasted with observed survivorship, *Biometrics,* Vol. 3, 1947). This is reprinted by permission of the Editor of *Biometrics*

5.13 Morbidity

While studying the morbidity (sickness) patterns in a community one has to distinguish between the prevalence and incidence of a disease. The former refers to the frequency of a disease in a population at a given moment in time, while the latter refers to the new cases of the disease diagnosed during a specified period of time. The subtle difference between these two concepts could also be explained by considering prevalence as equivalent to current balance in one's bank account while incidence corresponds to additions (deposits).

There is a significant relationship between prevalence and incidence, as is expressed below:

$$P_t \propto I_t \times d$$

where P_t is prevalence of a disease at the end of time period t, I_t is the incidence (new cases) of a disease diagnosed during time t, and d is the average duration of disease from its onset (usually measured from the time when the disease is positively diagnosed) to its termination resulting in cure or death.

Morbidity data may be collected at a census, by a survey of the population or as part of a registration procedure. The best known survey is the U.S. National Health Survey which has now been conducted continuously for twenty-five years. Reporting systems include the registration of certain notifiable diseases, workers' compensation records and the analysis of hospital or doctors' records.

For further reading

1. Benjamin, B., *Social and Economic Factors in Mortality*, 1965.
2. Benjamin, B. and Pollard, J. H., *The Analysis of Mortality and Other Actuarial Statistics*, Heinemann, 1980.
3. Dublin, L. I., Lotka, A. J. and Spiegelman, M., *Length of Life*, 1949.
4. Spiegelman, M., *Introduction to Demography*, Harvard, 1968.
5. United Nations, *The Determinants and Consequences of Population Trends*, 1974.

Exercises

5.1

N.Z. population, 1966 census			Age specific death rates per 10,000, for 1966			
Age	Males	Females	Maori males	Non-Maori males	Maori females	Non-Maori females
0– 4	156,954	149,689	82.4	45.2	66.4	33.0
5–14	289,314	276,442	10.1	4.7	8.1	3.1
15–24	222,720	213,299	22.5	14.4	8.0	4.9
25–44	327,752	312,959	36.3	20.0	34.2	12.4
45–64	251,646	253,051	217.4	131.4	200.2	69.9
65+	95,357	127,736	1041.4	822.8	814.4	583.0
Total	1,343,743	1,333,176				
Crude death rates			71.3	100.4	55.8	80.9

(a) Using the 1966 N.Z. male age distribution as the standard, calculate standardized death rates for male Maoris and non-Maoris.

(b) Using the 1966 N.Z. female age distribution as the standard, calculate standardized death rates for female Maoris and non-Maoris.

(c) Using the 1966 N.Z. age-sex distribution as the standard, calculate standardized death rates for Maoris and non-Maoris standardized for age and sex.

5.2 The population, deaths and death rates in a given year in two countries A and B (recorded in age groups) are as follows:

Country A			Country B		
Population	Deaths	Death rate	Population	Deaths	Death rate
100,000	1,000	.01	100,000	2,000	.02
80,000	1,600	.02	90,000	900	.01
60,000	1,800	.03	70,000	2,800	.04
40,000	2,000	.05	30,000	1,500	.05
20,000	2,000	.10	10,000	1,500	.15

Calculate the crude death rate for both countries. Then using Country A as the standard population
(i)   Calculate the standardized mortality ratio for Country B.
(ii) Calculate the standardized death rate for Country B.
(iii) Calculate the indirect standardized death rate for Country B.

5.3 From information in the United Nations Demographic Year Book calculate single figure indices to compare the female mortality in U.K., U.S.A. and N.Z. with that in Australia (taken as 100).

5.4 A life assurance company bases its adult premiums on the following average death rates:

Age group	Average death rate
20–under 30	.001
30–under 40	.0015
40–under 50	.004
50–under 60	.010
60–under 70	.025
70–under 80	.050
80 and over	.100

Its experience in the above age groups for the last three years was as follows:

1978		1979		1980	
Number of policy-holders	Deaths	Number of policy-holders	Deaths	Number of policy-holders	Deaths
26,742	28	28,959	35	30,269	42
35,689	52	37,742	58	41,956	65
53,294	226	55,924	235	58,729	275
37,594	392	39,629	426	42,825	502
35,842	824	39,245	952	44,329	1,062
20,629	1,010	23,942	1,305	26,942	1,502
8,526	924	10,694	1,264	11,685	1,364

Calculate single figure indices to measure its mortality experience for each of these years using 100 as the index for the mortality on which its premiums were based.

5.5 Age specific male death rates in the U.S.A. from cancer of the lung for the years 1949, 1954, 1959 and 1964 for various birth cohorts are shown in *Figure 5.2*. What can you deduce about the time trend in the mortality at any given age from this disease? Draw a graph showing the variation with age in the mortality rate from cancer of the lung obtained by the calendar year method for the year 1964. Compare the variation with age obtained by the calendar year method with that obtained by the generation method for ages over 70.

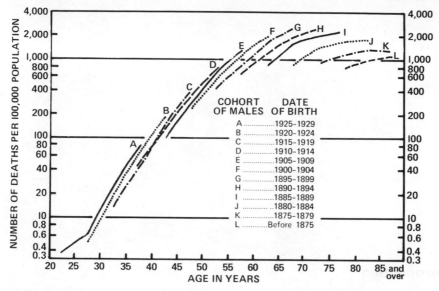

Figure 5.2: Age specific male death rates from cancer of the lung for U.S.A. for the years 1949, 1954, 1959 and 1964, for various birth cohorts.

(*Source:* U.S. Department of Health, Education and Welfare.
The health consequences of smoking, 1967)

6
Fertility

6.1 Introduction

Fertility is the term used in demography to indicate the actual number of children born alive. Contrary to popular usage it refers to actual reproductive performance not possible performance. The term *fecundity* is used to indicate the physiological ability to bear children and thus it is fecundity (not fertility) that is the direct opposite of *sterility*. Fertility is the measure of the reproductive performance of women as obtained from statistics of the number of live births.

The number of births occurring in any year in a population is determined partly by demographic factors such as the age and sex distribution, the number of married couples and their distribution by age, duration of marriage, and number of children already born. The number is also partly determined by many other factors related to the social and economic environment of that particular time, such as housing conditions, education, income, religion and current attitudes towards family size.

When studying fertility trends in a given country, or the differences in fertility between different countries, the demographer aims to determine the extent to which differences in the number of births have been caused by differences in these demographic factors and hence to deduce what differences remain to be explained by social and economic conditions. It is very difficult to isolate and measure the effect of each of these factors as they are so closely interrelated. Consequently the study of fertility involves the use of a number of methods of fertility measurement, each with advantages and disadvantages, each suitable under certain circumstances and unsuitable under others.

The purpose of this chapter is to introduce these various ways of measuring fertility. No single form of fertility measurement is suitable for all purposes and it is necessary to appreciate the merits and demerits of each method so that a realistic appraisal can be made of any figure quoted.

6.2 Family size from census data

While certain information of use in fertility studies is obtained from demographic surveys (e.g. intervals between births, attitudes to family planning, average family size of different socioeconomic groups) the two main sources of information concerning fertility are the population census and the birth registration system.

Some of the quite simple tabulations which are presented in the reports of the censuses of developed countries give a clear indication of the long-term trend of fertility over the previous half-century or more. The average number of children born to married women aged 45–49, 50–54, etc. at the census date indicates whether the average size of family has altered. The distribution of married women in each of these age groups according to number of children born indicates whether the changes which have taken place are due to a reduction in the proportion of large families or an increase in the proportion of childless families, etc. *Figures 6.1* and *6.2* present some graphs of data from censuses only which illustrate the fall over the years in family size in Australia and the substantial reduction in the proportion of large families.

Family data from censuses are not available for publication until many years after the date of the census and in any case give an indication of the level of fertility years before the census. For a study of current fertility it is necessary to turn to the annual birth registration data which are published within a shorter period after birth and which present schedules of births according to a wide range of characteristics of the parents. Ways in which this information may be used to measure fertility changes will be considered later in this chapter.

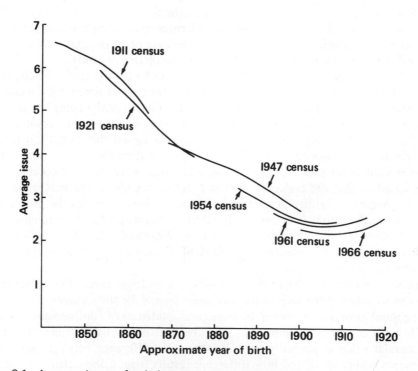

Figure 6.1: Average issue of existing marriages by approximate year of birth of mother for mothers over age 45.

(*Source:* Censuses of Australia, 1911–1966)

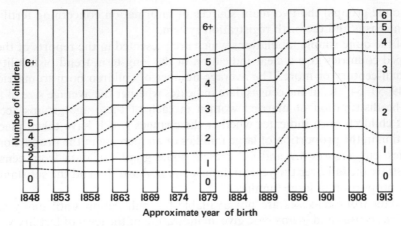

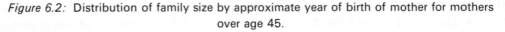

Figure 6.2: Distribution of family size by approximate year of birth of mother for mothers over age 45.

(*Source:* Censuses of Australia, various years)

6.3 Problems of fertility measurement

Fertility is a considerably more difficult characteristic to measure than mortality. Although birth rates are computed in the same way as death rates by dividing the number of events by the appropriate population exposed to risk, in the case of birth rates neither is uniquely defined and there are many problems which apply to birth rates only.

(i)   A birth rate normally refers to births over a particular time period. The choice usually settles down to two alternatives. One is to consider a short time period usually of one calendar year. The alternative is to measure fertility over the complete period of reproductive life. In effect this measures the number of births per person (or couple) by the end of their reproductive lives or what is called the completed family size.

(ii) A birth involves two parents so that it might be desirable to measure fertility by mother's characteristics, by father's characteristics or by the couple's characteristics. The statistics that are collected, however, relate mainly to the mother so that it is usual to measure fertility in relation to women. This eliminates the problems which occur when the father is unknown. In addition the shorter and more clearly defined reproductive period of females is often of arithmetical advantage. Nevertheless the procedures adopted in measuring fertility of women are applicable in every case to the fertility of men.

(iii) Roughly one confinement in eighty results in a multiple birth. This raises complications as to whether the unit of measurement should be the number of children born or the number of confinements. In some cases, statistics of confinements are collected but in most countries the emphasis is on the statistics of live births and hence this is the standard that is generally used. However the difference between births and confinements is very small and little difference results from using either approach.

(iv) The denominator of the birth rate, namely the population exposed to risk, is extremely difficult to measure. Parenthood is limited to only a selected portion of the population. The very young and the very old are easily excluded but not all those in between are exposed. Some are sterile. Others are single, widowed or divorced; this however does not completely remove them from the exposed to risk group. About 5% to 10% of births occur out of wedlock and the percentage in many countries has been increasing.

(v) The distinction between a live and a still birth is hard to classify consistently in many cases, and customs do vary between countries and between doctors.

(vi) Unlike death, parenthood is an event which can happen more than once. There is thus an element of choice. Consequently personal preferences and attitudes, which in turn depend on education and many other factors, have a strong influence on the number of children desired, and in these days of efficient family planning, on the number of children actually born. In mortality it can be assumed that most persons want to live as long as possible, but there is not much unanimity about the desired number of children or when they should be born. Yearly observations fluctuate much more widely in fertility than in mortality largely because it is possible to defer births temporarily and this may be desired in circumstances such as a downturn in economic activity.

6.4 Basic measures of fertility

In this section we consider some of the more basic measures of fertility. The crude birth rate, age specific fertility rates and child-woman ratios were introduced in Chapter 2 as examples of demographic rates and ratios. They are the most commonly quoted fertility measures and are reconsidered here to show their role in fertility measurement. The other measures considered in this section are the general fertility rate and the standardized birth rate.

(i) *Crude birth rate*

The crude birth rate, namely the number of births per 1,000 persons in the population is the simplest measure of fertility requiring only total births and total population. Only the most general judgments can be made from crude birth rates as these figures make no allowance for variations in the ratio of the sexes, differences in the age distribution, postponements or accelerations of marriage, etc., all of which can produce misleading results if only a crude rate is used. However, in many cases when the data are limited the crude birth rate is the only rate that is available.

(ii) *General fertility rate*

In cases where information is available on the age and sex distribution of the population, some improvement over the crude birth rate can be obtained by using the general fertility rate. This is the number of births per 1,000 women aged 15 to 44. This measure corrects to some extent the abnormalities in the crude birth rate due to an abnormal sex ratio in the population or an abnormal age distribution. This is a first step towards restricting the denominator of the rate to the correct numbers exposed to the risk of having a baby.

(iii) *Age specific fertility rates*

If, in addition to the female population by age, births are available according to age of mother then a schedule of age specific fertility rates may be obtained by dividing the number of births to mothers of each age (or age group) by the number of females of that age (or age group) in the population. The rates are usually expressed as births per 1,000 women of that age. When, as is usually the case, 5 year age groups are used, the age specific fertility rates form a relatively convenient set of six or seven rates (depending upon the assumed length of the reproductive life span), and hence this is now the most common way of indicating fertility. This method of measuring fertility eliminates one of the disadvantages of single figure indices by removing the distortions produced by variations in the age composition of the population. Misleading indications of fertility can however still result if age specific fertility rates are used at times when marriages are postponed or accelerated.

Figure 6.3 shows the age specific fertility rates for four selected countries in 1968. The rates are low in the 15–19 age group, rise to a peak in the 20–29 age group, and then decline to moderate levels in the 30–39 age group, and to low levels in the 40–49 age group. The pattern of age specific fertility rates is reasonably similar in different countries but the age specific fertility rates for the developing countries are generally above those for the developed countries for all age groups.

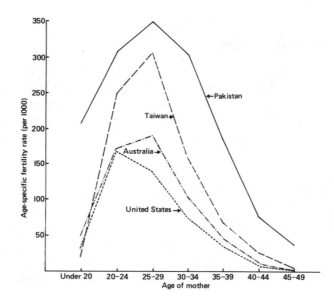

Figure 6.3: Age-specific fertility rates for Australia, United States and Taiwan in 1968 and Pakistan in 1965.

(*Source: United Nations' Demographic Year Book, 1970* and Yusuf, F. and Alam, I. Research Reports Nos 73 and 75, Pakistan Institute of Development Economics)

Age specific fertility rates are also calculated for certain subgroups of women, such as married women, ethnic women, working women and so on. *Figures 6.4* and *6.5* show the age specific fertility rates for married and unmarried women respectively in Australia during 1961 and 1966. Note the differences in the shape of the fertility schedules for married and unmarried women. An interesting point worth mentioning is that while the fertility of married women in Australia declined substantially during the 5 year period (1961–1966), that of unmarried women remained virtually constant.

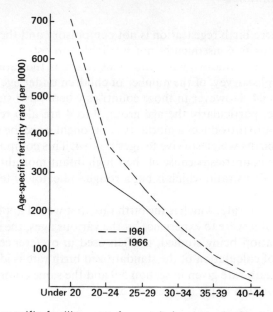

Figure 6.4: Age-specific fertility rates for married women in Australia, 1961 and 1966.

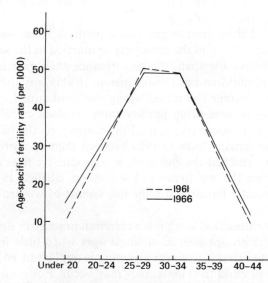

Figure 6.5: Age-specific fertility rates for unmarried women in Australia, 1961 and 1966.

(iv) *Child-woman ratio*

In populations where birth registration is not compulsory and the numerator of conventional birth rates is consequently not avaliable, an estimate of fertility can be obtained by use of the child-woman ratio. This figure is the ratio, usually obtained at a census or sample survey, of the number of children under age 5 to the number of females aged 15 to 44. However in those countries where birth statistics are lacking, census data by age, particularly the age group 0 to 4 are also relatively unreliable. Furthermore this ratio introduces a mortality component since the numerator depends on the number of births which survive to ages up to 4. This component is quite significant in developing countries because of their high infant mortality. Only limited use is therefore made of this ratio which is but a rough indicator of fertility levels.

(v) *Standardized birth rate*

The standardized birth rate, which is the birth rate that would apply to some standard female population if it were to experience, at the various ages, the age specific fertility rates of the population being studied, is often used in preference to the crude birth rate. The method of calculation of the standardized birth rate is identical with that of the standardized death rate given in section 5.9 and the same comments on the choice of a standard population apply (see section 5.9).

6.5 Generation versus calendar year approach

The various fertility measures can be applied in two distinct ways. It is possible to trace the same group of mothers year by year and record their fertility as they pass through each age. Alternatively we can study fertility by considering the fertility rates of mothers of all different ages during the one calendar year. *Table 6.1* gives the age specific fertility rates for Australia for each year in the period 1929–1970. We will illustrate the two ways in which these statistics could be analyzed.

The first method is called the cohort or generation method. Here, one group of women with common characteristics (born in the same year or married in the same year) is traced throughout their reproductive life span, the performance each year is recorded, giving finally the total number of children born to the group. In this way the 'mean number of children ever born' or 'the average completed family size' is obtained.

The generation method of measuring fertility rates involves calculating age specific fertility rates for single ages in successive years. For example, on the basis of these rates a group of 1,000 Australian females born in 1920 between them had produced 2,697 children by the time they had reached the end of their reproductive lives at age 50 in 1970. The diagonal starting from the top figure in the column labelled 1935 represents this particular cohort. Age specific fertility rates for this cohort of women have been underlined.

In order to reduce the arithmetical work it is a common practice in demographic studies to work with five year age groups instead of single ages when little inaccuracy is likely to result. It should be noted that if five year grouping is applied to both year of birth of mother and year of birth of child then inaccuracy may occur. For example, the cohort of women born in 1918–1922 spent the five years of life through ages 15–19 sometime in the ten year period 1933–1942. Most of this experience was concentrated in the middle of the period (say) 1935–1939. During this same period, 1933–1942, the cohort born in 1913–17 passed through ages 20–24, and so on.

Age specific fertility rates for Australia using the generation approach are given in the first part of *Table 6.2*. Rates in the triangle in the lower right hand side of the table are not yet available as these cohorts have not yet completed reproduction. One of the major defects of the generation approach is therefore obvious. The average completed family size is only available for those generations born up to about 1932. This method in 1980 (say) gives no indication of current fertility.

The second alternative mentioned above is the calendar year approach. Here the age specific fertility rates are calculated for mothers of different ages from births all of which occur in the same calendar year. These rates give an indication of current fertility levels. Age specific fertility rates for Australia using the calendar year approach are given in *Table 6.1* and in the lower panel of *Table 6.2*. If the fertility rates for mothers of different ages (and therefore of different cohorts) are added together to provide an indication of total fertility for a given calendar year misleading results can be obtained.

For example, if there is a trend towards younger childbirth without any change in final family size, total fertility obtained by summing the current year's rates for different women all of whom are now experiencing higher fertility assumes that they will, when they reach the higher ages, have the same fertility as the older women are now having. This is impossible if final family size is unchanged.

When considering age specific fertility by the calendar year approach it is never implied that women now aged 20–24 (say) will in 5 years' time experience the same fertility that women now aged 25–29 are experiencing. When age specific fertility rates by the calendar year method are added to obtain an estimate of the current level of fertility we are in fact considering a hypothetical situation.

Both approaches to fertility measurement are used. Each measures a different aspect of fertility. In *Table 6.2* where cohort and calendar year fertility rates for Australia are given, the figures are five year averages of single-year age specific fertility rates for the same group of women. It can be seen that the row of age specific fertility rates for the generation of women born in 1918–22 is identical with the downwards diagonal under the calendar year approach of women beginning with those aged 15–19 in 1935–39. Similarly the bottom row of age specific fertility rates for 1965–69 under the calendar year approach is identical with the lowest upwards diagonal of the age specific fertility rates under the generation approach.

6.6 Reproductivity formulae

Sometimes an indication of reproductivity rather than fertility is required. In this case we are endeavouring to measure the extent to which a population is replacing itself by births. This can be achieved by considering the number of daughters available to replace their mothers or the number of sons available to replace their fathers. Before introducing the usual reproductivity formulae we shall refer to the total fertility rate (TFR). It is not a reproductivity index but is a fertility measure since it considers children to mothers instead of daughters to mothers. It is mentioned in this section because of its close connection with reproductivity formulae.

Table 6.1

Age-specific fertility rates for Australia for the period 1929–1970

Age (years)	1929	1930	1931	1932	1933	1934	1935	1936	1937	1938	1939	1940	1941	1942	1943	1944	1945	1946	1947	1948	1949
15	3	2	2	2	2	2	2	2	2	1	2	1	2	2	1	1	2	1	2	2	2
16	9	9	8	8	7	7	6	7	7	6	6	6	5	6	6	6	6	6	7	8	7
17	25	23	21	19	19	18	19	18	19	18	18	16	17	16	18	16	16	18	21	22	25
18	45	46	41	40	38	37	35	39	38	38	37	35	37	36	34	32	34	37	46	48	51
19	69	71	64	60	58	56	58	59	62	60	60	57	60	59	62	56	59	66	78	83	85
20	89	87	82	74	73	70	73	76	75	78	77	80	82	83	89	83	86	95	111	113	118
21	109	108	101	92	91	89	88	91	96	94	99	98	108	107	117	108	115	130	147	145	149
22	129	125	116	106	105	103	106	107	111	113	113	117	128	132	142	135	138	158	176	170	177
23	141	138	124	115	113	112	114	118	123	123	127	130	143	144	156	150	158	182	197	188	191
24	149	146	134	120	119	119	120	127	129	131	133	138	148	149	164	158	164	189	199	197	199
25	151	147	133	123	122	121	124	130	135	133	136	140	151	150	166	163	170	190	201	195	198
26	149	150	139	127	125	122	128	131	134	135	136	138	149	151	164	162	172	196	195	187	191
27	145	143	132	124	125	123	122	128	134	133	135	139	147	144	155	159	165	184	186	179	179
28	151	142	127	123	124	122	123	127	131	132	135	136	139	142	152	157	160	178	183	174	171
29	145	143	121	113	121	115	119	120	119	122	127	131	130	132	142	147	154	167	165	162	164
30	133	136	124	107	108	107	111	114	117	118	117	124	128	121	134	140	144	155	155	154	149
31	118	110	114	103	93	93	97	99	103	104	103	106	112	111	119	128	129	139	138	133	133
32	116	115	104	105	105	90	94	100	98	101	99	100	105	107	117	122	126	135	130	127	122
33	103	103	92	85	92	90	82	86	91	88	88	89	93	94	108	115	114	119	120	112	111
34	102	95	87	81	82	86	86	77	78	82	82	81	84	86	94	105	110	108	107	100	97
35	89	93	82	76	76	71	78	79	69	69	73	74	77	78	80	95	98	102	97	92	89
36	85	84	75	70	66	64	61	72	70	60	63	66	65	68	75	81	86	91	86	80	77
37	72	75	65	62	61	58	53	54	62	59	52	54	57	59	63	71	75	76	74	69	63
38	74	67	63	59	56	54	51	53	49	52	51	46	49	51	55	64	65	68	64	62	60
39	64	59	53	48	47	45	42	43	43	41	44	42	40	43	47	51	53	53	52	50	50
40	51	50	44	39	40	39	36	35	34	33	34	33	36	31	35	40	40	44	41	39	36
41	38	35	34	31	28	28	25	26	24	25	23	23	24	26	24	26	31	32	30	28	26
42	32	32	28	28	24	25	23	22	22	20	18	20	17	21	21	21	22	23	21	22	21
43	21	21	19	18	17	17	15	16	14	14	13	12	12	12	14	15	15	15	15	13	13
44	15	13	13	11	12	11	10	10	9	9	8	8	8	7	7	9	10	8	9	8	9
45	8	7	8	7	6	6	6	6	5	5	5	5	4	4	5	4	5	6	5	5	4
46	4	4	3	4	3	3	3	3	3	3	3	2	2	3	2	2	2	3	3	2	2
47	2	2	2	2	2	1	1	2	1	1	1	1	1	1	1	1	1	1	1	1	1
48	1	1	1	1	1	1	1	1	1	0	1	0	0	0	0	0	0	1	0	0	0
49	0	0	0	0	0	0	0	0	0	0	0	0	0	0	0	0	0	0	0	0	0

Table 6.1 (continued)

Age (years)	1950	1951	1952	1953	1954	1955	1956	1957	1958	1959	1960	1961	1962	1963	1964	1965	1966	1967	1968	1969	1970
15	2	2	2	2	2	2	3	2	3	3	3	3	4	4	4	4	4	4	4	4	5
16	9	10	10	10	9	10	11	12	12	14	12	15	15	16	17	17	17	18	17	17	19
17	26	28	30	29	29	32	33	34	33	36	37	39	38	43	40	44	45	43	45	44	47
18	55	57	60	60	62	63	65	68	71	70	71	77	71	74	78	71	76	75	75	75	78
19	86	96	98	99	100	106	107	112	111	115	112	115	117	107	106	106	98	103	104	104	105
20	119	126	141	142	143	145	150	154	154	157	158	160	154	152	135	129	130	123	130	129	125
21	157	159	171	181	180	191	193	198	197	199	201	208	195	185	176	153	153	157	151	154	152
22	184	187	198	202	209	218	225	234	232	234	235	243	235	221	197	197	175	177	186	171	176
23	200	204	215	217	222	235	241	253	249	251	252	260	247	247	222	210	207	198	202	207	190
24	203	205	216	222	224	234	246	248	253	259	258	261	256	241	235	220	210	216	213	211	212
25	202	202	217	218	220	229	229	247	244	248	252	257	244	240	223	219	215	212	223	211	210
26	201	199	207	209	209	218	222	226	233	233	237	239	235	227	215	203	204	203	207	210	204
27	186	189	191	194	198	201	203	213	213	218	220	223	216	213	198	191	184	192	192	189	195
28	179	174	182	179	184	185	192	197	199	200	199	202	201	195	185	173	168	167	178	175	171
29	162	163	167	168	163	169	171	177	181	179	178	183	185	177	167	155	146	148	151	156	152
30	155	150	154	153	156	153	154	164	163	163	166	168	162	162	150	141	136	131	135	134	138
31	132	135	136	135	129	132	134	138	137	138	141	146	142	136	129	121	113	111	112	113	110
32	125	120	126	123	121	122	125	126	125	128	126	130	131	123	124	111	104	102	101	101	96
33	110	110	110	111	105	106	109	110	110	107	111	113	111	109	105	97	92	90	87	85	82
34	100	97	100	97	97	98	95	99	99	95	96	100	96	95	92	83	80	77	78	74	72
35	89	86	88	88	86	87	83	85	85	86	85	84	85	80	79	71	70	67	67	65	61
36	78	75	75	76	75	73	75	74	74	72	73	73	72	71	69	64	60	56	55	53	52
37	68	63	66	65	63	62	63	64	62	62	60	65	60	58	58	53	49	48	46	43	42
38	58	55	57	55	55	56	54	54	55	52	51	52	51	49	48	43	41	39	39	36	37
39	48	45	46	44	45	43	43	44	42	44	43	43	41	41	39	35	33	31	30	30	29
40	38	37	35	36	34	36	34	35	32	32	34	33	31	33	29	27	24	24	24	22	21
41	27	26	25	24	25	24	25	25	24	24	23	24	23	22	21	20	18	17	16	15	15
42	20	20	21	19	19	20	19	18	19	18	17	18	18	18	16	15	14	13	12	11	11
43	14	13	12	13	13	13	13	13	13	12	11	12	11	11	10	9	9	9	8	8	7
44	8	8	7	7	7	7	8	7	7	7	6	7	6	7	6	5	5	5	5	4	4
45	5	4	5	4	4	4	4	4	4	4	3	4	3	3	3	3	3	3	3	3	2
46	2	2	2	2	2	2	2	2	2	2	2	2	2	2	2	1	1	1	1	1	1
47	1	1	1	1	1	1	1	1	1	1	1	1	1	1	1	1	1	1	1	1	0
48	0	0	0	0	0	0	0	0	0	0	0	0	0	0	0	0	0	0	0	0	0
49	0	0	0	0	0	0	0	0	0	0	0	0	0	0	0	0	0	0	0	0	0

Table 6.2

Age specific fertility rates, average completed family size and total fertility rate

Generation approach

Approximate year of birth of mother	Age specific fertility rates at each age in the age group							Average completed family size
	15–19	20–24	25–29	30–34	35–39	40–44	45–49	
1903–07	26	127	128	97	62	23	2	2.325
1908–12	29	106	129	109	74	21	1	2.345
1913–17	26	106	147	126	66	19	1	2.455
1918–22	25	123	179	124	64	18	1	2.670
1923–27	24	156	190	125	61	14	1	2.855
1928–32	30	186	208	125	49	10	0	3.040
1933–37	39	213	213	105	38	5		
1938–42	44	212	188	93	24			
1943–47	45	174	179	74				
1948–52	48	166	147					

Calendar year approach

Calendar years of birth	Age specific fertility rates at each age in the age group							Total fertility rate
	15–19	20–24	25–29	30–34	35–39	40–44	45–49	
1920–24	26	134	168	138	98	41	4	3,045
1925–29	29	127	156	123	86	35	4	2,800
1930–34	26	106	128	100	65	27	3	2,275
1935–39	25	106	129	97	58	21	2	2,190
1940–44	24	123	147	109	62	20	2	2,435
1945–49	30	156	179	126	74	23	2	2,950
1950–54	39	186	190	124	66	21	2	3,140
1955–59	44	213	208	125	64	19	1	3,370
1960–64	45	212	213	125	61	18	1	3,375
1965–69	48	174	188	105	49	14	1	2,895
1970–74	51	166	179	93	38	10	1	2,690
1975–79	33	123	147	74	24	5	0	2,030

(i)   *Total fertility rate*

Despite the relatively convenient form of age specific fertility rates when expressed in five-year age groups, there are occasions when a single figure index is desirable. What is required is a convenient formula for combining the individual age specific rates.

The simplest of these is the total fertility rate (TFR) obtained by adding together the age specific fertility rates for women of each age. When 5-year age groups are employed the total must be multiplied by 5 since it is the sum of the rates at every individual age which is required. The total fertility rate thus represents the number of children that would be born (ignoring mortality) to a hypothetical group of 1,000 women who, as they pass through the reproductive ages, experience the particular age specific birth rates on which the index is based. Although the total fertility rate represents the same female population aged 15–49 as does the general fertility rate it is an improvement on the latter rate as it eliminates variations due to differences in the age distribution between 15 and 49. The total fertility rate can also be regarded as a standardized fertility rate where the standard population has the same number of women in each age group. The method of calculating the total fertility rate is illustrated in column 5 of *Table 6.3*.

The total fertility rate is in a sense analogous to the average completed family size concept in generation analysis in that it indicates, ignoring mortality, the average number of children produced by a hypothetical cohort of women experiencing the given age specific fertility rates.

(ii)   *Gross reproduction rate*

The gross reproduction rate (GRR) and the net reproduction rate (NRR) are the most commonly used reproductivity formulae. The GRR, which is simply the sum from ages 15 to 49 of the age specific fertility rates calculated for female births only, represents the average number of daughters which, ignoring mortality, will take the place of their mothers, assuming that the rates for the current year continue indefinitely. It is a measure of the average number of daughters produced by women during their complete lifetime. The calculation of the GRR is set out in column 6 of *Table 6.3*. The calculation of the GRR is similar to the calculation of the TFR but because the GRR is limited to one sex it is about half the size of the TFR. The TFR and the GRR are both obtained by adding age specific rates; in the case of the former it is age specific rates based on all children whereas the latter uses age specific rates for daughters only. Sometimes an approximation to the GRR is obtained by multiplying the TFR by the ratio of female births to total births. This makes the reasonable assumption of a constant sex ratio at birth for all ages of mother. The GRR is usually expressed as a rate per woman rather than a rate per 1,000 women. It may be expressed symbolically by the formula

$$\text{GRR} = \sum f_x$$

where f_x is the fertility rate at age x specific for sex (i.e. female births to females or male births to males) and the summation is over all ages in the reproductive life span.

(iii)   *Net reproduction rate*

The omission of mortality in the calculation of the GRR produces on overstatement of the reproductivity. A female born will only replace her mother provided she lives

Table 6.3

Calculation of age specific fertility rates, total fertility rate, gross reproduction rate
and net reproduction rate – Australia – 1961

Age group	Female births in 1961 to mothers in each age group	Total births in 1961 to mothers in each age group	Female population 1961 in each age group	Age specific birth rates per 1,000 women	Age specific birth rates daughters only	Probability of daughters surviving from birth to age group of mother	Expected survivors of female births per woman
(1)	(2)	(3)	(4)	1000 (3)/(4) (5)	(2)/(4) (6)	(7)	(7) × (6) (8)
15–19	9,015	18,670	394,119	47.37	.0229	.97417	.0223
20–24	36,956	75,651	335,924	225.20	.1100	.97131	.1068
25–29	33,785	69,048	313,611	220.17	.1077	.96827	.1043
30–34	22,383	46,193	351,825	131.30	.0636	.96438	.0613
35–39	11,377	23,559	372,637	63.22	.0305	.95866	.0292
40–44	3,131	6,409	334,594	19.15	.0094	.95000	.0089
45–49	226	456	321,900	1.42	.0007	.93642	.0007
Total	116,873	239,986		707.83	.3448		.3335
Multiply by 5 for single age figures				3,539	1.724		1.668
Total fertility rate (per 1,000 women) = 3,539							
Gross reproduction rate = 1.724							
Net reproduction rate = 1.668							

Note: Births to mothers under 15 have been included in age group 15–19, births to mothers
over 50 have been included in age group 45–49 and births to mothers whose ages
were not stated have been distributed proportionately.

to the age her mother was on the day that she was born. Consequently, it is desirable
to use a measure of reproductivity which makes some allowance for this mortality
element. The net reproduction rate (NRR) is such a measure. It is obtained by multiplying the age specific fertility rate (female only) at a given age by the chance of a
female child surviving from birth to the age group of mother and summing for all
ages of the mother.

The NRR may be expressed symbolically by the formula

$$\text{NRR} = \sum f_x l_{x+1/2}/l_0 \doteqdot \sum f_x L_x/l_0$$

where f_x is the fertility rate at age x specific for sex, $l_{x+1/2}/l_0$ is the probability of surviving from birth to age $x + \frac{1}{2}$ and the summation is over all ages in the reproductive life span.

The NRR is also expressed as births per woman rather than births per 1,000 women. In the case of five-year age groups, we calculate the probability that a female child will survive from birth to age $x + 2\frac{1}{2}$. This probability is

$$l_{x+2\frac{1}{2}}/l_0 \doteqdot L_{x+2}/l_0 \doteqdot (T_x - T_{x+5})/5l_0$$

The population will increase, remain stationary or decrease according to whether the net reproduction rate exceeds, equals or is less than unity.

Strictly speaking what we have described is the female NRR. A male NRR could be obtained in exactly the same way by using the corresponding male data throughout.

Neither the GRR nor the NRR allow for variations in marriage patterns. A more accurate measure would allow for variations in the proportions married by age and for fertility variation by duration of marriage. Both the gross and net reproduction rates therefore give misleading results if marriage conditions are abnormal.* A sudden temporary increase in marriages (e.g. after a war) would be followed, because of the high fertility in early marriage, by increased births and consequently a reproduction rate calculated from the age specific fertility rates obtained by the calendar year method would overstate reproductivity because it assumes that the abnormally high fertility rates will continue forever. It is indirectly assuming that the abnormal number of marriages taking place will continue every year forever, which is impossible. A fall in the number of marriages (e.g. during a depression) will produce the opposite effect.

(iv) *Replacement index*

The replacement index, of which there are several forms, is obtained by dividing the number of children in a given age group in the actual population by the number of women in the actual population who would have been in the reproductive age group when these children were born and then dividing this quotient by the corresponding quotient in the life table stationary population.

This index gives a very simple measure of reproductivity which can be used as an approximation to the net reproduction rate, when age specific fertility rates are not available. It requires only a knowledge of the population in age groups and a suitable life table.

A replacement index of one would indicate that the actual population had the same ratio of children to women as the stationary population. This corresponds to a net reproduction rate of one and the actual population is thus also stationary. A replacement index greater than one indicates a greater ratio of children to women in the actual population than in the stationary population and hence a net reproduction

*Pollard, A. H., The Measurement of Reproductivity, *Journal of the Institute of Actuaries*, Vol. 74, 1948.

rate greater than one and an increasing population. Similarly a replacement index less than one indicates a decreasing population.

The most common form of the replacement index is obtained by using in the above formula the children under age 5 and the females aged 15 to 44 (i.e. the child-woman ratio). If age groups ten years older are used, namely children 10–14 and women 25–54, then a replacement index for ten years earlier is obtained.

In developed countries the data necessary to produce the GRR and the NRR are generally available and as these rates are to be preferred the replacement index is not often used.

6.7 Rates of natural increase

The rate at which a population is increasing as a result of natural increase (i.e. an excess of births over deaths) is a matter of great national importance and measures of it need to be published. The crude rate of natural increase is defined as the difference between the crude birth rate and the crude death rate. This rate suffers all the disadvantages of the crude birth rate and of the crude death rate already discussed, in particular, problems associated with varying age distributions. It should be realized that as the rate of natural increase is the difference between two rates, it is possible for two countries to have equal rates of natural increase yet one may have high fertility and high mortality and the other low fertility and low mortality.

Some of the disadvantages of the crude rate of natural increase for comparing the population growth of two countries can be avoided by using the standardized rate of natural increase, which is the difference between the standardized birth rate and the standardized death rate. The standardized rate of natural increase however still depends on the age distribution of the standard population selected.

This problem was neatly overcome by Sharpe and Lotka when they proved that a population subject to a given age schedule of mortality and fertility will, no matter what its original age distribution, eventually approach a stable age distribution which they called the 'ultimate distribution' and will eventually increase at a fixed rate called the 'true or inherent or intrinsic rate of natural increase'. This rate depends entirely on the age specific mortality and fertility of the population for the year under consideration. It avoids the problems involved with abnormal age distributions and in the choice of a standard population and indicates the rate of population growth which will result if current mortality and fertility rates were to continue indefinitely. This inherent rate of increase reveals, by comparison, the misleading character of the observed rate of increase. The method of calculating the true rate of natural increase will be dealt with in section 7.5.

6.8 Fertility schedules

We have been dealing so far with the attempts which have been made to obtain single figure indices which measure fertility. In view of the many variables it is of course impossible to sum up fertility movements accurately in a single figure. Nevertheless single figure indices have the great merit of simplicity. The demographer must however be aware of their limitations in varying demographic circumstances. We shall now deal with more extensive statistical tabulations of fertility data. The full picture can only be seen by studying a number of these fertility schedules.

(i) *Age specific fertility schedules*

The rate of childbearing (i.e. fertility not fecundity) starts from zero at about age 15, rises to a peak in the late 20's, and then tapers off to zero again at about age 49. The actual peak age and the rate of decline after this peak vary from population to population and in any one population varies from time to time depending on marriage habits, incidence of sterility, the practice of family planning and other factors. However, most of the variation in fertility takes place in the level of this curve rather than in its general shape which remains fairly constant from population to population and from time to time. The variations with time can readily be seen by studying the age specific fertility rates in *Table 6.1*. This is the most commonly used fertility schedule.

(ii) *Duration of marriage specific fertility schedules*

All the measures of fertility so far introduced can give misleading results at a time when marriage rates are abnormal. If, for any reason, marriages are temporarily postponed, then because most fertility occurs early in marriage, a drop in the number of births occurs, followed by a compensating rise, provided the total fertility of marriage remains constant. Similarly, if marriages are temporarily accelerated a rise in the number of births occurs followed by a fall. It may be desirable to eliminate these short term fluctuations due to marriage by considering fertility of marriage instead of fertility of all women. In most countries of the world over 90% of births take place within wedlock and the remaining births can be treated separately.

One common fertility schedule is that of duration of marriage specific fertility rates showing the number of births to 1,000 women during the 0, 1, 2, ... years after marriage. This schedule is obtained by dividing the births to mothers of marriage duration x by the number of marriages x years earlier for values of $x = 0, 1, 2, \ldots$. This table, an example of which is *Table 6.4*, can be read two ways. When read vertically the figures represent the confinements to a given marriage cohort as it progressed from year to year. When read horizontally the figures represent the fertility for a fixed duration of marriage as we move from earlier cohorts to later ones. When single years are used on both scales the table can also be read diagonally upwards in which case the figures are fertility rates for successive marriage durations experienced during a given calendar year.

This schedule makes no allowance for age of mother and obviously the chance of having a child 10 years after marriage is very different if marriage occurs at 20 rather than at 30. Hence this schedule also has to be used with care in abnormal demographic conditions. In addition, particularly at the longer durations, figures may be affected by mortality changes and by migration.

(iii) *Marriage age and marriage duration specific fertility schedules*

The obvious development of the rates mentioned in the previous paragraph is to measure fertility according to age at marriage as well as marriage duration. The method of calculation is the same but applied to specific ages at marriage instead of all ages. The objection to this method is not only the large number of figures to be comprehended (each year requires a separate schedule) but the fact that data in this form cannot generally be obtained from the annual registration statistics which are published.

Table 6.4

Fertility by duration of marriage – Australia

(Number of confinements per 1,000 marriages at various durations)

Duration of marriage (years)	Year of marriage						
	1909–1910	1919–1920	1929–1930	1939–1940	1949–1950	1959–1960	1969–1970
Under 1	500	468	443	280	322	389	285
1	232	271	272	276	318	346	256
2	289	258	234	224	293	339	277
3	318	282	198	210	271	303	263
4	280	237	173	189	240	247	232
5	252	213	149	173	212	202	184
6	218	182	133	169	185	167	154
7	197	163	115	139	161	139	120
8	177	143	98	113	137	118	95
9	152	114	84	95	116	102	
10	140	98	74	85	102	86	
11	125	77	61	70	84	58	
12	108	65	54	59	71	47	
13	95	53	51	51	58	30	
14	77	45	49	41	45	20	
15–19	247	136	140	118	105	40	
20–24	64	34	36	30	17		
Total	3,471	2,839	2,364	2,422	2,805		

(iv) *Parity specific fertility schedules*

With the development of family planning, attention has increasingly been focussed on the desired ultimate family size. Economic and social disturbances may defer births for a period but it is likely that the desired family size will eventually be achieved and that the population will tend towards a certain frequency distribution by size of family. The number of first, second, third, etc., births per 1,000 women aged 15–49 is sometimes quoted as shown in *Table 6.5*. Changes in fertility can then be determined as being due to changes in the relative number of low order births (also called low parity births) or changes in the frequency of large families.

It should be noted that these parity specific fertility rates make no allowance for marriage nor for the existing number of children. The denominator is simply the *total* number of women aged 15–49. If there are few mothers in the population with *x* children, few *x* + 1 children can be born. These rates are therefore as much a reflection of the existing population structure as an indication of current fertility.

Table 6.5

Parity specific fertility rates – Australia

Year	Nuptial births per 1,000 women aged 15–49 of order					
	1	2	3	4	5–9	10 and over
1920–24	26.4	20.1	13.6	9.3	17.3	1.7
1925–29	23.9	18.2	12.5	8.4	15.9	1.5
1930–34	20.0	15.3	9.8	6.4	11.8	1.1
1935–39	23.2	15.4	8.9	5.2	8.8	0.8
1940–44	27.6	19.1	10.3	5.4	7.6	0.6
1945–49	31.9	25.1	13.9	6.8	7.8	0.5
1950–54	30.2	26.7	16.7	8.4	7.7	0.5
1955–59	28.8	25.4	17.8	9.8	9.3	0.4
1960–64	27.7	23.6	16.9	9.8	9.9	0.4
1965–69	27.9	21.7	13.3	6.9	6.7	0.3
1970–74	28.9	23.9	12.3	6.4	4.3	0.2
1975–79	22.8	20.8	9.9	3.3	1.9	0.1

(v) *Marriage duration and parity specific fertility schedules*

For a number of countries, annual births are published according to parity and marriage duration. By tracing the cohort of marriages of a given year through year after year, we can determine (ignoring mortality and migration), by subtracting the number of first births year by year to this cohort, the number of married women of this marriage duration who still have no children. Using these figures as 'exposed', and the number of first births this year to this cohort, first birth rates by duration of marriage can be calculated. Second, third etc. births rates for each marriage duration cannot however be obtained in this way without making assumptions about the distributions of the interval between births.

The calculations are complex, mortality and migration have to be ignored, and approximations to reconcile year of marriage and marriage duration have to be made, and accordingly this approach, though theoretically possible, is seldom adopted.

(vi) *Parity progression ratio*

Parity progression ratio is the term used for the proportion of women of given parity (*x* children) who advance to the next parity (*x* + 1 children). Parity progression ratios cannot be obtained from the data generally published by official statisticians without making assumptions about the intervals between births. Hence they are seldom published.

6.9 Inconsistencies between male and female rates

One of the problems with birth data mentioned in section 6.3 was whether the male or the female data should be used. The GRR, NRR, the true rate of natural increase, etc. may be calculated from the data for either sex. For various reasons mentioned earlier female data are commonly used. Different results are obtained for the two sexes due to differences between males and females in the age distribution, in proportions married by age, in fertility by age, etc. The male sex usually gives appreciably higher values because the average length of a generation (difference in age between parent and child) is a couple of years greater for males. The concept of the male sex indefinitely replacing itself at a higher rate than the female sex is, of course, untenable. Some rate between the two is a necessary compromise. Several theoretical attempts have been made to reconcile this apparent conflict.

6.10 Differential fertility

Differential fertility is the name given to the study of fertility differences between specific population groups. Common analyses are by socio-economic group, by religion, by education level, by race, by occupation, by urban/rural region, by wife's work experience and by husband's income. Such analyses are carried out in order to throw light on the causes of reproductive behaviour, to interpret the changes which have taken place in the birth rate and as a guide to changes likely to take place in the future. If, for example, residents of urban areas or persons with higher education experience lower fertility, and if the proportions of the population in these classes are increasing, then this could be a factor causing the overall birth rate to fall.

Differences in the fertility of specific population groups arise mainly from three sources, namely, differences in the number of children which couples in the various population groups want, differences in their knowledge, attitude and practice of fertility control which enable them to obtain these desires, and differences due to the demographic characteristics of each population group.

In analyzing cultural differences in fertility one should examine the factors, the 'intermediate variables' of Davis and Blake,* through which cultural conditions can affect fertility. These include age at entry into sexual unions, proportion of women never entering sexual unions, periods of abstinence (voluntary or involuntary), fecundity or infecundity, use of contraception, foetal mortality, etc.

Some of the earliest studies of differential fertility were carried out in the United Kingdom associated with population censuses. Fertility differences by religion and work status of woman have been noted in many studies conducted in the United States and other countries. Most of the differential fertility studies are based on sample demographic surveys. Since 1973 the World Fertility Survey, which is a project of the International Statistical Institute in collaboration with the International Union for the Scientific Study of Population, has been collecting valuable fertility data on a comparable basis for many countries of the world.

---

*Davis, K. and Blake, J., Social Structure and Fertility: an Analytic Framework, *Economic Development and Cultural Changes*, Vol. 4, 1955.

For further reading

1. Pollard, A. H. and Pollard, G. N., Fertility in Australia. *Transactions of the Institute of Actuaries of Australia and New Zealand*, Vol. 17, 1966.
2. United Nations, Recent Trends in Fertility in Industrialized Countries. *Population Studies*, No. 27, 1958.
3. United Nations, *Population Bulletin*, No. 7, 1965.
4. United Nations, *Determinants and Consequences of Population Trends*, 1974.
5. Yusuf, F. and Eckstein G., Fertility of Migrant Women in Australia, *Journal of Biosocial Science*, Vol. 12, 1980.

Exercises

6.1   It is possible for one population to have a higher gross reproduction rate than another population and yet for it to have a lower crude birth rate and a lower rate of increase. Explain how this can happen.

6.2   From the population and births listed respectively in the latest *Yearbook Australia* or *Births, Australia* and using the most recent Australian Life Table, calculate for that year:
   (i)   the age specific fertility rates
   (ii) the total fertility rate
   (iii) the gross reproduction rate
   (iv) the net reproduction rate
   (v)   the replacement index.
   Using five-year age groups 15–19, 20–24, etc., make the calculations both for males and for females and compare the results. (The corresponding data for another country may be used if they are more readily available.)

6.3   Calculate the ratio of illegitimate births to total births for the years 1950, 1955, 1960, 1965, 1970, 1975, 1980, for any country for which data are available. Repeat these calculations for mothers aged 15–19 and 20–24, and comment on the results.

6.4   For the latest year for which data are available, calculate for Australia the probability that a confinement results in a multiple birth. Repeat the calculation for ages of mother 15–19, 20–24, 25–29, 30–34, 35–39, 40–44, 45–49, and comment on the results.

6.5   For the latest year for which Australian data are available calculate the sex ratio at birth. Then compare the sex ratio at birth
   (i)   for various age groups of mother
   (ii) for legitimate and illegitimate births
   (iii) for single and multiple births
   (iv) for first and subsequent births
   and point out what you consider to be significant differences.

6.6   Using the Australian population in age groups as at the 1961 census and the 1960–62 Life Tables, calculate the replacement index for earlier years.

6.7   For a certain animal population the values of q_x (for females) and f_x (age specific fertility rates for females born to females) were as follows:

x	q_x	f_x
0	.3	0
1	.1	1
2	.2	2
3	.4	2
4	.7	1
5	1.0	0

Calculate
   (i) the gross reproduction rate
   (ii) the net reproduction rate.

6.8   From the U.N. Demographic Year Book, obtain the latest birth rates for some developing and some developed countries. In addition to the crude birth rate obtain some of the more refined birth rates mentioned in this chapter. Compare these rates with the corresponding rates five and ten years ago. Then use this information to write an essay on recent trends in fertility in developed and developing countries.

6.9 Comment on the following data. (You may make additional calculations if you wish.)

	Country				
	Ireland 1968	Great Britain 1967	U.S.A. 1967	Netherlands 1968	Poland 1968
Crude birth rate	21.0	17.2	17.8	18.6	16.2
General fertility rate	81.0	66.1	62.8	66.6	52.6
G.R.R.	1.91	1.28	1.26	1.33	1.08
N.R.R.	1.83	1.24	1.21	1.29	1.04
Age specific fertility rates					
15–19	6.7	25.3	32.6	10.8	14.8
20–24	135.2	165.4	174.0	139.3	163.8
25–29	221.1	164.9	142.6	190.5	128.3
30–34	197.0	92.0	79.3	114.2	74.0
35–39	133.9	43.4	38.5	55.0	38.9
40–44	48.4	11.3	10.6	16.5	12.3
45–49	4.1	0.8	0.7	1.5	1.3

6.10 In 1967 the crude birth rate for urban areas of Finland, namely 18.5 births per 1,000 females, was higher than that for rural areas, namely, 14.8 births per 1,000 females. Corresponding general fertility rates were 58.8 and 52.9. Using the following data calculate standardized general fertility rates for urban and rural Finland to see whether the different age structures have any effect.

Age	Estimated female population 1.7.67	1967 age specific fertility rate (per 1,000 women)	
		Urban	Rural
15–19	231,784	23.9	14.7
20–24	199,739	132.4	139.2
25–29	160,435	123.0	147.2
30–34	139,230	72.2	92.6
35–39	149,065	36.4	54.6
40–44	151,051	10.8	21.5
45–49	141,170	0.9	2.4

7
Stable populations and population models

7.1 Introduction

It was stated in Chapter 3 that the life table was probably the demographer's most useful tool. It was explained also in Chapter 4 how the life table can be used to solve a variety of problems concerning stationary populations. However, most human populations are not stationary. National populations, with which the demographer is frequently concerned, are almost always increasing populations. Some modification to the approach we have adopted so far is therefore required.

7.2 Stable populations

In 1911 Sharpe and Lotka proved what is probably the most important theorem in the mathematics of population, and yet one which at the same time has important practical uses.* The proof requires a knowledge of mathematics greater then that expected of the reader of this book, and so we will merely quote the result in words and without proof.

A closed population which experiences constant age specific fertility and mortality will, *no matter what its initial age distribution*, eventually develop a constant age distribution and will eventually increase in size at a constant rate. Any population with a constant age distribution and which is increasing at a constant rate is called a stable population. A stationary population is thus the special case of a stable population in which the rate of growth is zero and the age distribution is the life table L_x column. *Figure 7.1* shows, in the form of a series of population pyramids, the gradual development of the stable age distribution for two populations with completely different initial age distributions but subsequently experiencing constant age specific fertility and mortality rates. Initial 'gashes' in these pyramids, due probably to wars or periods of abnormally low births, gradually work their way up the pyramids until they disappear through the vertex. When these 'gashes' in the female pyramid pass through the reproductive ages a lowering of births will result producing a less pronounced 'gash' at ages about 30 years younger, but eventually these will all disappear and the stable age structure will be established.

*Sharpe, F. R. and Lotka, A. J., A Problem in Age Distribution, *Philosophical Magazine*, Vol. 21, 1911.

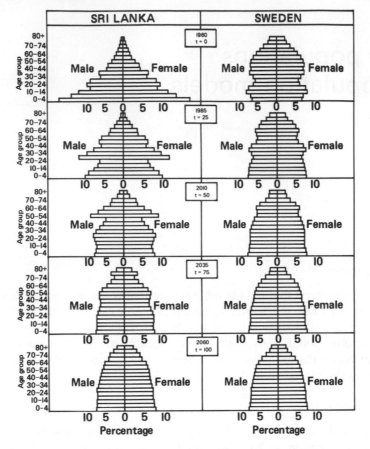

Figure 7.1: Approach towards the stable distribution for Sri Lanka and Sweden assuming both countries experience in future Sweden (1960) mortality and fertility.
(†= years after 1960)

A stable population has certain characteristics which, although probably obvious, are too important not to be specifically set out. Since the age distribution is constant, but the total population is increasing at a rate of $r\%$ per annum (say), the numbers in each age group must be increasing at $r\%$ per annum, the number of births, both to mothers of a given age and also in total, must be increasing at $r\%$ per annum and the number of deaths in each age group must be increasing at $r\%$ per annum. The demographic parameters of the population (i.e. the death and birth rates, the expectation of life, the average age at death, the average age of mother at the birth of her daughters, the average number of children to a mother, etc.) remain unchanged but the absolute numbers in each category increase at the rate of $r\%$ per annum. The probability of living or dying in the population is determined purely by the life table constructed from the underlying constant age specific mortality rates, and the rate of growth r is determined purely by the fertility and mortality rates. The method of calculating r from the age specific fertility and mortality rates will be demonstrated in section 7.5.

7.3 The stable age distribution

Consider a stable population increasing at a rate of $r\%$ per annum and currently producing births at the rate of l_0 per annum. The number of persons currently in this population aged x to $x + 1$ will be the survivors of one year's births on the average $x + \frac{1}{2}$ years earlier. If the number of births had been constant at l_0 per annum the population aged x to $x + 1$ would have been L_x. However, since the population is not stationary but is growing at $r\%$ per annum, one year's births $x + \frac{1}{2}$ years ago must have been less than l_0 by a factor of

$$(1 + r)^{-(x+1/2)}$$

and hence the population now aged x to $x + 1$ is

$$(1 + r)^{-(x+1/2)} L_x \text{ or } (1 + r)^{-(x+1/2)} l_{x+1/2} \qquad \text{.....................(1)}$$

It may be noted that the age used in the second formula of (1) is the age in the middle of the interval being used. This is often called the central or pivotal age. If we were using five year intervals x to $x + 5$ then the age to be used in this formula would be $x + 2\frac{1}{2}$.

For a stationary population $r = 0$, and formula (1) gives L_x as it should. It can be seen from this formula that the age distribution depends on two items, namely on $l_{x+1/2}$ (i.e. on the underlying mortality rates) and on the rate of growth r. The higher the mortality the more rapidly the age distribution falls with increasing age and also the higher the rate of growth the more rapidly the age distribution falls with age. This is illustrated in *Figure 7.2*,

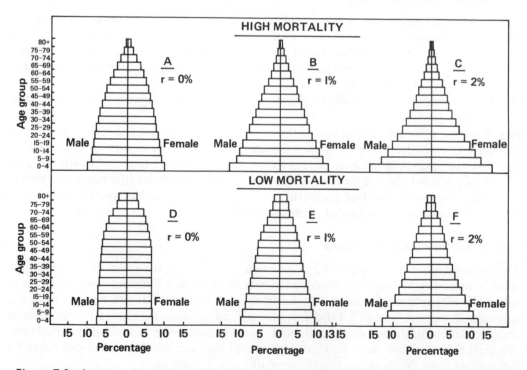

Figure 7.2: Age sex distribution of female stable populations with high mortality ($\mathring{e}_0 = 40$) and low mortality ($\mathring{e}_0 = 70$) and rates of growth $r = 0$, 1 and 2% p.a.

where the age distribution of a female population is shown for two levels of mortality corresponding to expectations of life of 40 and 70 years and, for each of these levels of mortality for three levels of fertility corresponding to annual growth rates of 0% (or stationary), 1% and 2% per annum. With a stationary population and light mortality (pyramid D) the numbers at each age are almost constant up to above age 40 and fall off fairly rapidly over age 60, whereas with a stationary population and heavy mortality (pyramid A) the numbers at each age fall steadily with increasing age right from birth. With average and high growth rates the numbers in the population fall steadily with age whatever the level of mortality (pyramids B, C, E and F). With both high mortality and high growth (pyramid C) which is typical of developing countries, the distribution falls sharply with age and takes the shape of a 'sagging tent'.

A comparison of each of the graphs A, B and C in *Figure 7.2* in each case with the graph below it shows that, if r is kept constant, even though the expectation of life might change from 40 to 70 years the age distribution does not change and the age pyramid is still of the same general shape. If mortality remains unchanged but the growth rate increases from 0% to 2% per annum then a substantial change in the age distribution occurs. These graphs suggest what has in fact been established by demographers, namely, that changes in fertility generally have a much greater effect on the age distribution than changes in mortality.

7.4 Other characteristics

Other characteristics of the stable population can be readily determined following the approach of section 7.3. Three examples follow.

(i)   Deaths aged x last birthday would be occurring at the rate of $(1 + r)^{-(x+1/2)} d_x$ per year. By substituting numerical values in this expression the average age of these deaths can be determined.

(ii) From formula (1), by substituting numerical values, the average age of the population can be calculated.

(iii) If we use y for the central age of the interval x to $x + 1$ and f_y for the age specific fertility rate (daughters only) then female births would be occurring to women in this age interval at the rate of $(1 + r)^{-y} l_y f_y$ per annum. From this distribution of female births by age of mothers at the birth of their daughters (the mean of which is called the mean length of generation), the crude birth rate, the average number of births per woman, etc. can all readily be determined.

7.5 The true rate of increase

The theorem quoted in section 7.2 stated that a closed population with constant age specific mortality and fertility would ultimately increase at a constant rate. This rate is called the true rate of increase or the intrinsic rate of increase. It can be seen from the formulae in sections 7.3 and 7.4 that it is necessary to calculate the true rate of increase in order to determine the age distribution and other characteristics of the stable population. We shall therefore now show how this true rate of increase, which we shall call r, can be determined from the given age specific mortality and fertility rates.

Since the number of births occurring to women in the year of age with central age y is currently at the rate of $(1 + r)^{-y} l_y f_y$ (see section 7.4) and the total number is currently at the rate of l_0 births per annum, we have

$$\Sigma(1 + r)^{-y} l_y f_y = l_0.$$

Expanding $(1 + r)^{-y}$ by the binomial theorem we have, approximately,

$$R_0 - rR_1 + \frac{r^2}{2}R_2 = 1 \qquad \dots\dots\dots\dots\dots(2)$$

where $\qquad R_0 = \dfrac{\Sigma l_y f_y}{l_0} \qquad R_1 = \dfrac{\Sigma y \, l_y f_y}{l_0} \qquad R_2 = \dfrac{\Sigma y^2 \, l_y f_y}{l_0}$

Taking logarithms to the base e of both sides of equation (2) and expanding by means of the expansion for $\log(1 + r)$ we obtain a quadratic equation from which r may be obtained. It is

$$\frac{r^2}{2}\left(\frac{R_2}{R_0} - \frac{R_1^2}{R_0^2}\right) - r\frac{R_1}{R_0} + \log_e R_0 = 0 \qquad \dots\dots\dots\dots\dots(3)$$

It can be seen from the definitions above of R_0 and R_1 that R_0 is the net reproduction rate and $\dfrac{R_1}{R_0}$ is the mean length of a generation. Since R_0 is the ratio of the number in one generation to the number in the preceding generation we can write down an approximate connection between R_0, the annual rate of increase r, and the length of a generation $\dfrac{R_1}{R_0}$. With annual compounding this relationship is

$$(1 + r)^{\frac{R_1}{R_0}} = R_0$$

and with continuous compounding

$$e^{\frac{R_1}{R_0}r} = R_0 \text{ giving } r = \frac{\log_e R_0}{R_1/R_0}$$

A better approximation which is due to Coale[*] and which avoids the calculation of R_2 by taking advantage of the fairly standard age distribution of $l_x f_x$ for human populations is

$$r \doteqdot \frac{\log_e R_0}{\dfrac{R_1}{R_0} - 0.7 \log_e R_0}$$

Since R_1/R_0, the mean length of a generation, is fairly constant for human populations at about 28 years, these three formulae can be used to write down, with the help of compound interest tables or logarithm tables a good approximation to the value of r given the net reproduction rate R_0. If an accurate value is required then the quadratic equation (3) should be solved. The working sheet for doing this, using as is the common practice, five-year age groups instead of individual ages, is presented as *Table 7.1*. In it the age specific fertility rates are those for Australia in 1966 and the mortality that of Australian females

[*] Coale, A. J., A New Method of Estimating Lotka's r, *Population Studies*, Vol. 11, No. 1, 1957.

Table 7.1

Calculation of the true rate of increase for Australian females using 1966 fertility
and 1961 mortality

Age group	Central age y	$\dfrac{l_y}{l_o}$	f_y (daughters only)	$\dfrac{f_y l_y}{l_o}$ = (3) × (4)	$\dfrac{y f_y l_y}{l_o}$ = y × (5)	$\dfrac{y^2 f_y l_y}{l_o}$ = y^2 × (5)
(1)	(2)	(3)	(4)	(5)	(6)	(7)
15–19	17.5	.97417	.02372	.02311	.404	7.077
20–24	22.5	.97131	.08402	.08161	1.836	41.315
25–29	27.5	.96828	.08892	.08610	2.368	65.113
30–34	32.5	.96439	.05082	.04901	1.593	51.767
35–39	37.5	.95867	.02478	.02376	.891	33.413
40–44	42.5	.95000	.00738	.00701	.298	12.662
Total			.27964	.27060	7.390	211.347
Multiply by 5 for single age figures			1.39820	1.35300 = R_o	36.950 = R_1	1056.735 = R_2

G.R.R. = 1.398

N.R.R. = R_0 = 1.353

R_1/R_0 = 27.310 R_2/R_0 = 781.031 $\log_e R_0$ = .30230

Hence $17.598r^2 - 27.310r + .30230 = 0$

Therefore r = 1.114% per annum.

in 1961. The three approximate formulae give 1.114, 1.107 and 1.116 respectively compared with 1.114 obtained by using the more complicated formula.

7.6 Calculation of the age distribution of a stable population

Using the true rate of natural increase found in *Table 7.1*, survival rates from the female life table, and formula (1), the stable female population in age groups may be determined. The sex ratio at birth enables the number of male births to be determined and then using the same rate of increase, male survival rates and formula (1), the male population in age groups can also be determined. The calculations are given in *Table 7.2* in which the last column gives the distribution of the population assuming a total population of 100,000.

7.7 Model life tables

The United Nations published a set of 24 life tables in 1955–56. They were not life tables for any particular country but were rather hypothetical life tables. To build up these tables 158 life tables were collected from a wide selection of countries representing different

Table 7.2

Calculation of the age-sex distribution of the stable population based on $r = 1.114\%$ per annum, Australian 1960–2 mortality and sex ratio at birth = 1.05.

Age group x to x + 5 last birthday	Central age y	Stationary population		$(1 + r)^{-y}$	Stable population			
		Males $_5L_x$	Females $_5L_x$		Males $1.05 \times (3) \times (5)$	Females $(4) \times (5)$	Number per 100,000	
							Males	Females
(1)	(2)	(3)	(3)	(5)	(6)	(7)	(8)	(9)
0– 4	2.5	488,383	490,761	.97269	498,798	477,358	5,053	4,836
5– 9	7.5	485,913	488,743	.92027	469,530	449,776	4,756	4,556
10–14	12.5	484,767	487,983	.87068	443,181	424,877	4,489	4,304
15–19	17.5	482,857	487,059	.82376	417,646	401,220	4,231	4,064
20–24	22.5	479,064	485,655	.77937	392,037	378,505	3,971	3,834
25–29	27.5	475,410	484,119	.73737	368,081	356,975	3,729	3,616
30–34	32.5	471,700	482,155	.69763	345,526	336,366	3,500	3,408
35–39	37.5	467,153	479,276	.66003	323,752	316,337	3,280	3,204
40–44	42.5	460,373	474,900	.62446	301,859	296,556	3,058	3,005
45–49	47.5	449,603	468,067	.59081	278,913	276,539	2,825	2,801
50–54	52.5	432,343	457,639	.55897	278,911	255,806	2,570	2,591
55–59	57.5	405,080	442,385	.52885	253,750	233,955	2,279	2,370
60–64	62.5	364,219	419,684	.50035	224,938	209,989	1,938	2,127
65–69	67.5	307,642	384,954	.47339	191,349	182,233	1,549	1,846
70–74	72.5	237,984	333,296	.44788	152,916	149,277	1,134	1,512
75–79	77.5	161,221	260,340	.42374	71,732	110,316	727	1,118
80–84	82.5	89,527	170,721	.40090	37,686	68,442	382	694
85–89	87.5	36,641	84,655	.37930	14,593	32,110	148	325
90–94	92.5	9,844	28,397	.35886	3,709	10,191	38	103
95+	97.5	1,727	6,589	.33952	616	2,237	6	23
Total		6,791,451	7,417,378		4,902,528	4,969,065	49,663	50,337

100,000

periods of time. The relationship between the value of q for one age group and the value of q for the next higher age group was studied and for each value of q which might occur in one age group the most appropriate value of q for the next higher age group was determined by using regression equations. Commencing then with a particular value of q_0 the most appropriate value of $_4q_1$ was determined. In the same way the most appropriate value of $_5q_5$ corresponding to the value of $_4q_1$ just found was chosen. Proceeding in this way a complete set of values of q originating from the selected value of q_0 was obtained and from these a model life table was constructed. The 24 model life tables published by the United Nations were all constructed in this way, and they provide a range of tables with varying mortality so chosen that the expectation of life at birth varies from 20 for the table with heaviest mortality to 73.9 years for the table with lightest mortality. The underlying assumption in this approach is that death rates in different age groups are inter-related i.e. if they are high in (say) middle age groups they usually have high infant and childhood mortality. In general, level of mortality is closely related to health conditions and if these are poor for one age group they are usually poor for all. There are of course exceptions to this situation but it is a reasonable statement of the position in many countries. A range of life table functions has been published for each of these model life tables.*

In 1966 a further set of model life tables was published by Coale and Demeny.[†] They collected over 300 life tables, each for males and females separately, reflecting actually recorded mortality experienced in various countries. These were divided into four groups. The 'West' tables covering 20 countries (including Australia, New Zealand, U.S.A., South Africa, Israel, Japan and Taiwan) showed a mortality experience which did not deviate in general pattern from the world average. The 'East' tables covered mainly Central European countries and the 'North' and 'South' tables were derived mainly from life tables from Scandinavian and Southern European countries respectively. These three groups were separated out because they revealed age patterns with substantial and significant deviations from the world average. Within each of these four sets which have their own characteristic mortality pattern there are 24 tables, for males and females separately at different mortality levels, with values of the expectation of life at birth for females equally spaced from 20 years (called level 1) to 77.5 years (called level 24). In both groups of model life tables the number of tables published is sufficiently large to justify linear interpolation should values based on some other expectation of life be required.[‡]

It is appropriate to comment here that the expectation of life at birth is selected as the most appropriate parameter available to indicate mortality levels because it is the only life table function which depends on the mortality of the whole life span. The lighter the mortality the greater the expectation of life and hence the latter is a reasonable indicator of mortality levels. A problem which illustrates how a model life table may be used follows.

Problem 1

For a certain country where the population is thought to be in a stable state it is estimated that one quarter of all babies born die before reaching age 1. Use the United Nations model

---

*United Nations, *Age and Sex Patterns of Mortality, Model Life Tables for Under-developed Countries*, 1955.

[†]Coale, A. J. and Demeny, P., *Regional Model Life Tables and Stable Populations*, Princeton University Press, 1966.

[‡]Since Coale and Demeny's work many other sets of model life tables have been prepared, see, for example, Brass' model life tables in Carrier N. and Hobcraft, J., *Demographic Estimation for Developing Societies*, 1971.

life tables to estimate the expectation of life at birth for females.

Solution

We require the mortality level for which $q_0 = .250$. From the female tables we find

$$\text{at level 15 where } \mathring{e}_0 = 27.5 \quad q_0 = .25101$$
$$\text{at level 20 where } \mathring{e}_0 = 30 \quad\quad q_0 = .23373$$

By linear interpolation the required value of $\mathring{e}_0$ is

$$27.5 + \frac{.25101 - .250}{.25101 - .23373} \times 2.5 = 27.65 \text{ years.}$$

7.8 Model stable populations

Coale and Demeny produced, in addition to their model life tables, a set of model stable populations. With each level of mortality they associated a range of levels of fertility as measured either by the GRR or by the true rate of natural increase. For each of these mortality-fertility combinations the age distribution and many parameters of the stable population are set out. The tables were originally used to estimate population characteristics for countries where the data available were incomplete, by selecting from the limited information available what appeared to be the most appropriate table. Further consideration will be given to this use of model stable populations in Chapter 12. The tables are useful for illustrating the relationship between demographic variables. For example, the 'West females' table with an expectation of life of 72.5 shows that the crude death rate per 1,000 for the stationary pupulation is 13.8, but is only 6.92 if the population increases at 2% per annum. A population with expectation of life of 55 but growing at 2% per annum has a lower crude death rate than a stationary population with an expectation of life of 72.5. The tables also demonstrate the relatively small effect of mortality and the relatively large effect of fertility on the proportion of the population under 15 or over 65, or on the mean age of the population. A problem which illustrates the use of stable population tables follows.

Problem 2

A certain female population thought to be in a stable state has an expectation of life at birth of 58.3 years and a growth rate of 2.36% per annum. Using the 'West' model life tables of Coale and Demeny estimate
(a) the crude birth rate
(b) the proportion of the population between 15 and 45
(c) the gross reproduction rate, and
(d) the net reproduction rate.

Solution

Expectations of life of 57.5 and 60 years correspond to mortality levels of 16 and 17 respectively. Hence, by linear interpolation we require the answers to (a) — (d) for mortality level 16.32.
(a) From the level 16 table crude birth rates of 32.18 and 36.54 per 1,000 correspond to growth rates of 2% and 2.5% per annum respectively. Hence a growth rate of 2.36%

corresponds to a birth rate of 35.32 per 1,000 under level 16 mortality. From the level 17 table, in the same way, we find a growth rate of 2.36% corresponds to a birth rate of 34.18 per 1,000. Hence by interpolation between these two values the crude birth rate for our problem, (namely mortality level 16.32), is 34.96 or 35 (say) per 1,000.

(b) By interpolation between growth rates of 2% and 2.5% we obtain, for level 16 with a growth rate of 2.36% the proportion of the population between 15 and 45 = .4335. In the same way, at level 17, the proportion = .4333. Interpolating between these two values the proportion required (namely mortality level 16.32) = .4334.

(c) The gross reproduction rate for a given rate of increase per annum will depend on the average age at maternity. Figures are provided in the model tables for four values of the average age at maternity, namely 27, 29, 31 and 33. We shall assume age 29. On this assumption, interpolating as before, first between growth rates of 2% and 2.5% and then between levels 16 and 17 we obtain

$$GRR = 2.38.$$

(d) A rough approximation to the relation between the net and gross reproduction rates is

$$NRR \doteqdot GRR \frac{l_m}{l_0}$$

where m is the average age at maternity (say 29). Interpolating between levels 16 and 17 we obtain $l_{29} = 82,431$ giving

$$NRR = 2.38 \times .82431 = 1.96$$

7.9 Quasi-stable populations

The model stable population tables of course produce exact numerical results in the case of analytical problems where the demographer is able to postulate stability of the population with which he is dealing. When applied to populations about which very little is known they cannot, of course, perform the miracles which they appear to have performed in section 7.8. The accuracy of the results in these situations depends on how nearly the assumed stable population matches the population being studied. There is firstly the problem of selecting the most appropriate table using the scanty information available about the actual population. However, the basic assumption that the population is in a stable state has also to be satisfied. Most of the developing countries have shown an approximate constancy in fertility over many decades. The absence of major trends in mortality was also a common characteristic of developing countries until the past few decades when rapid declines in mortality have been common. Where there have been no major trends or fluctuations in fertility and no sustained changes in mortality the use of stable population techniques is appropriate. The term quasi-stable population has been used for populations in which fertility has been nearly constant for a long time and mortality has been falling. Because of the frequent occurrence and importance of such populations a good deal of work has been done to show how estimates from stable population tables may be modified to compensate for this decline in mortality. With these modifications model stable population tables may be used effectively to obtain data for developing countries.

For further reading

1. Carrier, N. and Hobcraft, J., *Demographic Estimation for Developing Societies*, 1971.
2. Coale, A. J. and Demeny, P., *Regional Model Life Tables and Stable Populations*, Princeton University Press, 1966.
3. United Nations, *Age and Sex Patterns of Mortality. Model Life Tables for Under-developed Countries*, 1955.
4. United Nations, *The Concept of a Stable Population. Applications to the Study of Populations of Countries With Incomplete Demographic Statistics*, 1965.

Exercises

7.1 At the height of the great economic depression in the early 1930's the crude birth rate reached an all time low in many countries, e.g. U.K., U.S.A. and Australia. At that time the gross reproduction rate for females was the 'sophisticated' measure of fertility. In some countries it fell below unity and as a result 'the economics of declining populations' became a common subject for research. By calculating both the male and female true rates of natural increase for one of the above countries for this period show that if male rates had been used there would probably not have been the same concern. Did the male rate of increase ever become negative? The abovementioned attitude shows an ignorance of other weaknesses of the gross reproduction rate. What are they?

7.2 Use model stable population tables to obtain a rough numerical measure of the difference between male and female true rates of natural increase. Does this difference vary in any particular way with
(a) level of mortality and
(b) level of fertility?

7.3 Using data from model stable population tables draw graphs to show the effect of
(a) level of mortality and (b) rate of population growth on
  (i)   the proportion of the population aged under 15
  (ii) the proportion of the population aged over 65
  (iii) the dependency ratio.

7.4 A population in which the expectation of life for both males and females is 70 years is in a stable state with a growth rate of 2% per annum. The number of births in a particular year is 1,000. Estimate
(i)   the total population of the country
(ii) the total amount payable in this year under a national scheme which provides a death benefit of $50 for each death under age 10 and $100 for each death over age 10
(iii) the total amount payable this year under the national old age pension scheme which provides a pension of $1,000 per annum to every person over age 65
(iv) the number of school children and the number commencing school this year, given that schooling is compulsory from age 5 to age 15.

7.5 In the population of exercise 7.4 there are two political parties. Voting is compulsory after age 20. Sixty percent of the voters under 45 and forty percent of the voters over age 45 support party A and the remainder support party B.
(i)   Which party has majority support?
(ii) What percentage of voters would have to change allegiance to deny the majority party its advantage?
(iii) Estimate the crude death rate of supporters of party A and of party B.

7.6 You have been asked to estimate from model life tables the value of q_0 corresponding to values of the expectation of life at age 5 of 45, 55 and 65 years. You were not told which pattern of mortality was appropriate and hence made estimates using each of the regional tables. Show that the values of q_0 are

Regional table	Value of $\mathring{e}_5$		
	45	55	65
North	.200	.112	.048
South	.238	.154	.092
East	.331	.178	.070
West	.234	.126	.048
United Nations	.210	.140	.058

Comment on the problems of estimation when there is no clear indication as to which pattern of mortality is appropriate.

8
Population estimates and projections

8.1 Estimates and projections

In developed countries usually every ten years, or in some cases every five years, the best possible estimate of the total population size is obtained by means of a population census. In many developing countries census enumerations have also been made, but because of their cost and because in these countries censuses are often somewhat less accurate, sample surveys are being used to obtain demographic information. In one or other of these ways, information about the size and characteristics of populations is available as at specific points in time. However, populations are continually changing and estimates of the population size are often required at times other than census dates. For example, in order to compute the crude birth rate or crude death rate, an estimate of the total mid-year population is required for the year under investigation. Estimates are also often required of the future population size and structure. These estimates are used mainly for purposes of economic and social planning to determine future requirements of such items as food, fuel, manufactured goods, schools, teachers, etc.

Although in many cases the procedures are the same, population estimates are generally described as being of three types:
(i) inter-censal estimates
(ii) immediate post-censal estimates
(iii) future estimates or population projections.

The procedures adopted for making these estimates include:
(i) *mathematical methods*, the fitting to census data of any one of a variety of mathematical curves in the hope that the curves will accurately describe how the population has changed between the censuses, and when extended how the population will change in the future; and
(ii) *component method*, the use of annual registration data on births, deaths, immigrants and emigrants and also future estimates of these components to adjust the census populations to provide estimates of the inter-censal, post-censal or future population.

Demographers are rather meticulous in distinguishing between results which they describe as estimates and those which they describe as projections. The term 'estimate' is generally used for inter-censal periods or immediate post-censal periods when there is a high degree of confidence that the results obtained are likely to be very close to the actual figures at the time. The term 'projection' indicates that future population trends are unknown and that the figures quoted for future years are meant as an indication of what the future population would be if certain likely rates of mortality, fertility and migration were to apply. Because of the uncertainty about future rates it is usual to prepare several projections on the basis of different sets of rates. It is possible to make fairly reliable short term estimates but because of changes, particularly in fertility and migration patterns, actual populations in the long term may depart quite widely from projections made. As there is always a tendency in later years to compare earlier population projections with actual performance, it is usual to stress that in some cases population projections are little more than formal calculations showing the implications of the mortality, fertility, migration or growth rates on which they are based. The very publication of a population projection can influence future events as knowledge of the projections can lead to changes in individual attitudes and behaviour and in government policies. This destroys the assumptions on which the projection is based but is not a reason for criticizing the accuracy of the projections.

8.2 Inter-censal and immediate post-censal estimates

Given the total population at two (or more) different dates it is a relatively simple process to fit some mathematical curve to the data and on the basis of this curve obtain estimates of the total population at other dates. The choice of possible curves is considerable but care should be taken in applying the method, particularly over longer time periods. The appeal of the method is its simplicity rather than its theoretical justification and large discrepancies may be expected if curves are projected into the future. This type of projection is generally used for total population size only and in such cases important information, such as the age distribution, is not obtained. More accurate results are usually obtained with the component method which updates a census population by allowing for births, deaths, and net migration in the intervening period. This method should therefore be used if the data are available and are of sufficient accuracy.

(a) *Linear interpolation*

The simplest curve to use is the straight line

$$P_t = P_0 + (P_n - P_0)\frac{t}{n}$$

It is possible to employ linear interpolation to estimate the population between two censuses and to extrapolate into the future. The method is sometimes used where the interval is small but as actual observation has shown that populations do not usually grow linearly other curves should generally be used.

(b) *Polynominals*

If population counts are available for three or more censuses it is possible to fit a quadratic or higher degree curve to the data e.g. $P_t = a + bt + ct^2$. The results obtained are usually more accurate than if linear interpolation is used. Satisfactory results are obtained for inter-censal estimates or immediate post-censal estimates but projections become more unreliable the further into the future the projection is made.

(c) *Geometric*

The geometric or compound interest formula method is commonly used and was introduced in Chapter 2. If it can be assumed that population growth continues at a constant percentage r each year, then P_t, the population in year t, and P_0, the population in year 0, are connected by the formula

$$P_t = P_0(1 + r)^t$$

This curve also provides satisfactory estimates for inter-censal and immediate post-censal periods but care should be taken in using it for future projections as growth rates do not generally remain constant for long periods.

The above equation represents a growth of a constant percentage r each year, the addition being made regularly every twelve months. In practice however, growth is a continuous process rather than an annual increase, in which case the formula becomes

$$P_t = P_0 e^{rt}$$

The meaning and the value of r is thus slightly different in the two formulae. However, for human populations the growth rate is small and there is virtually no difference in the answers obtained by the two.

(d) *Logistic*

The above mathematical relationships all imply that there is no limit to the ultimate population size and consequently should only be used over a restricted range. It is possible to use a curve called the logistic curve which assumes the rate of growth does not stay constant but gradually drops to zero so that the population tends towards a finite size. As most populations have not yet reached the zero rate of growth all the suggested curves give reasonable current estimates, but when projections are required the logistic curve is useful when one might expect a limit to the ultimate population. Various modifications can be made to the logistic curve to achieve greater conformity with observed data.*

(e) *Component method*

It was explained in Chapter 2 that P_t the population in year t can be calculated from P_0, the population in year 0 (the date of the previous census), and from the components of population growth in the intervening period, namely the births (B), deaths (D), immigrants (I) and emigrants (E). The relationship is

$$P_t = P_0 + B - D + I - E.$$

Provided the above data are reliable and complete then this method is the most accurate for making inter-censal and immediate post-censal estimates.

However, it should be noted that even in countries like Australia, England and Wales and the U.S.A., where registration of vital events is reliable and relatively complete, some differences will be found between the population enumerated at the next census and that obtained by the component method applied over the whole period from the previous census. Adjustments incorporating the new information are then usually made retrospectively to any estimates which have been made.

---

*Croxton, F. E., Cowden, D. J. and Klein S., *Applied General Statistics*, Pitman, 1968.

8.3 Population projections

The methods used for projecting the population into the future are essentially the same as those introduced in section 8.2 for preparing inter-censal and post-censal estimates. For projections only a couple of years ahead any method, even linear extrapolation, may be sufficiently accurate for most purposes. Within this short period the differences between the results obtained by all methods are but a small percentage of the total population. However as the projection is carried further into the future these differences are magnified and become significant.

Attention was originally directed to mathematical methods, in the belief that it might be possible to find some relatively simple law of population growth. Subsequent changes in the birth rate and growth rate showed that such methods were quite unsatisfactory and projections are now almost exclusively carried out by the component method. The major advantages of the component method are, firstly, that it enables one to appreciate the effect of each of the separate assumptions about fertility, mortality and migration, and secondly, that the projected population is available by age and sex distribution and not just the total population obtained by mathematical curve fitting methods.

8.4 Component method for population projections

The basic principle of the component method is that the number of persons of a given age and sex who will be alive in the population in any year is the number in the population one year earlier and one year younger, less any deaths during the year and plus or minus any migrants. The number of children under age 1 must be the survivors of the births estimated to occur during the year, again adjusted for migration. Given the starting population and assumptions about future mortality, fertility and migration, the process can be repeated indefinitely. This type of projection is obviously most suited to calculation by computer and can be carried out with data in single years of age or in age groups.

The component method by age and sex in five-year age groups involves
(i)   taking a base population distributed by sex and age in five-year age groups
(ii)   applying survival ratios (usually $\frac{_5L_{x+5}}{_5L_x}$ or in the highest age group $\frac{T_{x+5}}{T_x}$) to each sex and age group to obtain the population still alive five years later and thus five years older
(iii) obtaining the number of births during the intervening period by applying age specific fertility rates to the female population; these births must be divided into male and female births by multiplying by $\frac{105}{205}$ and $\frac{100}{205}$ respectively (assuming sex ratio at birth is 105), and then converted to survivors aged 0–4 at the end of the five year period by multiplying by the appropriate survival ratio $\frac{_5L_0}{5 \times l_0}$
(iv)   adjusting for migration
(v)   repeating the process again and again to obtain the projected population ten years after the starting date, 15 years afterwards, 20 years afterwards, and so on.

Age-sex projections of this type can also be carried out by single years of age and for any time interval, but it is usually most convenient to project the population by time intervals equal to the age interval. Projections by the component method can be carried out with respect to any tabulated characteristic, not necessarily only sex and age, without any change to the basic method. British projections, for example, have been calculated with respect to marital status and duration of marriage. Where the population consists of sub-groups with decidedly different characteristics it is usually desirable to project for each sub-group separately. For example, the population projections for the United States are based on separate projections for whites and non-whites.

8.5 An example

As a detailed example consider the projection as at 1981 of the Australian male population based on the 1976 census population. In *Table 8.1* this base population is given in quinquennial age groups in column (2) and is multiplied by the five-year survival ratios in column (3) to give the expected number of male survivors in 1981 shown in column (4). The survival factors used are those derived from the A^{M61} Life Table in the Appendix, the assumption

Table 8.1

Estimating survivors of mid-1976 Australian population to mid-1981

Age last birthday	Number of males in mid-1976 ($\times 1,000$)	Proportion surviving to next higher age group	Expected number of males in mid-1981 ($\times 1,000$)
(1)	(2)	(3)	(4) = (2) × (3)
0– 4	630.5	.994942	(586.2)*
5– 9	654.0	.997642	627.3
10–14	646.9	.996060	652.5
15–19	638.2	.992145	644.4
20–24	588.1	.992373	633.2
25–29	594.8	.992196	583.6
30–34	499.6	.990360	590.2
35–39	430.8	.985487	494.8
40–44	382.4	.976606	424.5
45–49	407.6	.961611	373.5
50–54	389.5	.936941	392.0
55–59	319.4	.899129	364.9
60–64	278.6	.844662	287.2
65–69	215.4	.773574	235.3
70+	303.5	.556781	335.6**
Total	6,979.4		7,225.2

* *From Table 8.2*

***This figure is the number of survivors of both age groups 65–69 and 70 + (166.6 + 169.0)*

being made (for illustrative purposes) that this mortality will continue for the following five years. The survivors of the female population are obtained in the same way.

Table 8.2 shows the calculation of the expected number of births during the period 1976–81. Age specific fertility rates for 1976 have been used, the assumption being made that 1976 fertility levels will continue for the following five years. The expected number of births during the five-year period 1976–81 is taken as five times the average of the number expected in 1976 and the number expected in 1981. Changes in the female age distribution during the five-year period are thus allowed for although this refinement is not really necessary when projecting by single years. The figures in column (3) for the projected number of females in mid-1981 allow for mortality using the method of *Table 8.1*. Assuming a sex ratio at birth of 105 males per 100 females the expected number of male births is $\frac{105}{205}$ times the total births during the five-year period and the number of these surviving at the middle

Table 8.2

Expected births 1976–81, Australia

Age group	Number of females in mid-1976 (×1,000)	Projected* number of females in mid-1981 (×1,000)	Age specific fertility rates per 1,000 for 1976	1976 expected births	1981 expected births
(1)	(2)	(3)	(4)	$(5) = \dfrac{(2) \times (4)}{1,000}$	$(6) = \dfrac{(3) \times (4)}{1,000}$
15–19	610.9	609.7	35.55	21,717	21,675
20–24	576.3	609.1	129.22	74,469	78,708
25–29	579.2	574.5	147.34	85,339	84,647
30–34	468.7	576.9	73.06	34,243	42,148
35–39	406.6	465.9	24.28	9,872	11,312
40–44	360.2	402.9	5.57	2,006	2,244
45–49	399.6	355.0	0.41	156	146
Total				227,802	240,880

Expected births during the period 1976–81 $= 5 \times \frac{1}{2}(227,802 + 240,880)$

$= 1,171,705$

Expected male births during the period 1976–81 $= \frac{105}{205} \times 1,171,705$

$= 600,142$

Expected male population aged 0–4 in mid-1981 $= .976766 \times 600,142$

$= 586,198$

Using the same method as Table 8.1

of 1981 is obtained by applying the survival ratio $\frac{5L_0}{5l_0} = .976766$. These survivors become the expected male population aged 0–4 in 1981 and can be added to the top of column (5) of *Table 8.1*. When projecting by single years the appropriate survival ratio is $\frac{L_0}{l_0}$.

Migration to Australia is relatively large and the next step is to estimate the net gain by migration. A basis of 50,000 net immigrants per annum has been selected as this is roughly the target set by the government (since increased to 70,000), is a very easy radix should a projection be desired on some other basis (for 70,000 basis multiply by 1.4) and is in fact very close to actual experience (average net gain 1972–76 from permanent and long term movement was 50,037). An estimate of the age-sex distribution of migrants can best be obtained from the past five years' experience and it is reasonable to assume this distribution in the case of migrants during the next five years. The statistics on migrants are published by ages at arrival in or departure from Australia and it is necessary to adjust these to age at the beginning or end of the five-year period. A reasonable estimate of the age distribution in 1976 for all migrants during the period may be obtained by assuming that the numbers at each age within a quinquennial age group are equal. On this assumption, of the numbers in any particular age group one half should remain in that age group and one half should be placed in the next lower age group. A method of achieving this is to average the figure for each age group and the immediate older one. This leaves a residual group of half the children aged 0–4 at time of migration who were not yet born in 1976 and whose survivors will be in the 0–4 age group in 1981. The migrants are, on the average, exposed to the risk of death for 2.5 years only of the five-year period. Assuming that after arrival they experience the same mortality as the native population, the survival ratio may be approximated by $\frac{1}{2}(1 + P_x)$ where P_x is the five year survival ratio. For the 0–4 age group a modified survival ratio such as $\frac{1}{3}(1 + 2P_x)$ might be used to allow for the uneven distribution of deaths by age in this age group and to allow for the fact that children do not usually migrate immediately after birth.

The detail of this adjustment for migration is not illustrated here because there are other simpler methods for adjusting for migration that may be more appropriate under certain circumstances. When projecting for single years instead of five-year periods the above adjustment from age at date of migration to age at 30th June next is not really necessary. Births to migrants could be estimated by applying age specific fertility rates to the migrant female population. In many cases the level of net migration is relatively small and an assumption of zero migration may be reasonable or, alternatively, the assumption that the additional constant number or percentage of migrants per annum have the same age structure as the existing population may be sufficient. This simplifies the calculations considerably, while the error involved is likely to be small compared with the error in the fertility basis. Whatever method is used, the migration component should be added to the last column of *Table 8.1* to give the total projected population at 30 June 1981, and the process repeated again and again if projections further into the future are required.

8.6 Mortality basis for projections

The decline in mortality rates has been one of the outstanding demographic features of the 20th century. In all countries the decline is continuing, although at different rates, and in making projections it is generally assumed that further falls in the death rates will eventuate. The most significant improvement can be expected in those countries where the rates are still relatively high, e.g. the new African nations. Progress can still be expected in those areas where mortality is low, e.g. Sweden, but the small rate of decline means that satis- factory projections may be achieved even if constant mortality is assumed. Overall it is certain that the effects of further reductions in mortality will be less striking than in the past but sufficiently important that some allowance should be made.

The actual projections involve the use of survival factors and where the assumed mor- tality is constant these may be calculated from a life table. Model life tables prepared by the United Nations or by Coale and Demeny may be used for this purpose.

A presentation of various methods of mortality projection including generation and calendar year methods, methods involving extrapolation of trends over time and methods using some theories of mortality and mathematical curves is given by A. H. Pollard.* Changes in mortality are relatively slow and usually consistent in direction and conse- quently mortality bases can be estimated fairly accurately.

8.7 Fertility basis for projections

When carrying out population projections fertility rates specific for age of mother are generally used. These may be assumed to remain constant in the future or to follow some trend. For each five-year age group, the estimated female population is multiplied by the assumed age specific birth rate and summed for all ages to give the total number of births. To enable the projection to continue it is necessary to separate births into males and females by assuming some value for the sex ratio at birth. A similar procedure can be adopted to obtain the number of births if cruder fertility measures, e.g. general fertility rate or crude birth rate, are used. On the other hand, if the population is available by age, sex, marital status and duration of marriage and it is desired to use both ex-nuptial and nuptial fertility, the latter specified by age and duration of marriage, then this general approach can be modified to produce the number of births.

The estimation of the probable future trends in fertility rates is considerably more difficult than the estimation of mortality rates. We can assume a desire to reduce mortality rates but fertility levels depend largely on social customs and attitudes and these may change comparatively quickly. While a reasonable estimate may be achieved over a short period of time by an analysis of past trends, errors of considerable magnitude may arise if attempts are made to estimate fertility for long periods ahead. Errors in fertility estimation have considerably greater effect on estimates of future growth and population composition than do errors in mortality estimation.

The difficulties arising in the interpretation of past trends so that they may be used to estimate future fertility can be seen in *Figure 8.1* which is taken from the official projections for the United Kingdom. In 1955 it was assumed that, after a temporary increase in births after the war, fertility had returned to the lower pre-war levels; however, there immediately followed five years of increasing fertility. In 1960 it was considered unlikely that any further increase would occur, so the 1960 projection was based on a continuance of current fertility levels; however, births continued to increase for another five years. In 1965 it

*Pollard, A. H., Methods of Forecasting Mortality Using Australian Data, *Journal of the Institute of Actuaries*, Vol. 75, 1949.

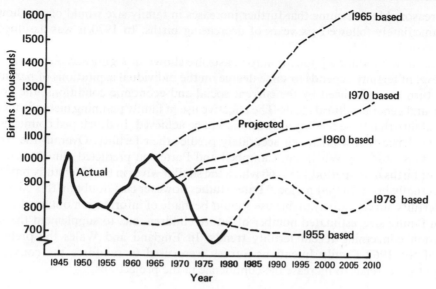

Figure 8.1: Actual and projected live births for the United Kingdom
(*Source:* Government Actuary, *Population Projections,* H.M.S.O. various years)

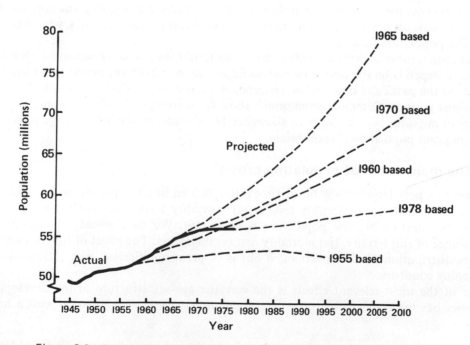

Figure 8.2: Actual and projected total population for the United Kingdom
(*Source:* Government Actuary, *Population Projections,* H.M.S.O. various years)

seemed reasonable to assume that further increases in family size would occur; however, there immediately followed six years of decreasing births. In 1970 it was assumed that fertility would settle down at 1970 levels but fertility in fact continued to fall. The large differences in the resulting population forecasts are shown in *Figure 8.2*.

The level of fertility depends to some degree on the individual aspirations of parents and these in turn are influenced by the current social and economic conditions, the political situation and general cultural ideals. The effective use of family planning methods increases the probability that these fertility aspirations will be achieved. In developed countries there is some evidence that women can accurately predict their fertility. Overall, the wives in the 1955 U.S. study by Whelpton, Campbell and Patterson predicted almost exactly the number of births in the period 1955–60 which the similar wives in the 1960 study reported as having actually borne in that period.* Later studies however cast doubt on this conclusion. Where fertility surveys are available use should be made of information obtained concerning ideal family size, estimated number of future children, etc. to supplement the factual information concerning recent fertility trends. In England and Wales the preliminary results of the 1967 Family Intentions Survey were used to reinforce the conventional analysis of past trends to increase the confidence in the projections.[†]

8.8 Migration basis for projections

For many countries net migration is not significant and may be neglected for population projection purposes. Where this is not so, some allowance should be made for it. Apart from its effect on the total number in the population, migration also affects the age-sex distribution because of the usually different age-sex structure of the migrant population. Migrants may also have different mortality and fertility characteristics which could affect the population figures.

Migration is more difficult to predict than either fertility or mortality because the level of migration depends on the economic and social situation in both the donor and recipient country at the particular time and on government policy. These all change markedly over quite short periods. Common assumptions allow for a constant number or constant percentage of migrants per annum, with allowance being made for the different age structure of the migrant population if appropriate.

8.9 The momentum of population growth

The size of a population at any future time is determined by (i) its present number, (ii) its age-sex composition, (iii) fertility levels, (iv) mortality levels, and (v) net migration. Clearly the starting or base population is important. We have already discussed the significance of (iii) fertility, (iv) mortality and (v) migration. The effect of (ii) the current age-sex distribution is often overlooked but is of great significance, particularly in the developing countries.

One of the most relevant effects is the way the age-sex structure in the developing countries has the tendency to perpetuate population growth. A population with a high

---

*Whelpton, P. K., Campbell, A. A. and Patterson, J. E., *Fertility and Family Planning in the United States*, Princeton University Press, 1965.
[†] Woolf, M., *Family Intentions*, Office of Population Censuses and Surveys, 1971.

proportion of young dependents (0–14) and young adults (15–29) has an in-built impetus for future growth. This *momentum of population growth* refers to the fact that because of the existing age-sex structure, even if we were able to reduce fertility rates down to replacement levels (NRR = 1) immediately, we cannot stop population growth in the foreseeable future (up to 60 years). Although this momentum of population growth is very strong in the developing countries, it is also present in the majority of populations of the developed world.

Any closed population when subjected to constant age specific fertility and mortality rates for a sufficiently long period of time will, no matter what its original age distribution, eventually become stable. If we have assumed that NRR = 1 immediately so that eventually the population becomes stationary, it would take around 60 years to reach this stationary state, during which time the population will have increased substantially (over 60% in some developing countries). It should be stressed that the assumption NRR = 1 immediately is unrealistic for most of the developing countries, so that a doubling (at least) of their population appears inevitable.

8.10 Ageing of the population

As discussed earlier, one of the main advantages of the component method of population projection is that one obtains not just the total projected population, but the age and sex structure of the population as well. The recent substantial decline in fertility has caused a corresponding decline in the proportion of children relative to their parents, and projections show that this trend will continue. 'Ageing' of the population involves a consideration of the proportion of the population aged 65 and over, and the way this proportion is continuing to increase, mostly due to the decline in fertility and the projected low fertility rates compared with those acting previously. Mortality and migration are of less importance because the effects are usually spaced over all ages. Further, it should be noted that the initial effects of declining mortality are to produce a 'younging' of the population (increase in proportion of population aged 0–14), since the experience has been that mortality improvement has mostly been at the younger ages and more children are surviving.

A variation in age structure would pose little problem if the attitude and behavior of the population did not vary with age. However, ageing of the population has important social, economic and political implications. The conservatism of its members, the lower consumption patterns, the greater use of health services, etc. are all important characteristics of an ageing population.

8.11 Internal migration

Internal migration is defined as the movement of people within the political boundaries of the nation being considered. This contrasts with international migration which is the movement of people across political boundaries. Internal migration includes moving across the street, from one suburb or statistical division to another in the same city, from one city to another, from country to city or vice-versa, and from one state to another. The success in measuring each of these types of internal migration depends on the data available. The problem with internal migration measurement is that, unlike international migration, the movement is unlikely to be recorded officially and must be estimated from other data.

Under the component method of population projection the estimated population of one state (say) at the date of a second census is equal to the population of that state at a first census plus the births in the state during the intervening period minus the deaths, plus the international immigration minus the international emigration. The difference between the actual population enumerated at the second census and that expected under the component method is the estimated net internal migration. The method requires complete birth, death and international migration statistics and two equally complete census enumerations. It is also desirable that the volume of migration both internal and international be small compared with the total population because births and deaths of the migrant population are generally included with those of the original population and this can distort the results. However, this defect is only rarely of any importance.

If the number of births and deaths is unknown an estimate of the internal migration can still be obtained if the age-sex distribution of the population is known at the two censuses and if international migration is negligible. The deaths can then be estimated by applying life table death rates, while the number of births is not required if only the population aged 5 and over at the second census (assuming quinquennial censuses) is used. In this way the migrant population by age and sex can be obtained.

Internal migration can also be estimated by other methods. At a census it is a common procedure to obtain place of birth and this can be tabulated against place of current residence giving an indication of the movement since birth between particular areas. Another method is to tabulate place of current residence against place of residence at some particular previous date by including a question to that effect in the census. An indication of movement between particular areas within a given time may thus be obtained. Another approach is to record at two censuses taken at time t and time $t + h$ those who were not living in the area in which they were born. Let I_t and I_{t+h} be the number of lifetime immigrants to a given area at times t and $t + h$ respectively, and E_t and E_{t+h} be the number of lifetime emigrants from this area at times t and $t + h$ respectively, then, if international migration is negligible, an estimate of the intercensal net migration for the area is given by

$$M = (I_{t+h} - E_{t+h}) - (S_I I_t - S_E E_t)$$

where S_I and S_E are the intercensal survival ratios for immigrants to and emigrants from the area giving the proportion of I_t and E_t that will survive the intercensal period. Since the survival factors vary with age the calculation will need to be carried out on an age basis.

For further reading

1. Cox, P. R., *Demography*, Oxford University Press, 1970.
2. United Nations, *Methods for Population Projections by Sex and Age*, 1956.
3. United Nations, *Methods of Measuring Internal Migration*, 1970.

Exercises

8.1 A country conducts a census every 10 years. Crude birth and death rates are constant but births, deaths and the total population size are all growing by 2% per annum. Show that by the time the next census is due the incorrect use of the previous census population unchanged in calculating the birth rate 10 years later will result in an overstatement of the crude birth rate by 22%.

8.2 At the Australian censuses on 30th June, 1971 and 30th June, 1976 the Australian population was 12,937,200 and 13,915,500 respectively and the population of the Australian Capital Territory was 145,600 and 203,300 respectively. Calculate the growth rates of the Australian and

A.C.T. populations. Use the geometric method to project both populations to 30th June, 1981 and 1st January, 2000. In what year by this method would the population of the A.C.T. equal the population of Australia?

8.3 An island has a population of 70,000 dogs of which 34,300 are females. Given the following age distribution, life table death rates and female-to-female age specific fertility of the dogs, calculate and draw a graph of the female dog population over the next five years assuming current birth and death rates remain constant.

Age (x)	Current female population aged x to $x + 1$	Female life table death rate q_x	Female-to-female age specific birth rates f_x
0	8,000	0.20	0.00
1	6,500	0.05	0.15
2	5,500	0.10	0.50
3	4,500	0.10	0.50
4	3,500	0.20	0.50
5	2,700	0.20	0.30
6	2,000	0.50	0.10
7	1,000	0.80	0.00
8	500	0.90	0.00
9	100	1.00	0.00

8.4 You have been asked to project the population of your country for the next 50 years by the component method using, inter alia, fertility rates specific for mother's age and duration of current marriage. For the purposes of this question migration should be ignored. What additional information do you require apart from the fertility rates in order to make the projection? Set out drafts of the calculation schedules you would use.

9
Demographic sample surveys

9.1 Introduction

Demographic sample surveys are conducted in many countries for one or more of the following reasons:
(i)   to collect vital statistics where the official registration system is inadequate or non-existent
(ii) to collect supplementary demographic and other data, where it is not feasible to collect the same from the population census, and
(iii) to test the accuracy of the traditional sources of demographic data, viz. the population census and vital registration systems.

Perhaps some of the topics most frequently studied in surveys are the social, economic, psychological and other factors affecting fertility and the knowledge, attitude and practice of family planning methods (called KAP surveys). These topics are usually covered by most of the general demographic surveys and quite frequently surveys are conducted solely to obtain information on these topics. Topics such as invalidity, labour force and to a lesser extent, mortality, sickness, migration and social mobility have also been studied by the use of sample surveys. In some of the developing countries regular demographic sample surveys are conducted to fill in the gaps in statistical information resulting from the inadequacy of demographic data from the traditional sources. Examples are the Population Growth Survey in Pakistan and the Turkish Demographic Survey. Even in developed countries, demographic sample surveys have been used to collect demographic data during the intercensal periods, for example, the Current Population Survey and the National Health Survey in the United States and the quarterly labour force survey in Australia. The Australian labour force survey has included additional items on an ad hoc basis. Topics covered include annual leave, child care, chronic illness, income, internal migration, school leavers, multiple jobholding, etc.

9.2 Defining the objectives and scope

One of the most important aspects in the planning of any demographic sample survey is to define clearly its objectives and scope. In other words, one must determine exactly why the survey is being conducted, what use will be made of its results, whether the survey should cover the whole population or be limited to some parts of it and whether it is going to be a single-round or multi-round survey. In defining the objectives and scope of the survey one must consider the limitations of cost, time, staff and other facilities available. For example, the objectives of a Family Formation Survey conducted by the authors were to study:*

(a) the inter-relationships between fertility and various social, economic, cultural and other factors;
(b) birth intervals;
(c) the aspirations of Australian couples with regard to the number of children they intend to have;
(d) the practice of various family planning methods; and
(e) opinions regarding selected aspects of the ideal family cycle.

Moreover, the scope of the survey was limited to ever-married females under the age of 55 years who were living in metropolitan areas or in urban and rural towns of 2,000 or more population, within the state of New South Wales. It was further decided to interview 10,000 respondents once only. These limitations on the scope of the survey were necessitated by considerations of cost, time and field problems.

9.3 Questionnaire design

The importance of questionnaire design is generally underestimated by persons who have not learned from experience the extra cost incurred, the extra time involved, the confusion caused and the loss in accuracy all resulting from a not-very-well-designed questionnaire. All questions must be so worded as to elicit the required information completely and accurately, and at the same time must maintain the co-operation and goodwill of the respondent. A good question must be easily comprehended by the respondent, clear in meaning, and identical in meaning to both the researchers and the respondents; it must be unidimensional, absolutely relevant to the topic being investigated, completely lacking in suggestion (i.e. not a 'leading question') and directly applicable to the respondent. These requirements are not easy to satisfy when the respondents include, for example, migrants of various nationalities and persons of various backgrounds and educational levels.

The answers can be elicited in two ways – by open and by closed questions. A closed question calls for a response of predetermined type, i.e. it contains a number of mutually exclusive and mutually exhaustive answers from which the respondent is free to choose. An open question leaves the wording of the answer to the respondent and the exact response given is recorded in full. Open questions are useful when little is known about the range of answers to be given, or the range is hard to precode; they avoid leading the respondent into a selected group of answers. However, they are time-consuming for the interviewer, they require more skill on his part, they can introduce interviewer bias, and can cause embarrassment when the respondent has no ideas or opinions on the subject. The advantages and disadvantages of closed questions are somewhat the complements to those for open questions. The great advantage of closed questions is that they lend themselves

---

*Pollard, A. H., Yusuf, F. and Pollard, G. N., Survey of Family Formation in Australia, *Transactions of the Institute of Actuaries of Australia and New Zealand*, 1972.

to rapid processing. It is possible to combine open and closed questions to take some advantage of the strengths of each. This is achieved by not showing the coded responses to the respondent and always keeping the last alternative answer open under some heading such as 'others (please specify) . . . .'.

Once the questions have been settled it is important that they be arranged in an order that is mutually satisfactory to the respondent, the interviewer, the office staff and the researchers. For the respondent it is important that the sequence of the questions appears logical, and that there is a gradual progression from easy to hard questions, with the most sensitive questions at the end so that refusal to answer these will not affect the earlier responses if they can be independently used. Such a sequence usually also helps the interviewer but he, in addition, requires the questionnaire to be well laid out, easy to handle, easy to read, etc., to help him in sometimes trying conditions. If, for example, he is required to check the answers to two questions for consistency they should, if at all possible, be on the same page. For the office staff it is important that the questionnaire should be designed to facilitate editing, coding, punching, identification, filing and storage. All these activities should be achieved with the minimum amount of turning from one page to the next and back again.

When what appears to be a satisfactory draft of the questionnaire has been prepared it should be tested in the field and in the office. The results of the pre-test should be examined closely, the views of the test interviewers and office staff sought, and the questionnaire modified appropriately. If necessary, this process should be repeated again and again until it can be reasonably certain that the questionnaire will successfully elicit the required information from the respondents with maximum efficiency.

9.4 Sample design

By sample design is meant the process of reaching decisions on the sampling techniques to be employed. Decisions have to be made regarding sample size, type of sampling, amount of clustering, estimation procedure for characteristics and their variances. We wish to emphasize immediately that a wide range of alternative designs is available and we wish to stress also the importance of selecting the design which is most appropriate to the special circumstances of the particular enquiry. The general aim of sample design is to produce in good time the most accurate statistics possible within the permitted expenditure, or to produce results with a specified accuracy at minimum cost. Enlisting as a consultant a sampling statistician with this special knowledge and experience will, in any large survey, pay high dividends. In fact, it would be dangerous to carry out an important survey without such advice.

Having decided on the statistical information which is to be produced by the survey and the accuracy which is required in that information, the next step is to estimate roughly the size of sample which is necessary to achieve that accuracy so that an estimate can be made of costs. For a sample of given size, both the accuracy obtained and the costs involved depend on the particular sample design chosen – whether it be a simple random sample, or stratified sample, or cluster sample. Assume, for purposes of illustration, that we are using simple random sampling and that we wish to estimate a percentage – say the percentage of married women aged 15–44 using the contraceptive pill. If we require the chance to be 0.95 that the true percentage P lies within the range ± 1 on either side of our sample figure p, then since p is normally distributed with standard deviation $\sqrt{\dfrac{pq}{n}}$, the sample size required to give us this accuracy is $4pq$. This is nearly 10,000 since p and q in this case are not far from 50. Clearly quite large samples are required for such accuracy.

Table 9.1 shows the accuracy of estimated population percentages based on simple random samples of different sizes. If from simple random samples we are estimating numbers that are assumed to be normally distributed, say numbers of children per family and we require the population value to be within ± 0.1 of our sample value with 95% confidence then the required sample size can easily be shown to be about $400S^2$ where S is the standard deviation of the number of children per family. As S is of the order 1 to $1\frac{1}{2}$ the required sample size is (say) 750. In both of these cases, and generally, to estimate sample size or accuracy we require some population parameter which we do not in fact know.

Table 9.1

Range of error with 95% confidence in estimating population percentages
from simple random samples of various sizes

Percentage	Sample size			
	100	500	1,000	5,000
2 or 98	±2.80	±1.25	±0.88	±0.40
5 or 95	±4.36	±1.95	±1.38	±0.62
10 or 90	±6.00	±2.68	±1.90	±0.84
25 or 75	±8.66	±3.87	±2.74	±1.22
50	±10.00	±4.47	±3.16	±1.41

When estimating required sample size it is usually near enough to make an educated guess at the parameter or to use a value obtained in a similar survey. When estimating the accuracy of the results we have obtained we can often use an estimate of the required parameter obtained from the survey itself. In *Table 9.2* we include some figures concerning accuracy of family size taken from the report on the British Family Intentions Survey.

Simple random sampling is not generally used in large surveys. Stratified sampling, multi-stage sampling, cluster sampling or combinations of these and other designs are used. The appropriate theory for these designs and the associated complicated formulae are given in specialist sampling texts such as *Sampling Techniques* by W. G. Cochran. Stratification usually results in a smaller variance in the estimate of population parameters; the extra accuracy obtained by stratification depends on the extent to which a heterogeneous population is divided up into sub-populations each of which is internally homogeneous. The use of clustering instead of simple random sampling reduces cost but also reduces precision. The loss in accuracy depends on the particular population and on the particular sample design used, and calculations would have to be made in each case. Accuracy based on simple random sampling can be used only as a very rough guide and will need adjusting. It may be noted that the British Family Intentions Survey, which used both stratification

Table 9.2

Range of error with 95% confidence in estimating expected family size
assuming simple random sampling

Date of marriage	Wife's age at marriage	Effective sample size (children)	Expected family size	Standard deviation (children)	Range of error
All dates	All ages	6,192	2.58	1.32	±0.04
	<20	1,759	2.91	1.36	±0.06
	20–24	3,536	2.53	1.26	±0.04
	25–29	741	2.23	1.24	±0.10
	30+	149	1.58	1.24	±0.20
1960–1964	All ages	1,536	2.49	0.98	±0.06
	<20	495	2.66	0.92	±0.08
	20–24	783	2.51	0.92	±0.06
	25–29	185	2.37	1.04	±0.16
	30+	73	1.38	1.11	±0.26

(*Source:* Woolf, M., *Family Intentions*, 1971)

and clustering in its design, suggested as a rough formula to add 50% to the range of error obtained assuming simple random sampling.

Calculations of the type mentioned earlier in this section result in a large number of values for the required sample size; some parameters can be accurately estimated from relatively small samples; others require very large samples. Accuracy and cost have to be balanced and when deciding on this balance the relative importance of those parameters which require a comparatively large sample has to be taken into consideration. Usually it is a good idea to adopt the working rule that each of the major 'cells' in the tables produced in the analysis should contain at least 50 persons in the sample.

9.5 Organization of the field work

The first task in the organization of the field work consists of the recruitment and training of interviewers and field supervisors. Personality traits like honesty, interest, accuracy, adaptability, intelligence, education and a pleasant but businesslike approach are important in selecting the appropriate field staff. As far as possible both the interviewers and field supervisors should be given monetary and other incentives for doing their job efficiently and constant evaluation of their work should be made at least during the initial stages so as to exclude workers who are not up to the required standard of efficiency. Feedback between the field staff and the principal investigators and the headquarter's staff responsible for the processing and analysis of the data should be encouraged. Where the survey is non-repetitive and where there are market research organizations or university research centres which have the necessary expertise in conducting sample surveys, it is perhaps cheaper and more convenient to employ such organizations to do the field work. However, in the case of repetitive surveys it is much better to set up a special survey unit for the purpose, and to hire interviewers who can work at the headquarters as coders, editing clerks, etc. during the period when the field work is not being conducted. With short period assignments it often happens that full-time interviewers are not available and part-time interviewers must be used. In planning the field work a balance has to be achieved between extending unduly the duration of the field work and keeping the number of interviewers and other field staff to a minimum. It is usually better to complete a demographic sample survey in the shortest possible time rather than extend it for months; nevertheless, the team of interviewers should be not so large that poorer interviewers need to be included and supervision becomes ineffective. Before commencing field work, the procedures for distributing questionnaires, in what manner and how frequently completed questionnaires are to be transmitted to headquarters, the steps to be taken in case of refusals or non-contact of the respondents, etc. have all to be clearly set out.

9.6 Data preparation

The preparation of data involves the editing of questionnaires, coding of the data and punching it on cards, paper tape or any other input device compatible with the data processing equipment on which the actual processing will be done. Editing is usually carried out in two stages. First, the questionnaires are edited to check that all relevant questions have been answered and that there are no major inconsistencies. The second stage of editing can be done mechanically by using the coded input data on punch cards or paper or magnetic tape. In this second editing process more thorough checks can be made. For example, in a fertility survey one may check that the birth intervals are not less than nine months, that ages of parents are consistent in relation to the ages of children, etc.

The coding of questionnaires involves assigning codes to non-numerical information. The scope and definition of each code should be clearly specified and understood by the coders. With questionnaires which are predominantly precoded the task of coding is quite minimal. However, if the questionnaire has many open-ended questions coding will be a time-consuming job.

9.7 Data processing

With the help of modern electronic data processing equipment, the tabulation and further processing of the data have become relatively easy and routine jobs. In preparing tables for publication it is important to consider each table in the light of what it contributes to the objectives of the survey. Unless active steps are taken in this direction many tables may appear which have little relevance to the purpose of the survey.

9.8 Report on the survey

It is often advisable for results of the survey to be presented progressively in the form of preliminary reports or research papers so that they become available to interested users of the data as soon as possible. Reports should contain the methodology of the sample survey, the results and some estimates of sampling and non-sampling errors. These preliminary reports can later be combined to form a final complete report of the survey.

9.9 Retrospective and prospective studies

Doll and Hill in 1950 published the results of a survey which they had carried out into the smoking habits of patients in a London hospital.* They found a much higher proportion of heavy smokers and a much lower proportion of light smokers and non-smokers among lung cancer patients (the test sample) than among the remainder of patients in the hospital (the control sample). Some association between lung cancer and smoking was thus suggested. Such studies are called retrospective studies, because the test sample being analyzed consists solely of persons who, at the time of the survey, were already victims of the disease being studied. Some scientists criticized this approach suggesting that there were ways in which bias may have been introduced. They suggested that the control group may not have been typical of the general population and that a knowledge of the illness from which patients were suffering may have biased their replies. Within 15 years after this work of Doll and Hill some 29 retrospective studies into the association of smoking and lung cancer were carried out in nine different countries. With the larger samples it was possible to divide the total sample into groups according to the amount of smoking and study the incidence of lung cancer in each of these groups. These studies consistently showed a significant association between smoking and lung cancer and an association which increased with the amount of smoking.

As a check on these results and because of the criticisms made about the retrospective method a more protracted, more expensive and more difficult approach to the problem was made – called a prospective study. Under this method a large random sample of persons is selected, divided into groups according to their smoking habits, and all traced for a number of years and the cause of death recorded for those who died. Several such studies including one of British doctors by Doll and Hill have been carried out involving well over a million persons and over 100,000 deaths. With such large samples it is possible to study the effect of such factors as the amount of smoking, age, degree of inhalation, duration of smoking, age when smoking commenced, the giving-up of smoking, etc. These prospective studies consistently confirmed the association suggested by the retrospective studies. The following comments on the prospective method are relevant:

(i)   the mortality ratios used to measure the relative mortalities of the test group and the control group depend mainly on the number of deaths from lung cancer among the non-smokers. As these are few the ratios fluctuate fairly widely,

(ii)   bias could be introduced if a high proportion of the subjects do not reply to the initial questionnaire,

(iii) bias could be introduced if the sample includes an abnormal proportion of smokers or non-smokers who are initially in a state of ill-health,

(iv)   bias could be introduced if there were a tendency for doctors to record lung cancer as a cause of death in the case of heavy smokers. (If this were so, deaths from other causes would be reduced.)

The Framingham study in Massachusetts U.S.A. is one of the largest and most important of prospective studies. It aims to determine the factors which are associated with the development of cardiovascular disease. A large random sample of the population was selected in 1950 and in the case of those free from cardiovascular disease a record of age,

*Doll, W. R. and Hill, A. B., Smoking and Carcinoma of the Lung, *British Medical Journal*, 1950.

educational status, smoking and drinking habits, cholesterol count, etc. were all recorded. The subjects have since been regularly brought in for clinical examination to observe the first symptoms of disease and to study the conditions associated with the onset of disease. The length of disability, capacity for work during disability and survival prospects in cases of chronic illness are also being studied. Such studies are obviously long-term and costly projects but ones which give great promise of success in furthering our knowledge of the factors which cause incapacity and death.

9.10 Population growth estimation surveys

One form of survey which has been frequently conducted in many developing countries is the so-called population growth estimation (PGE) survey.* These surveys enable an estimate to be made of the extent of under-registration and under-enumeration and permit a more accurate estimate of (say) the birth rate to be made. They involve establishing two 'independent' systems of data collection. For example, in selected areas one may have a registrar collecting information about vital events as they occur and in the same area demographic sample surveys may be conducted once in every quarter to obtain the same information about vital events and in addition some demographic and other characteristics of the population. The vital events collected by both systems can be compared and events which were reported by both systems can be separated from those reported by registration but not by the survey and from those reported by survey but not by the registration system. Under the assumption of 'independence' between these two systems, one can estimate the vital events which were missed by both systems. The adjusted birth and death statistics can then be used for estimating various demographic parameters.

The importance of the assumption of independence between the two systems should be stressed and checks should be made to see that the assumption is valid.† Population growth estimation studies have been conducted in many of the developing countries such as Pakistan, Thailand, Turkey and Morocco.

9.11 KAP surveys

The KAP survey is a classic example of the use of the demographic sample survey for the purpose of understanding some of the problems of society and helping to influence government actions to overcome these problems. In this case KAP is an abbreviation for surveys which attempt to determine the extent of knowledge, attitudes and practice of family planning in a community, region or country. Actual fertility questions are often included as well, and demographic background characteristics must also be obtained. It is extremely difficult to ascertain attitudes towards such items as family size and surveys often distinguish between desired, expected or ideal family size as applied to the respondent herself or to someone with similar socioeconomic characteristics. Answers often differ, depending on whether the questions are asked of the wife alone, the husband alone or of both together. The final questionnaire may well exceed 200 questions and take longer than an hour for each interview.

*Chandrasekaran, C. and Deming, W. E., On a Method of Estimating Birth and Death Rates and the Extent of Registration, *Journal of the American Statistical Association*, Vol. 44, 1949.
†Yusuf, Farhat, Population Growth Estimation: Studies in Methodology 1, Matching of Vital Events, *Pakistan Institute of Development Economics Research Report No. 67*, 1968.

9.12 World Fertility Survey

The World Fertility Survey is an international population research programme designed to determine current fertility levels throughout the world, particularly in the developing countries where there is no satisfactory birth registration system. The Survey began in 1972 and is being undertaken by the International Statistical Institute with the collaboration of the United Nations and in cooperation with the International Union for the Scientific Study of Population. Financial aid is being provided by grants from the United Nations Fund for Population Activities and the United States Agency for International Development. As a result of the Survey, which is still continuing, an increasing number of countries have now conducted scientifically designed, nationally representative and internationally comparable surveys of human fertility behaviour. Another advantage of the Survey is that developing countries will acquire the capacity for conducting further demographic surveys and the trained personnel to see that the results are properly used for national economic and social planning.

For further reading

1. Caldwell, J. C., Choldin, H. M., Nora, L. F., Sills, D. L. and Stephan, F. F., *A Manual for Surveys of Fertility and Family Planning: Knowledge, Attitudes and Practice*, 1970.
2. Cochran, W. G., *Sampling Techniques*, 1953.
3. United Nations, *The Mysore Population Study*, 1961.
4. United Nations, *Methodology of Demographic Sample Surveys*, 1971.

Exercises

9.1 The government of a particular territory uses a stratified sample of dwellings for a quarterly work force survey. Discuss the appropriateness of using this same sample for a fertility survey in which the respondents are ever-married women aged 15 to 45. Would the sample be suitable for a survey of retired persons?

9.2 A fertility survey is being carried out in which the respondents are ever-married women aged 15 to 65. One of the aims of the survey is to estimate the relationship between fertility and income. Outline the problems which you expect to encounter with the collection of data on 'income' and set out the instructions you would give interviewers in order to achieve a consistent approach. (You will, of course, need to set out the particular questions to be answered by respondents if your instructions to interviewers are to be understood.) What difficulties arise in the interpretation of the data?

9.3 It has been suggested that the following question might be interpreted by respondents in several ways.
'How many children do you have?'
What are thse different interpretations and what steps would you take to avoid misinterpretation?

9.4 The government of a country which already provides compensation benefits for injury due to motor vehicle accidents and due to accidents resulting from employment wishes to extend those benefits to persons injured under any circumstances (e.g. in the home, at sport, on holiday, etc.). The benefits take the form of payment of all medical, etc. costs and payment of 80% of salary while unable to work. What sampling investigation would you suggest in order to obtain a rough estimate of the annual cost of the proposed benefit?

9.5 The number of deaths in motor vehicle accidents as a percentage of the population is much higher in the 17–25 age group than in other age groups and is higher for males than for females. This may suggest a greater propensity in the young to take risks or a lesser ability to control motor vehicles. The explanation could, of course, be a greater use of such vehicles by the young, particularly young males, or the use of older vehicles by the young. Design a survey to provide an estimate, on an age and sex basis and by age of car, of the chance per 1,000 miles of driving that a driver will be involved in (a) a fatal accident and (b) an accident. Mention any problems which arise.

9.6 A government which has declared itself to be more concerned with 'quality of life' than with 'economic growth' wishes to publish a series of social indicators (analogous to the economic indicators) which will measure the progress which is being made. The indicators are to be published quarterly. What indicator or indicators would you suggest as a measure of community health and how would you obtain them?

10
Multiple-decrement tables

10.1 Introduction

In our study of the life table so far we determined the number of survivors at each age (l_x) out of a group of $l_0 = 100,000$ (say) births as this number was diminished by deaths. In this case there is only one form of decrement, namely mortality, and hence what we studied was in fact a single-decrement table. The entries in the d_x column represent the decrements (deaths) at each age.

Frequently in demographic problems we wish to determine the number of survivors from a group which is deminished as a result of two or even more factors operating. For example, a group of bachelors may be diminished by death and by marriage. A group of employees may be diminished by death, age retirement, ill health retirement or resignation. Tables similar to the life table, and to serve similar purposes, may be constructed in these cases also. If there are two causes of decrement only, then such tables are called double-decrement tables; if there are more than two causes of decrement then the term multiple-decrement table is used. The multiple-decrement table is very similar to the life table in the columns constructed, except that we now have a number of d_x columns representing the number of persons leaving the population by each type of decrement, and similarly a number of columns for the corresponding rates of decrement.

10.2 Net nuptiality table

The net nuptiality table, an example of which is *Table 10.1*, is probably the most commonly used example of a multiple-decrement table, and traces the single population as it is decreased by marriage and death. It is perhaps the most refined device for investigating nuptiality. The data required are age-sex specific first marriage rates and age-sex specific mortality rates for single persons. From this table we can obtain the probability of marriage at each age, average age at marriage, proportion of single persons and ever married persons at each age, and the average years of single life remaining. A gross nuptiality table where mortality is not considered, only marriage rates being used, is also constructed, the method being identical with a single-decrement life table.

Table 10.1

Net nuptiality table for women of all races – U.S.A., 1960

Age	Rate per 1,000		Of 100,000 born alive			Stationary population of *single* persons		
	Mortality	Marriage	Survivors at age x and still single	Deaths aged x while single	Marriages aged x	Aged x	Aged x & over	Average years left before marriage or death
x	$1{,}000Q'_x$	$1{,}000Q''_x$	l_x	d'_x	d''_x	L_x	T_x	$\overset{\circ}{e}_x$
0	22.56	—	100,000	2,256	—	98,109	2,173,829	21.74
14	0.38	3.37	97,053	37	327	96,871	810,876	8.35
15	0.44	12.33	96,689	43	1,192	96,072	714,005	7.38
16	0.50	48.01	95,454	48	4,583	93,139	617,933	6.47
17	0.55	72.73	90,823	50	6,606	87,495	524,794	5.78
18	0.59	198.62	84,167	50	16,717	75,784	437,299	5.20
19	0.61	214.34	67,400	41	14,447	60,156	361,515	5.36
20	0.64	212.03	52,912	34	11,219	47,286	301,359	5.70
21	0.67	276.83	41,659	28	11,532	35,879	254,073	6.10
22	0.70	286.75	30,099	21	8,631	25,773	218,194	7.25
23	0.73	244.02	21,447	16	5,233	18,823	192,421	8.97
24	0.76	212.90	16,198	12	3,449	14,468	173,598	10.72
25	0.79	187.45	12,737	10	2,388	11,538	159,130	12.49
26	0.82	168.74	10,339	8	1,745	9,463	147,592	14.28
27	0.87	149.76	8,586	7	1,286	7,940	138,129	16.09
28	0.92	128.81	7,293	7	939	6,820	130,189	17.85
29	0.98	116.31	6,347	6	738	5,975	123,369	19.44
30	1.06	101.65	5,603	6	570	5,315	117,394	20.95
31	1.14	86.31	5,027	6	434	4,807	112,079	22.30
32	1.22	74.14	4,587	6	340	4,414	107,272	23.39
33	1.31	66.49	4,241	6	282	4,097	102,858	24.25
34	1.40	61.97	3,953	6	245	3,828	98,761	24.98
35+			3,702	2,023	1,679	94,933	94,933	25.64

(*Source:* Grabill, W. H., Some demographic implications of nuptiality rates,
International Population Conference, London, 1969, Vol. 3, p. 1828)

The first six columns of the net nuptiality table are completed in the same manner as the early columns of a life table. For example,

deaths aged 20 last birthday while single
d'_{20} = number of single women aged 20 multiplied by the rate of mortality at age 20
$(l_{20} \times Q'_{20})$
= 52,912 × .00064
= 34

Similarly, the number of marriages at age 20 last birthday $(l_{20} \times Q''_{20})$
d''_{20} = 52,912 × .21203
= 11,219

Hence the number of survivors at age 21, both alive and single $(l_{20} - d'_{20} - d''_{20})$
l_{21} = 52,912 − 34 − 11,219
= 41,659

From *Table 10.1* we can deduce that the chance that a woman now aged 23 and single will marry when aged 27 last birthday is 1286/21,447 or .06. The chance that a woman now aged 23 and single will die at age 29 while still single is 6/21,447 or .00028.

This table may be extended to produce a stationary population of single persons (i.e. L_x functions) from which the relative numbers of single women in age groups in a stationary population, and the expected number of future years of single life may be calculated. These figures are set out in the last three columns of *Table 10.1*. Attention is drawn to the shape of the curve representing the average number of years left before leaving the single state through marriage or death, as given in the last column of *Table 10.1*. Care must be taken in using these tables. For example, the average age at marriage for single women now aged 25 is not 25 + 12.49; this is the average age at *death or marriage* (whichever event occurs first) of single women now aged 25.

If we assume that single females and married females experience the same mortality, and also if we are given that the expectation of life at birth for a female is 73.24 years then it follows from *Table 10.1* that the expectation of 'ever-married' life for a newborn female is 73.24 − 21.74 or 51.5 years. Some other results which follow from *Table 10.1* are now given without explanation.

The ratio in a stationary population of single women aged 30–34 to those 20–24 is

$$\frac{T_{30} - T_{35}}{T_{20} - T_{25}} = \frac{117,394 - 94,933}{301,359 - 159,130} = 0.158$$

The chance that a single woman aged 32 will eventually marry is:

$$\frac{340 + 282 + 245 + 1,679}{4,587} = 0.555$$

The chance that a single woman aged 32 will die single therefore is 1 − 0.555 or 0.445, since she must either die single or marry. Alternatively, the chance is

$$\frac{6 + 6 + 6 + 2,023}{4,587} = 0.445$$

The chance that a single girl aged 18 will

(i)   be single at age 21 $= \dfrac{l_{21}}{l_{18}} = \dfrac{41,659}{84,167} = 0.495$

(ii)   die single before age 21 $= \dfrac{50 + 41 + 34}{84,167} = 0.001$

(iii)   marry before age 21 $= \dfrac{16,717 + 14,447 + 11,219}{84,167} = 0.504$

These three chances total unity since one of the three outcomes must take place.

It should be noted that it is not possible to write down in simple form this table the chance that a single woman age 18 will die within (say) 10 years. A life table with the mortality decrement only is required for this purpose. However, if it can be assumed that the mortality of single persons used in the multiple-decrement table is the same as population mortality, then it is possible to calculate the associated single-decrement table with mortality as the only decrement using the method of the following paragraphs.

10.3 Dependent and independent rates

It may be noticed that in *Table 10.1* a capital letter Q was used for rates of decrement instead of q which was used with single-decrement life tables. This was done deliberately, because there is an important difference between the two rates. Suppose that marriage and mortality are such that the rates in *Table 10.1* apply. Between ages 20 and 21 in that table there are 34 deaths and 11,219 marriages. Of these 11,219 women who marry some will die before age 21 but they will not be included in the deaths because these 34 deaths are deaths of single women only. Now suppose the tendency to marry between ages 20 and 21 falls considerably, then there would be some women who would have married under the previous system but now will not, and any deaths which occur among them, will have to be added to the 34 shown since they are now deaths of single women. Thus, even though there is no change in the intrinsic mortality of the population, a change in the tendency to marry will result in a change in the rate of mortality. Thus the rate of mortality used in *Table 10.1* is dependent on the rate of marriage. These rates of decrement are therefore called dependent rates. An independent rate of decrement is the rate of decrement which would be observed if only this one mode of decrement were operating. This rate which is independent of any other decrements is therefore the fundamental measure of the rate of decrement due to a particular cause. Dependent rates are designated by the capital letter Q and independent rates by q. For each of the causes of decrement in a multiple decrement table it is possible to calculate a single decrement table that shows the operation of that decrement independent of the others. Also it may sometimes be necessary to take two independent single decrement tables and combine these into a multiple decrement table where the rates are dependent on each other.

10.4 Relationship between dependent and independent rates

Using one and two dashes to refer to two different causes of decrement it is possible to obtain a measure of the way in which Q_x depends on q'_x and q''_x. The results are stated here without proof. The following formulae hold approximately if q'_x and q''_x are both small compared with unity:

$$Q'_x = q'_x(1 - \tfrac{1}{2}q''_x) \qquad Q''_x = q''_x(1 - \tfrac{1}{2}q'_x)$$

$$q'_x = \frac{Q'_x}{1 - \tfrac{1}{2}Q''_x} \qquad q''_x = \frac{Q''_x}{1 - \tfrac{1}{2}Q'_x}$$

With three causes of decrement the corresponding relationships are:

$$Q'_x = q'_x(1 - \tfrac{1}{2}q''_x - \tfrac{1}{2}q'''_x) \text{ and}$$

$$q'_x = \frac{Q'_x}{1 - \tfrac{1}{2}Q''_x - \tfrac{1}{2}Q'''_x}$$

These formulae are based on the assumption that lives being removed by the decrements were exposed to the operation of the decrement being studied for half a year on average.

10.5 The effect on mortality of the elimination of a disease

Deaths may be split up into deaths from specific causes, each cause of death being treated as a separate decrement. The effect of various diseases on total mortality may be studied in this way. The dependent rates of mortality for males in Australia in 1967 from diseases of the circulatory system (Q'_x), from neoplasms (Q''_x) and from all other causes (Q'''_x) for five-year age groups were:

Age (x)	Q'_x	Q''_x	Q'''_x
40–44	.00515	.00300	.01035
45–49	.01360	.00505	.01275
50–54	.02360	.00975	.01705
55–59	.04315	.01605	.02640
60–64	.06820	.02800	.04015

From these rates the following multiple-decrement table was constructed

Age (x)	l_x	d'_x	d''_x	d'''_x
40	10,000	51.5	30.0	103.5
45	9,815	133.5	49.6	125.1
50	9,506.8	224.4	92.7	162.1
55	9,027.6	389.5	144.9	238.3
60	8,254.9	563.0	231.1	331.4
65	7,129.4			

Thus the chance that a 40 year old male survives to age 65 according to these rates is 0.71294.

We might well ask what would be the probability of surviving this same period if deaths from diseases of the circulatory system could be eliminated. It was in fàct such a problem which stimulated interest in multiple-decrement tables. The problem then was to determine the probable effect on the increase in population of the extinction of smallpox. The mathematicians D'Alembert, Laplace and Bernouilli examined the problem and in 1875 Makeham set out a solution following a multiple-decrement table approach.*

If deaths from diseases of the circulatory system were eliminated there would be a greater exposure to other diseases and we would expect the death rates we are using (the dependent death rates) for other causes of death to increase. The method of tackling the problem is first to take the given dependent rates (Q) and from these calculate the equivalent independent rates (q) for the three causes of death, using the formulae in section 10.4. Second, the independent rates are adjusted as required. In this case diseases of the circulatory system are eliminated so q'_x becomes zero, but q''_x and q'''_x do not change as they are independent rates. Third, we then use these adjusted independent death rates to calculate new dependent death rates, again using the formulae in section 10.4. Finally, the adjusted multiple-decrement table can then be calculated.

The independent death rates so obtained are:

Age (x)	q'_x	q''_x	q'''_x
40–44	.00518	.00302	.01039
45–49	.01372	.00512	.01287
50–54	.02392	.00995	.01734
55–59	.04409	.01663	.02720
60–64	.07061	.02960	.04218

As an illustration of the method of calculation we show how the rate in the top left hand corner of the above table (.00518) was determined.

$$q'_x = \frac{Q'_x}{1 - \frac{1}{2}Q''_x - \frac{1}{2}Q'''_x}$$

$$= \frac{.00515}{1 - \frac{1}{2} \times .00300 - \frac{1}{2} \times .01035}$$

$$= 0.00518$$

The new dependent rates with diseases of the circulatory system eliminated are:

* Makeham, W. M., On an Application of the Theory of the Composition of Decremental Forces, *Journal of the Institute of Actuaries*, Vol. 18, 1875.

Age (x)	Q'_x	Q''_x	Q'''_x
40–44	0	.00300	.01037
45–49	0	.00509	.01284
50–54	0	.00986	.01725
55–59	0	.01640	.02697
60–64	0	.02898	.04156

As an illustration of the method of calculation we show how the rate in the top right hand corner of the above table (.01037) was determined.

$$Q'''_x = q'''_x(1 - \tfrac{1}{2}q'_x - \tfrac{1}{2}q''_x)$$

$$= .01039(1 - \tfrac{1}{2} \times 0 - \tfrac{1}{2} \times .00302)$$

$$= .01037$$

It can be seen that the new dependent rates are larger than the old, as we expected, although not greatly so. From these new values of Q''_x and Q'''_x the following double-decrement table was obtained in the usual way.

Age (x)	l_x	d''_x	d'''_x
40	10,000	30.0	103.7
45	9,866.3	50.2	126.7
50	9,689.4	95.5	167.1
55	9,426.8	154.6	254.2
60	9,018.0	261.3	374.8
65	8,381.9		

Thus, if deaths from diseases of the circulatory system were eliminated but mortality otherwise not changed, the probability of a 40 year old male surviving to 65 is 0.83819.

It might well be said that this is a very hypothetical situation. However it could well be of interest to determine the effect of reducing by one-third (say) the mortality both from diseases of the circulatory system and from neoplasms.

From both the old and new values of l_x the usual stationary population functions L_x, T_x and $\mathring{e}_x$ can be determined, and thus the extra number of years lived can be estimated.

10.6 Combined tables

In the tables considered so far we have traced the experience of a group of persons who remain members of a certain class (e.g. spinsters) and have not considered the subsequent experience of these persons once they have been removed by some cause other than death (e.g. marriage). Sometimes we require such a table, called a combined marriage and mortality table, which records both the number of bachelors and the number of married men, as well as the movement of both classes. *Table 10.2* is an extract from such a table.

Table 10.2

Hypothetical marriage and mortality table

Age	Number, at exact age x, of		Decrement between ages x and $x + 1$		
(x)	Bachelors	Married men	Bachelors dying	Married men dying	Bachelors marrying
.	.	.	.	.	.
.	.	.	.	.	.
.	.	.	.	.	.
28	9,487	7,426	80	52	665
29	8,742	8,039	76	54	605
30	8,061	8,590	75	58	563
.	.	.	.	.	.
.	.	.	.	.	.
.	.	.	.	.	.

Combined tables can be constructed in two ways. If we are given the rates of marriage and of mortality of bachelors and the rates of mortality of married men the decrement and survivor columns of the table can be constructed in the usual way commencing with a radix of (say) 100,000 bachelors at age 15. However, sometimes the incidence of marriage is not measured in terms of rates but rather by a column of 'proportion married' specified by age. If this is the case then the total number of males at each age has to be divided into bachelors and married men using the proportions married given and from these figures the 'bachelors marrying' column is the last to be filled in. A combined mortality and disability table and a working life table are further examples of combined tables which are in principle statistically identical with *Table 10.2*. We shall now consider a working life table which is constructed by means of the second of the methods described above for a combined marriage and mortality table, in this case dividing the total population at each age into two groups using work force participation rates.

10.7 Working life table

To construct a working life table such as that shown in *Table 10.3* we need (i) the mortality rates q_x from which a life table, particularly the l_x column, can be constructed, and (ii) the male work force participation rates at each age (p_x) so that l_x can be split into two parts, l'_x (alive and in work force) and l''_x (alive but not in work force) using the formulae

$$l'_x = l_x \times p_x$$
$$l''_x = l_x - l'_x$$

Table 10.3

Working life table – U.S.A. males 1960

Age	Number surviving to age x out of 100,000 births	Work force participation rates	Number of men in column (2)		Stationary population				Movement between the ages in column (1)			Expected future lifetime	
			in work force	not in work force	In work force		Not in work force		Deaths while		Joining work force (net)	in work force	not in work force
					between ages in col. (1)	age x and above	between ages in col. (1)	age x and above	in work force	not in work force			
(x)	(l_x)	(p_x)	(l'_x)	(l''_x)	(L'_x)	(T'_x)	(L''_x)	(T''_x)	(d'_x)	(d''_x)		$\bar{e}'_x$	$\bar{e}''_x$
(1)	(2)	(3)	(4)	(5)	(6)	(7)	(8)	(9)	(10)	(11)	(12)	(13)	(14)
14	96,102	.154	14,800	81,302	17,290	4,120,600	78,771	1,138,159	15	67	4,995	42.9	11.8
15	96,020	.206	19,780	76,240	25,524	4,103,310	70,445	1,059,388	27	75	11,516	42.7	11.0
16	95,918	.326	31,269	64,649	38,147	4,077,786	57,712	988,943	47	71	13,804	42.5	10.3
17	95,800	.470	45,026	50,774	53,509	4,039,639	42,224	931,231	75	59	17,041	42.2	9.7
18	95,666	.648	61,992	33,674	67,533	3,986,130	28,061	889,007	101	42	11,184	41.7	9.3
19	95,523	.765	73,075	22,448	76,070	3,918,597	19,379	860,946	119	30	6,109	41.0	9.0
20	95,374	.829	79,065	16,309	80,616	3,842,527	14,677	841,567	138	25	3,240	40.3	8.8
21	95,211	.863	82,167	13,044	83,328	3,761,911	11,797	826,890	151	21	2,474	39.5	8.7
22	95,039	.889	84,490	10,549	85,313	3,678,583	9,639	815,093	156	18	1,803	38.7	8.6
23	94,885	.908	86,137	8,728	86,721	3,593,270	8,057	805,454	158	15	1,327	37.9	8.5
24	94,692	.922	87,306	7,386	87,749	3,506,549	6,860	797,397	154	12	1,041	37.0	8.4
25	94,526	.933	88,193	6,333	447,230	3,418,800	23,328	790,537	788	41	3,294	36.2	8.4
30	93,697	.968	90,699	2,998	452,077	2,971,570	13,985	767,209	940	29	373	31.7	8.2
35	92,728	.972	90,132	2,596	446,110	2,519,493	14,025	753,224	1,359	43	−461	27.2	8.1
40	91,326	.967	88,312	3,014	435,080	2,073,383	16,000	739,199	2,141	79	−451	22.7	8.1
45	89,106	.962	85,720	3,386	417,590	1,638,303	19,165	723,199	3,356	154	−1,048	18.4	8.1
50	85,596	.950	81,316	4,280	386,335	1,220,713	27,705	704,034	5,203	373	−2,895	14.3	8.2
55	80,020	.915	73,218	6,802	338,020	834,378	43,500	676,329	6,585	847	−4,643	10.4	8.5
60	72,588	.854	61,990	10,598	242,990	496,358	94,813	632,829	7,233	2,822	−19,551	6.8	8.7
65	62,533	.563	35,206	27,327	134,360	253,368	147,908	538,016	5,788	6,371	−10,880	4.1	8.6
70	50,374	.368	18,538	31,836	70,440	119,008	147,458	390,108	4,393	9,196	−4,507	2.4	7.7
75	36,785	.262	9,638	27,147	33,857	48,568	116,218	242,650	3,055	10,485	−2,678	1.3	6.6
80	23,245	.168	3,905	19,340	11,935	14,711	73,683	126,432	1,707	10,536	−1,329	.6	5.4
85+	11,002	.079	869	10,133	2,776	2,776	52,749	52,749	550	10,452	−319	.3	4.8

(Source: Garfinkle, S., The Lengthening of Working Life and its Implications, *World Population Conference*, Belgrade 1965)

We then calculate

$$L'_x = \tfrac{1}{2}(l'_x + l'_{x+1})$$

$$T'_x = \sum_{t=0}^{\omega} L'_{x+t}$$

and similarly for L''_x and T''_x.

The total deaths $d_x = l_x - l_{x-1}$ are split in the ratio $L'_x : L''_x$ i.e.

$$d'_x = (l_x - l_{x+1})\frac{L'_x}{L'_x + L''_x}$$

$$d''_x = l_x - l_{x+1} - d'_x$$

The number joining the work force between ages x and $x + 1$ is $l''_x - l''_{x+1} - d''_x$. From general reasoning we can see that this number must also equal $l'_{x+1} - l'_x + d'_x$. Illustrating from the first line of *Table 10.3* we have

$$4{,}995 = 81{,}302 - 76{,}240 - 67 = 19{,}780 - 14{,}800 + 15.$$

Finally we can construct columns equivalent to $\mathring{e}_x$ as follows:

expected future years in work force $\mathring{e}'_x = \dfrac{T'_x}{l_x}$

expected future years not in work force $\mathring{e}''_x = \dfrac{T''_x}{l_x}$

total expectation of life $\mathring{e}_x = \dfrac{T'_x + T''_x}{l_x} = \dfrac{T_x}{l_x} = \mathring{e}'_x + \mathring{e}''_x.$

It is clear that the five columns 4, 5, 10, 11 and 12 of *Table 10.3* are statistically the same as the five columns in *Table 10.2* although the demographic problems they are tackling are different.

We now give examples of some of the useful information which may be obtained from *Table 10.3*.

(i)   The rate at which men join the work force at age $18 = 11{,}184/95{,}666 = 117$ per 1,000 men. Or, expressed relative to the number not in the work force, the rate $= 11{,}184/33{,}674 = 332$ per 1,000 men not in the work force.

(ii) The average number of years expected to be worked by males now aged $14 = 4{,}120{,}600/96{,}102 = 42.9$ years.

(iii) The average number of years expected to be spent out of the work force by males now aged $14 = 1{,}138{,}159/96{,}102 = 11.8$ years.

(iv) From (ii) and (iii), the future expectation of life for a male aged $14 = 42.9 + 11.8 = 54.7$ years.

(v)   By interpolation within columns 7 and 9 we can see that above age $57\tfrac{1}{2}$ there are approximately the same number of men in, and not in, the work force in the stationary population.

(vi) Men who reach age 65 spend thereafter on the average $253{,}368/62{,}533$ or 4.05 years in the work force, and $538{,}016/62{,}533$ or 8.60 years not in the work force.

(vii) Extensions as in Chapter 4 enable us to study the growth and change in the work force, estimate expected future lifetime earnings, estimate replacement needs for industry, etc.

10.8 Use of multiple-decrement tables

We now repeat the examples of multiple-decrement tables referred to so far in this chapter.

(i)   Single persons subject to the decrements of marriage and mortality.

(ii)   Persons subject to mortality from two or more causes.

(iii)   Combined marriage and mortality tables recording the number of bachelors and the number of married men and the deaths of each class and movement between classes.

(iv)   Persons subject to the decrements of mortality and disability.

(v)   Persons subject to the decrement of mortality and movement to and from the work force.

Other uses have been made of multiple-decrement tables of which the more important are:

(vi)   Measuring the contraceptive effectiveness of intra-uterine devices where the device may be considered ineffective if any one of three events (decrements) takes place, namely, removal of the device, expulsion of the device or the person becomes pregnant (see exercise 10.10).

(vii)   Failure of a machine through breakdown of two or more components.

(viii) 'Service tables' for employees subject to death, retirement, resignation or invalidity.

(ix)   The application of rates of fertility and dissolution of marriage (due to death, divorce, etc.) to a cohort of marriages to obtain the proportion of marriages still infertile by duration of marriage.

For further reading

1. Benjamin, B. and Haycocks, H. W., *The Analysis of Mortality and Other Actuarial Statistics*, Cambridge University Press, 1970.
2. Benjamin, B. and Pollard, J. H., *The Analysis of Mortality and Other Actuarial Statistics*, Heinemann, 1980.
3. Hooker, P. F. and Longley-Cook, L. H., *Life and Other Contingencies*, Vol. II, Cambridge University Press, 1957, pp. 1–45.
4. Jordan, C. W., *Life Contingencies*, Chicago University Press, Chapters 14 and 15.
5. Neill, A., *Life Contingencies*, Heinemann, 1977, pp. 291–320.

Exercises

10.1   From the data in *Table 10.1* insert in the blank spaces of the following schedule the percentage of single women of given age who marry within the periods specified.

	Age					
	16	18	20	25	30	40
Within 1 year						3.6
Within 2 years						6.7
Within 3 years						9.4
Within 5 years						13.9
Within 10 years					48.3	21.3
Lifetime					63.4	29.7

10.2 Calculate the chance that a male aged 40 will survive to age 65 assuming the mortality rates given at the beginning of section 10.5 but with mortality from neoplasms eliminated.

10.3 Assuming that the population is stationary and that all men aged 40 to 65 are in the work force, find the percentage increase in the male work force between age 40 and age 65 if diseases of the circulatory system above age 40 were to be eliminated. (Use the information given in section 10.5.)

10.4 Explain clearly how you would estimate the percentage increase in the male work force if the mortality from heart disease and from cancer were both to be reduced by one-third.

10.5 'Diseases which affect the young result in relatively greater losses to the community than diseases which affect the aged'. What statistical approach would you adopt to support this statement?

10.6 Use the information in *Table 10.3* to answer the following questions:
  (i) What is the ratio of men under 21 in the work force to men under 21 not in the work force in the stationary population?
  (ii) At what age might a man expect to spend
      (a) one half; and
      (b) two-thirds of his future life in the work force?
  (iii) What is the median age of men
      (a) in the work force; and
      (b) not in the work force?

10.7 From the information in *Table 10.3* draw a graph showing how the rate at which employed men withdraw from the work force varies with age, for ages over 45. At what age does the rate reach a maximum? Comment on this result and on the graph generally and suggest what information you would need to investigate the matter further.

10.8 How would you determine the expected future working life and expected future retired life of a person now aged 24 and in the work force?

10.9 What information would you suggest should be included in a working life table for women?

10.10 R. G. Potter in a paper presented to the 1967 Conference of the Internation Union for the Scientific Study of Population used multiple-decrement tables to estimate the chance, month by month, of retaining an intra-uterine device and not becoming pregnant and thus to measure their contraceptive effectiveness. Construct part of such a table from the following information for women of a given age.

Month	Dependent probabilities of		
	expelling the I.U.D.	removing the I.U.D.	becoming pregnant
1	.02537	.03464	.00167
2	.01754	.01688	.00430
3	.01666	.01929	.00438

From this table determine:
(i) the probability of retaining the device for at least three months without falling pregnant,
(ii) the probability that a new user falls pregnant in the second month,
(iii) the probability of expulsion or removal of the device in the first three months.

(The following demographic comment is relevant. Younger women have higher fertility than older women but expel I.U.D.s more frequently. Multiple decrement tables for women of different ages may be used to determine whether population growth is retarded more by the use of I.U.D.s by younger women rather than by older women.)

10.11 Communication between two parties will break down in the event of transmitter failure, receiver failure or failure of the link between transmitter and receiver. Experiments were carried out on a number of these three components independently to determine their rates of failure. The following results were obtained:

Age x (years)	Rate of failure at age x of		
	transmitter	receiver	link
0	0.1	0.10	0.3
1	0.2	0.05	0.2
2	0.3	0.05	0.2
3	0.4	0.05	0.1

Construct the 'life table' for effective communication for 0 to 4 years and from it estimate the chance that effective communication is maintained for four years.

11
Testing the accuracy
of demographic data

11.1 Introduction

Even in the most developed countries, where considerable care is taken to ensure that the demographic data collected are both complete and accurate, errors do occur. They occur with greater frequency in the less developed countries where the skill and training of the data collection personnel and the education level of the respondents may all be lower. They occur in census data, in registration data and in survey data, but within the same country the type of error and the extent of the error will vary considerably between the different data sources.

All the demographic rates and ratios discussed in the earlier chapters have assumed that the data are complete and accurate. We must now consider how reasonable is such an assumption. Clearly before embarking on any detailed investigation of any demographic data it is essential to first consider how reliable the data are and, if possible, correct any errors or adjust the data so that they appear reasonable.

There is no unique general procedure to apply; what is needed is a large amount of personal experience and familiarity with the peculiarities of the data under consideration. Some guidelines about what to expect and ways to proceed are given here, but this must be modified to suit the actual situation.

11.2 Types and sources of errors

Errors may be divided into three broad categories described as:
(i)   sampling errors (including random fluctuations)
(ii) errors of coverage
(iii) errors of content (or response errors).

Sampling errors are those inaccuracies arising because data have been collected for only some and not all members of the population. The magnitude of error here is determined very largely by the number of persons covered. Generally speaking, the larger the sample the more accurate the results. However a doubling of accuracy is achieved only by a quadrupling of the size of the sample and this requires a near quadrupling of costs. The subject of demographic sample surveys was discussed in Chapter 9. Sampling errors are not considered here and are the subject of separate texts in sampling techniques.* It should be stressed that if sampling is to be employed, the services of a sampling expert should be sought.

Even when the total population is considered, chance or random fluctuations can occur from year to year or between different population groups. Thus some random fluctuation about a general trend is expected in the birth rate, death rate, cause specific death rate, etc. The magnitude of this variability again depends on population size. The existence of both sampling errors and random fluctuations should be noted. However, the purpose of this chapter is to consider defects in the data through the other causes.

Errors of coverage occur when a particular segment of the population is under-enumerated or counted more than once or even missed altogether. Countries may deliberately include or exclude certain relatively small classes of population from their census counts. Examples include merchant seamen, diplomats, armed forces, etc. Others may be excluded on the grounds of cost (e.g. nomadic tribes or full-blood aborigines in remote areas) or danger (e.g. indigenous population in the highlands of New Guinea). However, no matter how careful an approach is adopted some persons will inadvertently be omitted from the population or counted twice. For example, errors may arise in allocating the 'floating' population; that is, people travelling during the census period might be double counted or missed completely. In some Asian censuses it has been noted that the enumeration of females, particularly young unmarried women, is incomplete because of the reluctance on the part of householders to divulge information about their womenfolk. In vital statistics duplicate registration is negligible, but omission can be quite serious, even to the extent that the data are useless for measuring birth, death and marriage rates, and other techniques must be used. This is particularly true in developing countries and some of the techniques are discussed in Chapter 12.

Errors of content or response errors occur because of the inability or unwillingness of the respondent to give correct information. For example, many people do not report their income, and even if they do so, they do not give their correct income. In some countries people do not report their ages correctly, not because they do not wish to tell their age but because they in fact do not remember their correct age. This phenomenon of inability of the respondent to recall information is known as 'recall lapse'. The extent of recall lapse varies with characteristics such as age and may also vary according to the type of information needed to be recalled. Recall lapse not only tends to introduce response errors but may also result in errors of coverage. For example, in many censuses and surveys it has been found that older women have a tendency to forget to report their live-born children who were not alive at the time of interview.

The respondent is not the only source of errors. The interviewer or enumerator completing the census or registration form, the person who codes the data and the person who punches up the data for computer analysis can also make errors. Incomplete or incorrect classification by doctors of the cause of death is a well-known source of error for cause of death statistics. In open-ended questions there can even be disagreement among experts of the correct coding of certain items such as occupation. Success depends on adequate preparation and planning, design of questionnaire, training and supervision

---

*See for example, Cochran, W. G., *Sampling Techniques*, 1953.

of the field staff and office staff. Further examples of the various types of error are given in the following sections as we consider methods for detecting errors.

11.3 Some general testing procedures

As discussed earlier, there is no unique general procedure to apply but rather a search for a few familiar defects and examination of the reasonableness of the data should be made. No test is conclusive and the lack of detection of errors does not necessarily mean errors do not exist but does give some increased confidence in the data. All methods of appraising the data involve comparing two or more statistics which have a definite relationship (known or assumed) and to see whether the relationship holds. Methods of testing the accuracy of demographic data usually fall under one of the following headings:
(i)   Conducting a post-enumeration quality check.
(ii) Checking the internal consistency of the data, either on an individual record basis or on an aggregative basis for the tabulated data.
(iii) Comparing the data with some other body of data to check the plausibility of the data being tested.

The post-enumeration quality check is usually done following a population census or a large demographic sample survey. Such a check is performed by selecting a small sample of blocks and arranging for specially trained interviewers to re-interview respondents in those blocks. A comparison of the results of the post-enumeration quality check with the corresponding results for the selected blocks from the census or survey being tested gives an indication of the extent of errors of coverage, and also of the differences in response patterns between the actual census or survey and the post-enumeration quality check. For example, the 1976 census population of Australia of 13.5486 million was increased by 2.71% to 13.9155 million as a result of a post-enumeration quality check.

A number of checks should be applied to the raw data to test for internal consistency. First, it is necessary to check that all the answers given by each individual are internally consistent or at least plausible. For example, should both date of birth and age be asked, these should agree. Second, the total data should be checked for internal consistency. These include a check in each tabulation that the figures run smoothly from (say) age to age or duration to duration. If there are irregularities, an explanation should be found for them. For example, if the irregularities are thought to be due to age preference a check should be made to see whether similar preferences occurred at the previous census. The sex ratio at birth should be about 1.05 and at higher ages should change smoothly with age. The proportions married should increase steadily with age. A decrease in the parity of women with age should be viewed with suspicion. The number of currently married males should be approximately equal to the number of currently married females. If in a set of data the number of currently married males is, say, 20% more than the number of currently married females, if there is no evidence of emigration of married females from that population and if the number of polygamous marriages is relatively very small, we can argue that the above data are inconsistent and that they indicate the extent of under-enumeration of females. In recent population censuses and demographic sample surveys the internal consistency of data is usually tested by means of computer editing procedures.

The accuracy of a given set of demographic data may also be tested by comparing it with some other data pertaining to the same or related phenomenon. Thus, for example, in countries with compulsory education up to a certain grade, a comparison can be made between the school-going population recorded in a census or a demographic sample survey with the school enrolment statistics. Country of birth statistics from a census can be compared with immigration records. The population under the age of five can be compared with the births over the previous five years less any deaths. If the results of an earlier census are available the number of males and females in age groups should be compared with the number of survivors expected from the earlier census. The sex ratios at higher ages should be compared with those obtained at recent surveys or recent censuses.

Finally, researchers should not overlook examining the various rules of procedure used in gathering and compiling the statistics. These can lead to inaccuracies or inadequacies in the data which can be confirmed by analysis. Tests which depend on reference to individual records or on a post-enumeration quality check are beyond the resources or access of the ordinary researcher and are for the Census Bureau or Registration personnel only. We are therefore concerned only with an examination of the available published data. There do exist a number of tests for some of the more major flaws that occur and these are now considered.

11.4 Checking the accuracy of age and sex data

The age-sex distribution of a population at any point of time is a result of the interaction of the fertility, mortality and migration levels of the past seven or more decades. In a life table or stationary population, the number of persons at each age is greater than the number at the next older age. The sex ratio should commence at 105 males per 100 females at the youngest ages and decrease as age increases.

Actual populations, however, experience varying fertility and mortality rates and some of them (e.g. Australia) are subject to large migrant streams and as a result the above relationship may not hold and the population may not exhibit a smooth age distribution. Ups and downs in the age distribution which result from such variations are real and cannot be termed errors.

However, irregularities in the age and sex distribution cannot always be attributed to fluctuations in the fertility, mortality and migration levels in the population. It is well established that some people do not report their ages correctly and this can cause a lack of smoothness in the age distribution. Errors in age reporting do occur to some extent in developed countries but they are of real significance in many populations in Asia, Africa and Latin America. Some of the more common reasons for age misstatement include the omission of young infants, the rounding off due to lack of knowledge of exact age, the changing of age for reasons of schooling, voting, marriage, entitlement to age pension and legal permission to purchase alcohol or to gamble, understatement by young adult women or exaggeration by the elderly. In addition, a proportion of the population fail to report age at all, but these can be distributed in the same proportion as those who do state their age. The errors in age-sex distribution have been more closely examined than other errors because of the important effect age and sex have on other demographic characteristics.

11.5 Checking the accuracy of single-year age distributions

Table 11.1 shows the single-year age distribution of the male and female population of

Table 11.1

Age distribution by sex, for West Malaysia: 1970 Census

Age	Males	Females	Age	Males	Females
0	134,940	129,318	33	49,568	50,498
1	133,098	128,141	34	51,208	53,008
2	142,684	137,410	35	49,639	51,831
3	136,409	131,973	36	42,270	44,885
4	142,739	137,104	37	37,745	39,849
5	136,493	130,742	38	36,591	37,556
6	140,957	135,708	39	37,807	40,097
7	136,882	131,218	40	45,435	44,932
8	132,675	128,428	41	40,447	45,102
9	136,598	131,503	42	37,870	40,542
10	130,386	125,920	43	32,062	28,558
11	125,346	121,519	44	30,640	27,443
12	119,025	115,532	45	32,029	29,055
13	116,613	114,067	46	37,999	43,911
14	115,040	113,108	47	30,412	35,935
15	107,433	107,094	48	25,237	23,086
16	102,462	103,415	49	26,608	25,111
17	97,436	99,839	50	32,211	30,768
18	94,949	96,542	51	37,251	39,025
19	81,327	84,673	52	30,500	32,624
20	82,308	86,810	53	19,971	16,635
21	77,940	81,336	54	19,929	16,573
22	71,304	73,535	55	20,625	17,733
23	74,404	76,446	56	31,973	30,216
24	60,048	59,526	57	26,709	26,319
25	54,018	53,874	58	18,142	15,442
26	54,978	56,595	59	19,271	15,675
27	56,157	56,759	60	25,143	22,429
28	53,904	54,069	61	27,759	27,315
29	53,298	53,864	62	22,608	23,030
30	58,175	57,983	63	13,375	10,429
31	51,622	52,032	64	12,679	9,866
32	54,129	54,633	65 & over	145,439	134,259
			Unknown	23,827	22,227
			All ages	4,436,756	4,372,680

Note the relatively large numbers recorded at ages 46, 51, 56 and 61

(*Source:* 1970 Population and Housing Census of Malaysia)

West Malaysia according to the 1970 census. This same information is shown graphically in *Figure 11.1*. It is apparent that the population reported ages ending in certain digits more frequently than ages ending in the other digits. Note particularly the numbers recorded at ages 46, 51, 56 and 61. This phenomenon which is called 'digital preference' has been frequently observed in many countries and particularly in the developing countries. Common preference is for the digits 0 and 5 and for the even digits.

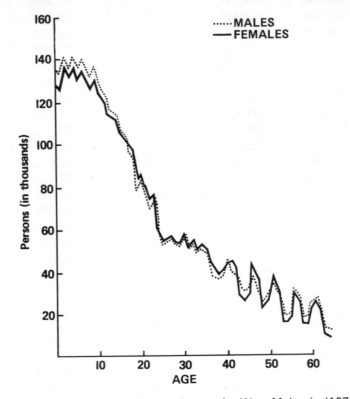

Figure 11.1: Single year age distributions by sex for West Malaysia (1970 Census)

Digital preference is usually apparent from a visual presentation of the data like *Figure 11.1*. Numerical methods of measuring it have been devised. However, as the numbers in the population fall with age a simple tabulation of the population according to final digit of the age would weight the smaller digits unduly, (see columns 2 or 5 of *Table 11.2*). Myers* in 1940 proposed a method which made an allowance for this factor.

His method involves calculating a 'blended' population of final digits in which, if the population numbers decrease linearly with age, the expectation is that in the absence of any digital preference about 10% of the population will have reported ages ending in digit 0, 10% ages ending in digit 1, and so on. Any deviations from the expected 10% for each

*Myers, R. J., Errors and Bias in the Reporting of Ages in Census Data, *Transactions of the Actuarial Society of America*, Vol. 41, 1940.

terminal digit are added (irrespective of sign) to arrive at the Myers' index. *Table 11.2* illustrates the computational procedure, using the 1970 census data for males in West Malaysia.

The first step in calculating the Myer's index is to derive the 'blended' population. For this, one has to decide the age range over which the extent of digital preference has to be measured. Any age range can be selected; however, in our example we have selected the age range of 10–59 years. The chosen age range is divided into two partly overlapping sub-ranges with a time lag of 10 years. In the example these will be age ranges 10–49 and 20–59 which have a 10-year time lag and have ages 20–49 as the overlapping part of the two ranges. Taking the 10–49 age range, population totals are computed for ages ending in each of the ten digits and are recorded in column (2).

These population totals are multiplied by the coefficients given in column (3) and the products recorded in column (4). This procedure is repeated in the age range 20–59 for which the population totals are given in column (5), the coefficients in column (6) and the products in column (7). It may be noted that for each digit the sum of the coefficients given in columns (3) and (6) is 10. It can easily be shown that the multiplication by these coefficients ensures that each digit is given equal weight.

In age distributions which are free from digital preference like those of life table populations, the blended population total for each digit would be close to 10 per cent of the total population for all digits. The percentages for each final digit for the West Malaysian males' data are given in column (9), and column (10) gives the absolute values of deviations from 10 per cent, the total of which is called the Myers' index. For West Malaysian males for the age range chosen the index was 3.62. Theoretically, the Myers' index can vary from 0 to 180. The smaller the value of the index the less is the extent of digital preference in the reporting of ages. The percentage of the blended population suggests that in this case the terminal digits in order of preference were 0, 1, 2, 6, 3, 4, 5, 7, 8 and 9.

The figures in column (9) of *Table 11.2* and the Myers' index of 3.62 suggest that there is little digital preference in West Malaysia. However a glance at *Figure 11.1* shows clearly that there is actually substantial digital preference at ages over 40, little between 10 and 40, and a different form of preference under age 10. This shows the need for a graphical inspection of the data before proceeding to mechanical methods. In this case a separate analysis should be made for the three age ranges in which different forms of preference apply. If mechanical methods are routinely applied to the whole age range in cases such as this significant preference in different age ranges may balance out.

The pattern of digital preference and the extent of age misreporting varies from country to country. For example, in Pakistan for the age range 10–79 years for data collected during 1965 for the Population Growth Estimation Project the Myers' index was 66 for males and 65 for females. The percentage of the blended population for each digit is given in *Table 11.3* which shows that digits 0, 5, 2 and 8 account for nearly three-quarters of the total blended population.

If fluctuations in numbers have been established as being due to digital preference it is necessary to correct the raw data in some way. It is a common practice in such a situation to use data in age groups with the ages appropriately selected. Otherwise graphical or mechanical methods of smoothing should be adopted. These include redistributing five year age groups into single year of ages according to the birth statistics to which they relate or according to the survivors of these births or according to the life table stationary

Table 11.2

Illustrative calculation of Myers' index for males in West Malaysia: 1970 Census

Terminal digit	Age group 10–49			Age group 20–59			Blended population (4) + (7)	%	Deviations from 10%
	Sum	Coefficient	Product (2) × (3)	Sum	Coefficient	Product (5) × (6)			
(1)	(2)	(3)	(4)	(5)	(6)	(7)	(8)	(9)	(10)
0	316,304	1	316,304	218,129	9	1,963,161	2,279,465	10.69	.69
1	295,355	2	590,710	207,260	8	1,658,080	2,248,790	10.55	.55
2	282,328	3	846,984	193,803	7	1,356,621	2,203,605	10.33	.33
3	272,647	4	1,090,588	176,005	6	1,056,030	2,146,618	10.07	.07
4	256,936	5	1,284,680	161,825	5	809,125	2,093,805	9.82	.18
5	243,119	6	1,458,714	156,311	4	625,244	2,083,958	9.77	.23
6	237,709	7	1,663,963	167,220	3	501,660	2,165,623	10.16	.16
7	221,750	8	1,774,000	151,023	2	302,046	2,076,046	9.74	.26
8	210,681	9	1,896,129	133,874	1	133,874	2,030,003	9.52	.48
9	199,040	10	1,990,400	136,984	0	0	1,990,400	9.33	.67
All digits	—	—	—	—	—	—	21,318,313		3.62

Table 11.3

Percentage of the blended population for each final digit: Pakistan 1965

Digit	Males	Females
0	28.72	29.02
1	2.71	2.39
2	9.86	10.52
3	4.03	4.01
4	5.00	5.94
5	24.02	22.79
6	7.79	7.73
7	4.82	4.83
8	10.24	10.18
9	2.81	2.59
All digits	100.00	100.00

(*Source:* Yusuf, Farhat, On the Extent of Digital Preference in Reporting of Ages in Pakistan, *Pakistan Development Review*, Vol. 7, 1967, p. 523)

population (L_x) distribution or by various forms of mathematical interpolation including Sprague's osculatory interpolation formula, quadratic interpolation or the Carrier Farrag ratio method.

11.6 Checking the accuracy of grouped age data

In many countries, because of errors in age reporting, populations are often tabulated as has just been pointed out, in five- or ten-year age groups. The detection of errors in grouped data is much more difficult than for single age data. Various methods exist such as re-interviewing or matching records, or more technical methods such as inter-censal cohort analysis and comparison with birth statistics. These all involve comparison with another set of data. The United Nations Population Division has developed a method* to check the accuracy of such grouped data using only the data collected. The method is based on the assumption that the sex ratio and the numbers in each age group should change smoothly with increasing age and it attempts to measure the differences which occur from a steady trend. As an illustration, this method is applied in *Table 11.4* to the age-sex distribution at the 1970 census of West Malaysia.

The sex ratio for each age group is determined, the first differences calculated and the average of these, irrespective of sign, gives what is called the sex ratio score. This makes no allowance for the fact that the sex ratio is expected to decline by age.

* United Nations, *Population Bulletin No. 2*, 1952.

Table 11.4

Computation of age and sex ratio scores for West Malaysia: 1970 Census

Age	Actual population		Sex ratio	Absolute value of difference	Average population*		Percentage by which actual population exceeds average population	
	Males	Females			Males	Females	Males	Females
0– 4	689,870	663,946	103.90	.05				
5– 9	683,605	657,599	103.95	1.19	648,140	627,046	5.47	4.87
10–14	606,410	590,146	102.76	4.36	583,606	574,581	3.91	2.71
15–19	483,607	491,563	98.40	1.48	486,207	483,900	0.53	1.58
20–24	366,004	377,653	96.92	2.06	377,981	383,362	3.17	1.49
25–29	272,355	275,161	98.98	.27	315,353	322,904	13.63	14.79
30–34	264,702	268,154	98.71	3.46	238,204	244,690	11.12	9.59
35–39	204,052	214,218	95.25	4.68	225,578	227,366	9.54	5.78
40–44	186,454	186,577	99.93	2.99	178,169	185,658	4.65	0.49
45–49	152,285	157,098	96.94	6.18	163,158	161,101	6.66	2.48
50–54	139,862	135,625	103.12	7.64	134,503	131,242	3.98	3.34
55–59	116,720	105,385	110.76	1.63	120,713	114,347	3.31	7.84
60–64	101,564	93,069	109.13					
Sex ratio score				2.99	Age ratio scores		6.00	5.00

* Average of population in next higher and next lower age group.

To obtain the age ratio score for a particular sex, the absolute value of the percentage by which the number in each age group differs from the average of the numbers in the next higher and the next lower age group is determined and the average of these percentages is the age ratio score.

A combination of these, called the joint score, is sometimes used. It is defined as three times the sex ratio score plus the sum of the male and female age ratio scores. Figures for the censuses of West Malaysia in 1970 and India in 1961 are:

	West Malaysia (1970)	India (1961)
Sex ratio score	3.0	7.8
Age ratio score, male	6.0	22.8
Age ratio score, female	5.0	29.2
Joint score	20.0	75.4

These scores do no more than give a rough indication of smoothness of the data which is affected by a number of items such as digital preference, age variations in under-reporting, etc. A study of the differences columns in *Table 11.4* by age group may suggest errors which warrant further investigation.

11.7 Use of life table in testing the accuracy of demographic data

Given an appropriate life table and complete birth statistics for the five years prior to a census, one can calculate the population expected to be enumerated at ages 0, 1, 2, 3 and 4 in the census by multiplying births by the appropriate survival ratios. Thus, for example, births in the year preceding the census will be multiplied by the survival ratio L_0/l_0, births two years prior to the census by the ratio L_1/l_0 and so on. More generally births x years prior to the census will be multiplied by L_{x-1}/l_0 to arrive at the expected population aged $x - 1$ to x at the time of the census. In this way we can check the accuracy of age reporting of children in the census.

On the other hand, the completeness of birth registration can also be tested by calculating the number of births which occurred, say, five years before the census by multiplying the population aged 4 in the census by the reciprocal of the survival ratio namely l_0/L_4. This is called the reverse survival ratio method.

For further reading

1. Barclay, G. W., *Techniques of Population Analysis*, Wiley, 1962, pp. 56–92.
2. Jaffe, A. J., *Handbook of Statistical Methods for Demographers*, 1951, pp. 85–179.
3. Shryock, H. S. and Siegel, J. S., *The Methods and Materials of Demography*, U.S. Government Printing Office, 1973, pp. 102–12, 203–30.
4. Spiegelman, M., *Introduction to Demography*, Harvard, 1968, pp. 43–79.
5. United Nations, Manual II, Methods of Appraisal of Quality of Basic Data for Population Estimates, *Population Studies No. 23*, 1955.

Exercises

11.1 Calculate the Myers' index for females for the age range 10 to 59 years for the 1970 West Malaysian data in *Table 11.1*.

11.2 On the basis of your analysis of digital preference in the above question, which scheme of quinquennial age groupings would you recommend (e.g. 0–4, 1–5, 2–6, ...) and why?

11.3 Calculate the age ratio scores, sex ratio score and joint score for the 1965 census of Turkey from the following data:

Age	Population (000's)	
	Males	Females
0– 9	4,770	4,512
10–19	3,603	3,174
20–29	3,266	2,294
30–39	2,136	2,069
40–49	1,150	1,106
50–59	1,062	1,006
60–69	711	773
70+	272	441
Unknown	28	18
All ages	16,998	15,393

11.4 The following statistics relating to births during 1956 in the United Arab Republic are taken from the 1959 edition of the United Nations Demographic Year Book.

Parity	Number of births
1	54,956
2	68,909
3	85,286
4	83,248
5	62,890

Comment on the accuracy and consistency of these figures.

11.5 Estimate the male and female population aged 0, 1, 2, 3 and 4 in the census of Australia taken on 30th June, 1961 by using the A^{M61} and A^{F61} life tables and the following birth statistics:

Calendar Year	Males	Females
1956	109,589	102,544
1957	113,237	107,121
1958	113,957	108,547
1959	116,241	110,735
1960	118,415	111,911
1961	123,112	116,874

11.6 The actual population recorded in the 1961 census of Australia at ages 0 to 4 was

Age	Males	Females
0	116,736	111,790
1	112,262	106,212
2	114,988	110,421
3	112,964	108,074
4	110,792	105,279

Assuming that the census and registration system constituted an accurate record, estimate from the answer to exercise 11.5 the extent to which the population at ages 0 to 4 has been augmented by migration.

12
Estimating demographic measures from incomplete data

12.1 Introduction

In previous chapters we described the population census, the vital registration system and other sources of demographic data and explained how they yield information which is used to construct life tables, to measure mortality and fertility changes, to estimate rates of growth and to prepare population projections. In developed countries the census and registration systems are well established and reliable statistics are available not only in respect of recent years but for many decades in the past. Outside the more advanced countries however such a system seldom exists; indeed the majority of the world's population lives in countries that are underdeveloped not only economically but from the point of view of demographic and other statistics as well. The effort being made in these countries to speed up economic and social advance requires for its planning information on demographic matters which the existing statistical sources cannot adequately supply. The demographer may be presented with a miscellaneous collection of field survey results, censuses, administrative records, incomplete registration material, socio-economic enquiries, medical records, etc., all incomplete to an unknown degree and referring to different periods of time. He is required to weigh the relevance and quality of the information from the various sources and make estimates of the basic demographic measures. Alternatively, he may be provided with limited funds to collect the minimum required information through specially designed field enquiries. Here he has to weigh the desirability, reliability, feasibility and cost of the various types of investigations on which he may spend the funds. The problem of estimating demographic measures from incomplete data is a challenging one, one for which there is no universal answer and one which therefore requires in the demographer the qualities of resourcefulness and imagination.

The estimates which are made are usually based on assumptions which can be accepted with different degrees of confidence. Some assumptions are based on fairly universal characteristics of human populations and can be taken to be fairly reliable, e.g. the assumption that the sex ratio of births is constant, that the average number of children born to a woman increases with increasing age, or that the distribution of fertility by age is constant. Other assumptions frequently used, often without any reliable justification, are that the shape of the mortality curve in the country being studied follows that of one of the model life tables or that mortality and fertility have been approximately constant over a long period of time justifying the use of stable population models.

It is not possible in a brief chapter to present a comprehensive survey of the various techniques which have been used, but enough examples will be given to enable the reader to ponder on the problems involved.

12.2 Two censuses by age and sex

In many countries vital statistics are non-existent or so deficient as to be useless for demographic purposes. Population counts may have been taken at two different times; in any case they usually can be organized more easily than establishing a registration system. In Fiji, for example, the population was enumerated by age and sex in 1956 and again in 1966. Can we estimate the crude birth and death rates and the crude rate of increase from these data? If we can assume that migration is negligible, the answer is 'yes'. The basic steps are:

(i)   The average growth rate r over the 10 years is obtained from the two total populations by the formula $P_{10} = P_0(1 + r)^{10}$.

(ii)   By following through each age cohort (e.g. females 10–14 in 1956 become females 20–24 in 1966) a set of ten-year survival ratios is obtained and from this the central death rate for each age group can be estimated.

(iii) By applying these death rates to the average population by age for the decade, the deaths in age groups are obtained, and hence the total deaths.

(iv)   Total deaths divided by the average population gives the crude death rate.

(v)   The crude birth rate is obtained by adding the crude death rate to the rate of population growth, r, estimated earlier.

Two practical difficulties with this method are soon apparent. Firstly, there are no cohorts of persons under 10 alive at both censuses and so some other method is required to estimate mortality under 10. Secondly, because of migration or age misstatements some 10-year survival ratios exceed unity, which is theoretically impossible. The second problem can be tackled by smoothing the data, or better still by the following method which at the same time solves the first difficulty.

This method is to use model life tables at various mortality levels to estimate the number of survivors after 10 years of the 1956 population 0 and over, 5 and over, 10 and over, etc. in order to find for each of these age groups which mortality level best fits the actual experience. A series of mortality levels, one for each age group, is thus obtained. The median of these levels is adopted for the population and by reference to the model life table the values of the age specific death rates, thence the deaths in age groups, total deaths and finally the crude death rate can be calculated. It will be noted that mortality under age 10 has in this way been obtained from the model life table appropriate for age 10 and over.

The accuracy of estimates such as these should always be assessed. One source of error results from the fact that for a given level of mortality over age 5, mortality under age 5 varies quite considerably with the regional model life table used. Moreover mortality under age 5 contributes substantially to the crude death rate and any error automatically affects the birth rate also. The fact is that there is no way of accurately determining mortality under age 5 from censuses alone. Another common source of error is underenumeration at a census. If the degree of underenumeration at the later census is greater then the growth rate is underestimated and the death rate overestimated. If such errors are likely, a range of estimates should be given to provide an indication of the extent to which the estimates are sensitive to the assumptions.

12.3 One census by age and sex

Information about the age-sex distribution of the population at one point of time is insufficient to produce sound estimates of birth or death rates. However, as fertility is the main factor in determining the age structure, a rough assumption about mortality level may be used to estimate whether fertility is 'high', 'medium' or 'low'. It would not, however, discriminate between 'very high' and 'moderately high'. If it could be assumed that mortality was the same for different socio-economic groups in the population then the age distributions of those groups could be used to provide an indication of differential fertility. A comparison of child-woman ratios would be appropriate for this purpose.

If it is justifiable to assume that the population is in a stable state it is possible to estimate birth and death rates from one census by age and sex. If, for example, the number of females aged 30–34 is divided by the number aged 20–24 we obtain the 10 year survival ratio multiplied by a 10 year growth factor. If we obtain a similar quotient for females 40–44 and 30–34 and divide the two quotients the growth factor cancels out leaving only the ratio of survival factors. This ratio may be used to identify the appropriate model life table. This model table and the census age distribution may be used to calculate the crude death rate, and the model life table mortality together with child-woman ratios from the census enable fertility rates to be calculated.

It should be noted that this method is just as appropriate with a sample survey as with a full census.

Where there is no vital registration system it is a common practice to ask questions about fertility at the census. These questions are of two types:
(i)   inquiries about the number of children born during the past 12 months, and
(ii) inquiries about the number of children ever born up to the time of the inquiry.
The first question enables the calculation of age specific fertility rates indicating current fertility. Answers to the second question give an indication of past fertility. By cumulating births during the past 12 months per mother by age of mother figures are obtained for current fertility comparable to the estimates of past fertility measured by the average number of children ever born obtained from (ii). If the former are systematically higher than the latter, fertility is rising and vice versa.

Unfortunately experience has shown that where no written record of a birth exists, as is often the case in developing countries, women are often several months in error in indicating the date of birth and consequently many births are incorrectly allocated within or outside the 12 month period. Also, with respect to children ever born, understatement is common, usually due to memory failure or omission of dead children or children who have left home. These latter biases particularly affect older women or women of higher parities.

It might be thought that death statistics could be obtained in a similar way by asking about deaths in the past 12 months but as yet this approach has not proved very successful.

12.4 Comparison of current and past fertility (P/F ratio)

Brass (1975) has suggested a method which uses statistics on current and past fertility to derive mutually consistent estimates of the pattern and level of fertility. According to this procedure, the *shape* of the fertility schedule is based on births in the previous twelve months, while the *level* of fertility is determined by the number of children ever born to women in younger age groups, such as 25–29, so as to minimize the problems of recall lapse. The actual procedure involves the calculation of synthetic average parities, F_i, based on cumulative age specific fertility rates to age i reported as by women at each age in the reproductive life span. Theoretically these synthetic average parities should coincide with the reported average parities if there are no problems of recall lapse, if ages of women are correctly reported, if the respondents had a proper perception of the reference period and if the female age at marriage and fertility levels were relatively constant. When the two sets of parities do not coincide, the ratio of the actual to the synthetic parity (i.e. P_i/F_i), for $i = 20$–24 or 25–29 is used to adjust the level of fertility implied by the data on births last year.

Let f_i be the age specific fertility rate for women aged i, where i takes values 0 through 7 corresponding to age group 10–14, 15–19, ..., 45–49. The cumulative age specific fertility rates to the end of age i, $\emptyset_i$, may be defined as:

$$\emptyset_i = 5\left(\sum_{j=0}^{i} f_j\right).$$

We have to convert these cumulated age specific fertility rates (which represent average parity at the *end* of age group i) into average parity for the group of ages i. Moreover, as data on current fertility are usually tabulated according to the age of mother at the time of interview, mothers may be assumed to be half a year younger at the birth of their child, provided births are uniformly distributed. A simple procedure for interpolation has been suggested (Barclay et. al., 1976). It involves fitting a second degree polynomial to every three consecutive points of the $\emptyset_i$. Each of these polynomials expresses $\emptyset_i$ as a function of age over a ten-year age span. Thus the average parity over any age interval within the ten-year span is obtained by integrating the polynomial over the particular interval and dividing by the length of the interval. Using the above procedure the following equations could be derived in order to convert $\emptyset_i$ and f_i into the synthetic average parities, F_i:

$$F_1 = \emptyset_0 + 3.392 f_1 - 0.392 f_2$$

$$F_j = \emptyset_{j-1} + 0.392 f_{j-1} + 2.608 f_j \text{ (for } j \geqslant 2).$$

12.5 The age distribution of deaths

If the population is in a stable state and if the under-registration of deaths does not vary from age to age, the rate of population increase and the crude birth and death rates may be estimated from the age distribution of deaths alone. It should be emphasized however that the assumptions specified are not likely often to be realized.

If D_{30-40} represents the proportion of the total deaths which are of persons aged 30 to 40, then D_{30-40} on the above assumptions equals $\dfrac{l_{30} - l_{40}}{l_0}$ from the appropriate life table multiplied by a factor depending on the growth rate. By calculating the ratio $\dfrac{D_{30-40} \times D_{50-60}}{D_{40-50}^2}$ the growth rate factor cancels out and this ratio should equal $\dfrac{(l_{30} - l_{40})(l_{50} - l_{60})}{(l_{40} - l_{50})^2}$ from the appropriate life table. By working out this ratio for several model life tables the appropriate life table can be selected. Having thus selected the life table the growth rate can be calculated from

$$\frac{D_{30-40}}{D_{40-50}} \times \frac{l_{40} - l_{50}}{l_{30} - l_{40}} = (1 + r)^{10}$$

From the growth rate and the mortality level the population characteristics can be obtained by reference to model stable population tables.

A range of ages covering most of the life span (e.g. 14 and under, 15–44, 45 and over) might be more appropriate to use than the particular ages just quoted.

12.6 Proportions living among children ever born

A census or survey may be used to collect data from women over 15 concerning the number of children ever born and the number still alive; these data may be used to estimate infant and child mortality. These ratios alone may be used to indicate differential mortality but for other purposes they need to be converted into probabilities $_xq_0$ of dying between age 0 and age x. A study covering a wide range of mortality and fertility levels showed that the proportion dead of children ever born to women now 15–19 is very close to $_1q_0$. For mothers 20–24 and 25–29 the proportion is very nearly equal to $_2q_0$ and $_3q_0$ respectively. For mothers 45–49 the proportion is very nearly equal to $_{20}q_0$ and similarly for other ages. Conversion factors to produce $_xq_0$ given the proportion dead of children ever born to mothers aged x have been tabulated. These factors depend to some extent on the shape of the fertility curve and hence different factors are provided for different shaped fertility curves, as indicated by the mean or median age of the fertility schedule or the ratio of children ever born to mothers 15–19 to the similar figure for mothers 20–24. Using model life tables the level of mortality corresponding to each value of $_xq_0$ can be obtained and the most appropriate table can thus be selected (for details see Brass, 1975).

From the numbers in the population by age found at the same census and using the selected mortality table the number of births each year in the past can be found by the reverse survival ratio method (*see* section 11.7). If we can make the further assumption that the population is in a stable state then birth rates, death rates, rates of natural increase and reproduction rates can also be estimated (*see* exercise 12.5).

12.7 Other approaches

Many other limited data sources have been used to estimate demographic measures. These include:

(i) a survey of expectant mothers, combined with foetal mortality rates

(ii)   the use of smallpox vaccination records where vaccination by a given age is compulsory

(iii) the ratio of first births to total births in a survey

(iv) the measurement in years of the average interval between births, the reciprocal of which is the number of births per woman per year or the fertility rate of women who have children

(v)   the census population by age together with birth and death statistics both of which are known to be under-registered to a different but constant degree

(vi) a census population by age plus the distribution by age of deaths which are known to be under-registered to a degree which does not vary with age.

12.8 Empirical formulae

In many countries where demographic statistics are lacking, and hence where considerable ingenuity is required in estimating demographic measures, use can be made of the fact that birth control is not practised. One might expect a fairly standard age pattern of fertility in these countries and might therefore expect that it would be possible to derive some empirical relationships between demographic measures which might enable some of the less easily measured quantities to be estimated from those which are normally obtained in a census or a survey. Three of the useful empirical formulae which have been commonly used will now be mentioned.

(i)   Age schedules of fertility for countries not practising birth control do in fact vary in shape in societies where there is little fertility outside marriage. The shape of the fertility curve at younger ages depends largely on the age pattern of marriage in that society. At the ages where fertility is falling the fall is largely due to declining fecundity and follows much the same pattern in different societies. This suggests that the parity P of women who have ceased childbearing might be estimated from the parity P_3 of women aged 25–29 adjusted in some way for early or late marriage. A likely adjustment is to multiply P_3 by P_3/P_2 where P_2 is the parity of women aged 20–24, since higher values of this ratio would occur with later marriages and hence later fertility. Empirical studies with data for countries where birth control is not practised and where reliable statistics are available showed that the relationship $P = P_3^2/P_2$ is a very close one. The parity of women is often obtained at a census and from values of P_3 and P_2 the average number of children P in a completed family can be obtained from the formula. It is often more accurate than using the parity of women over 50 at the census because older women frequently under-report the number of children they have had while younger women report parity accurately. It should be emphasized that this formula is only appropriate for societies where birth control is not practised and where fertility has been constant in the recent past.

(ii)   Another empirical formula which applies to populations of the kind just referred to and from which we may obtain the mean age of the fertility schedule, an essential quantity for converting reproduction rates to annual growth rates and vice versa is as follows:

$$\text{Mean age of fertility schedule} = 2.25\frac{P_3}{P_2} + 23.95$$

(iii) From the average experience of a number of populations in which either little or no birth control is practised, Louis Henry* derived the following pattern of female marital fertility, expressed in terms of the rate for age group 20–24 which is taken as unity:

Age	Index of marital fertility
15–19	$1.2 - 0.7\,m*$
20–24	1.000
25–29	.935
30–34	.853
35–39	.685
40–44	.349
45–49	.051

where $m*$ is the proportion of females aged 15–19 who are married.

If the fertility of non-married women is negligible and if the proportions of women who are married are available from a census, then by multiplying these proportions by the indices in the above table we obtain the shape of the schedule of fertility for women from which the mean age of the fertility schedule can be calculated. If the crude birth rate and the age distribution of the population are known the indices in the above table may be used to estimate the age specific fertility rates.

For further reading

1. Barclay, G. W. et. al., A Reassessment of the Demography of Transitional Rural China, *Population Index*, 42, 1976.
2. Brass, W. et. al., *Demography of Tropical Africa*, 1968.
3. Brass, W., *Methods of Estimating Fertility and Mortality From Limited Data*, University of North Carolina, Chapell Hill, 1975.
4. Musham, H. V., *Moderator's Introductory Statement on Vital Statistics From Limited Data*, International Population Conference, Ottawa, 1963.
5. Stolnitz, G. J., *Life Tables From Limited Data*, 1956.
6. United Nations, *Methods of Estimating Basic Demographic Measures From Incomplete Data*, 1967.

Exercises

12.1 For each of the methods referred to in paragraph 12.7 explain in detail how you would collect the necessary data, what demographic information you would expect to be able to obtain from it, and the assumptions which are involved in the method.

12.2 The United Nations suggest that when the distribution of fertility by age is not known appropriate weights for the six age groups 15–19 to 40–44 are 1, 7, 7, 6, 4, 1 respectively. (It might be mentioned in passing that several demographers have pointed out that quite significant departures from this pattern do occur.) Nevertheless, explain how you would use these particular weights together with the given crude birth rate and age distribution of a country to estimate its age specific fertility rates.

12.3 Use Coale and Demeny's stable population tables to illustrate the importance of the mean age of the fertility schedule as a factor in determining annual population growth rates.

*Henry, L., Some Data on Natural Fertility, *Eugenics Quarterly*, Vol. 8, 1961.

12.4 In the 1966 census of the female population of Fiji the following proportions married were obtained:

Age	Proportion married
15–19	.166
20–24	.672
25–29	.872
30–34	.910
35–39	.911
40–44	.883
45–49	.830

Use Louis Henry's indices of marital fertility (see paragraph 12.8) to show that the mean age of fertility may be estimated at 30.55 years.

12.5 From the proportions still living among children ever born as determined for a region of Turkey in 1966, the following values of $_xq_0$, the proportion dead by age x, were obtained by the method described in section 12.6:

Age x	$_xq_0$
1	.220
2	.262
3	.263
5	.275
10	.294
15	.311
20	.321

By using 'West' model life tables show that a mortality level of 9 or 10 approximates to this experience.

12.6 The female age distribution found for the population in exercise 12.5 was as follows:

Age (x)	Proportion of population up to age x
5	.1724
10	.3314
15	.4457
20	.5365
25	.6037
30	.6739
35	.7479
40	.8070
45	.8438

Using the mortality level found for this population in exercise 12.5 (i.e. 'West' level 9) and assuming the population is in a stable state, estimate (for each of the proportions given) the birth rate, death rate and rate of natural increase.

12.7 It has been stated that 'age specific mortality rates at ages above 1 year scatter widely among populations exhibiting the same infant mortality rate; and a corresponding remark applies to the expectation of life'. Can you find any evidence to support this statement from model life tables? If the statement is correct what conclusions follow regarding the use of model life tables?

Appendix

Australian Males Life Table (1960-62)—A^{M61}

Age	l_x	d_x	q_x	p_x	L_x	T_x	$\overset{\circ}{e}_x$	Age
0	100,000	2,239	0.02239	0.97761	98,433	6,791,451	67.91	0
1	97,761	177	0.00181	0.99819	97,655	6,693,018	68.46	1
2	97,584	117	0.00120	0.99880	97,525	6,595,363	67.59	2
3	97,467	88	0.00090	0.99910	97,423	6,497,838	66.67	3
4	97,379	64	0.00066	0.99934	97,347	6,400,415	65.73	4
5	97,315	56	0.00058	0.99942	97,287	6,303,068	64.77	5
6	97,259	53	0.00055	0.99945	97,233	6,205,781	63.81	6
7	97,206	52	0.00053	0.99947	97,180	6,108,548	62.84	7
8	97,154	49	0.00050	0.99950	97,129	6,011,368	61.87	8
9	97,105	43	0.00044	0.99956	97,084	5,914,239	60.91	9
10	97,062	40	0.00041	0.99959	97,042	5,817,155	59.93	10
11	97,022	41	0.00042	0.99958	97,001	5,720,113	58.96	11
12	96,981	45	0.00046	0.99954	96,959	5,623,112	57.98	12
13	96,936	51	0.00053	0.99947	96,910	5,526,153	57.01	13
14	96,885	60	0.00062	0.99938	96,855	5,429,243	56.04	14
15	96,825	73	0.00075	0.99925	96,789	5,332,388	55.07	15
16	96,752	92	0.00095	0.99905	96,706	5,235,599	54.11	16
17	96,660	119	0.00123	0.99877	96,600	5,138,893	53.16	17
18	96,541	157	0.00163	0.99837	96,463	5,042,293	52.23	18
19	96,384	169	0.00175	0.99825	96,299	4,945,830	51.31	19
20	96,215	166	0.00173	0.99827	96,132	4,849,531	50.40	20
21	96,049	163	0.00170	0.99830	95,968	4,753,399	49.49	21
22	95,886	158	0.00165	0.99835	95,807	4,657,431	48.57	22
23	95,728	151	0.00158	0.99842	95,652	4,561,624	47.65	23
24	95,577	145	0.00152	0.99848	95,505	4,465,972	46.73	24
25	95,432	140	0.00147	0.99853	95,362	4,370,467	45.80	25
26	95,292	138	0.00145	0.99855	95,223	4,275,105	44.86	26
27	95,154	140	0.00147	0.99853	95,084	4,179,882	43.93	27
28	95,014	143	0.00150	0.99850	94,942	4,084,798	42.99	28
29	94,871	145	0.00153	0.99847	94,799	3,989,856	42.06	29
30	94,726	149	0.00157	0.99843	94,652	3,895,057	41.12	30
31	94,577	152	0.00161	0.99839	94,501	3,800,406	40.18	31
32	94,425	158	0.00167	0.99833	94,346	3,705,905	39.25	32
33	94,267	164	0.00174	0.99826	94,185	3,611,559	38.31	33
34	94,103	172	0.00183	0.99817	94,017	3,517,374	37.38	34
35	93,931	182	0.00194	0.99806	93,840	3,423,357	36.45	35
36	93,749	195	0.00208	0.99792	93,651	3,329,517	35.52	36
37	93,554	211	0.00226	0.99774	93,448	3,235,865	34.59	37
38	93,343	231	0.00247	0.99753	93,228	3,142,417	33.67	38
39	93,112	253	0.00272	0.99728	92,985	3,049,189	32.75	39
40	92,859	279	0.00300	0.99700	92,720	2,956,204	31.84	40
41	92,580	306	0.00330	0.99670	92,427	2,863,484	30.93	41
42	92,274	336	0.00364	0.99636	92,106	2,771,057	30.03	42
43	91,938	369	0.00401	0.99599	91,753	2,678,951	29.14	43
44	91,569	404	0.00441	0.99559	91,367	2,587,198	28.25	44
45	91,165	442	0.00485	0.99515	90,944	2,495,831	27.38	45
46	90,723	485	0.00535	0.99465	90,481	2,404,887	26.51	46
47	90,238	533	0.00591	0.99409	89,971	2,314,406	25.65	47
48	89,705	587	0.00654	0.99346	89,412	2,224,435	24.80	48
49	89,118	645	0.00724	0.99276	88,795	2,135,023	23.96	49
50	88,473	711	0.00804	0.99196	88,118	2,046,228	23.13	50
51	87,762	783	0.00892	0.99108	87,370	1,958,110	22.31	51
52	86,979	860	0.00989	0.99011	86,549	1,870,740	21.51	52
53	86,119	944	0.01096	0.98904	85,647	1,784,191	20.72	53
54	85,175	1,033	0.01213	0.98787	84,659	1,698,544	19.94	54
55	84,142	1,127	0.01339	0.98661	83,578	1,613,885	19.18	55

Australian Males Life Table (1960-62)—A^{M61}

Age	l_x	d_x	q_x	p_x	L_x	T_x	$\overset{\circ}{e}_x$	Age
56	83,015	1,225	0.01476	0.98524	82,403	1,530,307	18.43	56
57	81,790	1,331	0.01627	0.98373	81,124	1,447,904	17.70	57
58	80,459	1,442	0.01792	0.98208	79,738	1,366,780	16.99	58
59	79,017	1,561	0.01975	0.98025	78,237	1,287,042	16.29	59
60	77,456	1,685	0.02176	0.97824	76,613	1,208,805	15.61	60
61	75,771	1,817	0.02398	0.97602	74,863	1,132,192	14.94	61
62	73,954	1,952	0.02640	0.97360	72,978	1,057,329	14.30	62
63	72,002	2,087	0.02899	0.97101	70,958	984,351	13.67	63
64	69,915	2,216	0.03170	0.96830	68,807	913,393	13.06	64
65	67,699	2,338	0.03454	0.96546	66,530	844,586	12.48	65
66	65,361	2,451	0.03750	0.96250	64,136	778,056	11.90	66
67	62,910	2,557	0.04064	0.95936	61,631	713,920	11.35	67
68	60,353	2,657	0.04402	0.95598	59,025	652,289	10.81	68
69	57,696	2,752	0.04770	0.95230	56,320	593,264	10.28	69
70	54,944	2,844	0.05177	0.94823	53,522	536,944	9.77	70
71	52,100	2,932	0.05628	0.94372	50,634	483,422	9.28	71
72	49,168	3,008	0.06118	0.93882	47,664	432,788	8.80	72
73	46,160	3,068	0.06646	0.93354	44,626	385,124	8.34	73
74	43,092	3,108	0.07212	0.92788	41,538	340,498	7.90	74
75	39,984	3,124	0.07814	0.92186	38,422	298,960	7.48	75
76	36,860	3,115	0.08451	0.91549	35,302	260,538	7.07	76
77	33,745	3,084	0.09140	0.90860	32,203	225,236	6.67	77
78	30,661	3,032	0.09888	0.90112	29,145	193,033	6.30	78
79	27,629	2,960	0.10713	0.89287	26,149	163,888	5.93	79
80	24,669	2,866	0.11617	0.88383	23,236	137,739	5.58	80
81	21,803	2,749	0.12607	0.87393	20,429	114,503	5.25	81
82	19,054	2,606	0.13679	0.86321	17,751	94,074	4.94	82
83	16,448	2,440	0.14836	0.85164	15,228	76,323	4.64	83
84	14,008	2,250	0.16062	0.83938	12,883	61,095	4.36	84
85	11,758	2,042	0.17363	0.82637	10,737	48,212	4.10	85
86	9,716	1,819	0.18726	0.81274	8,806	37,475	3.86	86
87	7,897	1,591	0.20151	0.79849	7,102	28,669	3.63	87
88	6,306	1,363	0.21620	0.78380	5,624	21,567	3.42	88
89	4,943	1,143	0.23133	0.76867	4,372	15,943	3.23	89
90	3,800	938	0.24675	0.75325	3,331	11,571	3.05	90
91	2,862	751	0.26241	0.73759	2,486	8,240	2.88	91
92	2,111	587	0.27821	0.72179	1,818	5,754	2.73	92
93	1,524	448	0.29415	0.70585	1,300	3,936	2.58	93
94	1,076	334	0.31023	0.68977	909	2,636	2.45	94
95	742	242	0.32649	0.67351	621	1,727	2.33	95
96	500	171	0.34294	0.65706	414	1,106	2.21	96
97	329	118	0.35963	0.64037	270	692	2.10	97
98	211	79	0.37654	0.62346	172	422	2.00	98
99	132	52	0.39364	0.60636	106	250	1.89	99
100	80	33	0.41087	0.58913	63	144	1.80	100
101	47	20	0.42822	0.57178	37	81	1.72	101
102	27	12	0.44565	0.55435	21	44	1.63	102
103	15	7	0.46310	0.53690	12	23	1.53	103
104	8	4	0.48057	0.51943	6	11	1.38	104
105	4	2	0.49799	0.50201	3	5	1.25	105
106	2	1	0.51533	0.48467	1	2	1.00	106
107	1	1	0.53253	0.46747	1	1	1.00	107
108	0	0	0.54953	0.45047	0	0		108
109	0	0	0.56630	0.43370	0	0		109

Australian Females Life Table (1960-62)—A^{F61}

Age	l_x	d_x	q_x	p_x	L_x	T_x	$\overset{\circ}{e}_x$	Age
0	100,000	1,757	0.01757	0.98243	98,770	7,417,378	74.17	0
1	98,243	169	0.00172	0.99828	98,142	7,318,608	74.49	1
2	98,074	100	0.00102	0.99898	98,024	7,220,466	73.62	2
3	97,974	63	0.00064	0.99936	97,942	7,122,442	72.70	3
4	97,911	57	0.00058	0.99942	97,883	7,024,500	71.74	4
5	97,854	49	0.00050	0.99950	97,829	6,926,617	70.79	5
6	97,805	43	0.00044	0.99956	97,784	6,828,788	69.82	6
7	97,762	37	0.00038	0.99962	97,743	6,731,004	68.85	7
8	97,725	32	0.00033	0.99967	97,709	6,633,261	67.88	8
9	97,693	29	0.00030	0.99970	97,678	6,535,552	66.90	9
10	97,664	27	0.00028	0.99972	97,651	6,437,874	65.92	10
11	97,637	26	0.00027	0.99973	97,624	6,340,223	64.94	11
12	97,611	27	0.00028	0.99972	97,598	6,242,599	63.95	12
13	97,584	28	0.00029	0.99971	97,570	6,145,001	62.97	13
14	97,556	31	0.00032	0.99968	97,540	6,047,431	61.99	14
15	97,525	37	0.00038	0.99962	97,507	5,949,891	61.01	15
16	97,488	45	0.00046	0.99954	97,465	5,852,384	60.03	16
17	97,443	52	0.00053	0.99947	97,417	5,754,919	59.06	17
18	97,391	56	0.00057	0.99943	97,363	5,657,502	58.09	18
19	97,335	57	0.00059	0.99941	97,307	5,560,139	57.12	19
20	97,278	58	0.00060	0.99940	97,249	5,462,832	56.16	20
21	97,220	59	0.00061	0.99939	97,190	5,365,583	55.19	21
22	97,161	60	0.00062	0.99938	97,131	5,268,393	54.22	22
23	97,101	59	0.00061	0.99939	97,072	5,171,262	53.26	23
24	97,042	58	0.00060	0.99940	97,013	5,074,190	52.29	24
25	96,984	60	0.00062	0.99938	96,954	4,977,177	51.32	25
26	96,924	63	0.00065	0.99935	96,893	4,880,223	50.35	26
27	96,861	67	0.00069	0.99931	96,827	4,783,330	49.38	27
28	96,794	71	0.00073	0.99927	96,759	4,686,503	48.42	28
29	96,723	74	0.00077	0.99923	96,686	4,589,744	47.45	29
30	96,649	79	0.00082	0.99918	96,609	4,493,058	46.49	30
31	96,570	85	0.00088	0.99912	96,528	4,396,449	45.53	31
32	96,485	93	0.00096	0.99904	96,438	4,299,921	44.57	32
33	96,392	100	0.00104	0.99896	96,342	4,203,483	43.61	33
34	96,292	109	0.00113	0.99887	96,238	4,107,141	42.65	34
35	96,183	118	0.00123	0.99877	96,124	4,010,903	41.70	35
36	96,065	129	0.00134	0.99866	96,001	3,914,779	40.75	36
37	95,936	139	0.00145	0.99855	95,866	3,818,778	39.81	37
38	95,797	151	0.00158	0.99842	95,722	3,722,912	38.86	38
39	95,646	165	0.00172	0.99828	95,563	3,627,190	37.92	39
40	95,481	179	0.00187	0.99813	95,391	3,531,627	36.99	40
41	95,302	195	0.00205	0.99795	95,205	3,436,236	36.06	41
42	95,107	214	0.00225	0.99775	95,000	3,341,031	35.13	42
43	94,893	235	0.00248	0.99752	94,775	3,246,031	34.21	43
44	94,658	258	0.00273	0.99727	94,259	3,151,256	33.29	44
45	94,400	283	0.00300	0.99700	94,529	3,056,727	32.38	45
46	94,117	308	0.00327	0.99673	93,963	2,962,468	31.48	46
47	93,809	335	0.00357	0.99643	93,642	2,868,505	30.58	47
48	93,474	365	0.00390	0.99610	93,292	2,774,863	29.69	48
49	93,109	396	0.00425	0.99575	92,911	2,681,571	28.80	49
50	92,713	430	0.00464	0.99536	92,498	2,588,660	27.92	50
51	92,283	466	0.00505	0.99495	92,050	2,496,162	27.05	51
52	91,817	503	0.00548	0.99452	91,566	2,404,112	26.18	52
53	91,314	541	0.00593	0.99407	91,043	2,312,546	25.33	53
54	90,773	582	0.00641	0.99359	90,482	2,221,503	24.47	54
55	90,191	625	0.00693	0.99307	89,879	2,131,021	23.63	55

Australian Females Life Table (1960-62)—A^{F61}

Age	l_x	d_x	q_x	p_x	L_x	T_x	$\overset{\circ}{e}_x$	Age
56	89,566	671	0.00749	0.99251	89,231	2,041,142	22.79	56
57	88,895	724	0.00814	0.99186	88,533	1,951,911	21.96	57
58	88,171	783	0.00888	0.99112	87,780	1,863,378	21.13	58
59	87,388	851	0.00974	0.99026	86,962	1,775,598	20.32	59
60	86,537	929	0.01074	0.98926	86,073	1,688,636	19.51	60
61	85,608	1,017	0.01188	0.98812	85,100	1,602,563	18.72	61
62	84,591	1,112	0.01314	0.98686	84,035	1,517,463	17.94	62
63	83,479	1,214	0.01454	0.98546	82,872	1,433,428	17.17	63
64	82,265	1,321	0.01606	0.98394	81,604	1,350,556	16.42	64
65	80,944	1,432	0.01769	0.98231	80,228	1,268,952	15.68	65
66	79,512	1,550	0.01950	0.98050	78,737	1,188,724	14.95	66
67	77,962	1,677	0.02151	0.97849	77,124	1,109,987	14.24	67
68	76,285	1,815	0.02379	0.97621	75,378	1,032,863	13.54	68
69	74,470	1,965	0.02638	0.97362	73,487	957,485	12.86	69
70	72,505	2,127	0.02933	0.97067	71,441	883,998	12.19	70
71	70,378	2,299	0.03266	0.96734	69,229	812,557	11.55	71
72	68,079	2,479	0.03641	0.96359	66,840	743,328	10.92	72
73	65,600	2,661	0.04057	0.95943	64,269	676,488	10.31	73
74	62,939	2,843	0.04517	0.95483	61,517	612,219	9.73	74
75	60.096	3,019	0.05024	0.94976	58,586	550,702	9.16	75
76	57,077	3,189	0.05587	0.94413	55,483	492,116	8.62	76
77	53,888	3,345	0.06207	0.93793	52,215	436,633	8.10	77
78	50,543	3,485	0.06895	0.93105	48,800	384,418	7.61	78
79	47,058	3,605	0.07660	0.92340	45,256	335,618	7.13	79
80	43,453	3,697	0.08507	0.91493	41,605	290,362	6.68	80
81	39,756	3,750	0.09432	0.90568	37,881	248,757	6.26	81
82	36,006	3,759	0.10440	0.89560	34,126	210,876	5.86	82
83	32,247	3,717	0.11526	0.88474	30,389	176,750	5.48	83
84	28,530	3,621	0.12692	0.87308	26,720	146,361	5.13	84
85	24,909	3,469	0.13927	0.86073	23,174	119,641	4.80	85
86	21,440	3,266	0.15231	0.84769	19,807	96,467	4.50	86
87	18,174	3,016	0.16597	0.83403	16,666	76,660	4.22	87
88	15,158	2,731	0.18020	0.81980	13,792	59,994	3.96	88
89	12,427	2,422	0.19486	0.80514	11,216	46,202	3.72	89
90	10,005	2,100	0.20990	0.79010	8,955	34,986	3.50	90
91	7,905	1,780	0.22521	0.77479	7,015	26,031	3.29	91
92	6,125	1,475	0.24079	0.75921	5,388	19,016	3.10	92
93	4,650	1,193	0.25656	0.74344	4,053	13,628	2.93	93
94	3,457	942	0.27255	0.72745	2,986	9,575	2.78	94
95	2,515	726	0.28875	0.71125	2,152	6,589	2.62	95
96	1,789	546	0.30523	0.69477	1,516	4,437	2.48	96
97	1,243	400	0.32197	0.67803	1,043	2,921	2.35	97
98	843	286	0.33899	0.66101	700	1,878	2.23	98
99	557	198	0.35626	0.64374	458	1,178	2.11	99
100	359	134	0.37380	0.62620	292	720	2.01	100
101	225	88	0.39152	0.60848	181	428	1.90	101
102	137	56	0.40942	0.59058	109	247	1.80	102
103	81	35	0.42744	0.57256	63	138	1.70	103
104	46	20	0.44557	0.55443	36	75	1.63	104
105	26	12	0.46374	0.53626	20	39	1.50	105
106	14	7	0.48195	0.51805	11	19	1.36	106
107	7	4	0.50010	0.49990	5	8	1.14	107
108	3	2	0.51816	0.48184	2	3	1.00	108
109	1	1	0.53608	0.46392	1	1	1.00	109

Solutions to selected exercises

2.1   (i)   19.3 births per 1,000 population
     (ii)   8.9 deaths per 1,000 population
     (iii) 3.9 persons per square mile
     (iv) 104 males per 100 females
     (v)   236,076
     (vi) .023
     (vii) 176 births per 1,000 women
     (viii) 1.9% p. a.

2.2   (i)   155 persons per square mile
     (ii)   105 males per 100 females
     (iii) 50 births per 1,000 population
     (iv) 150 deaths per 1,000 male births
     (v)   2.15% p. a.
     (vi) 137.7 million
     (vii) 500 children (0–4) per 1,000 women (15–44)

3.3   (i) l_5/l_0 0.750   0.981
     (ii) l_{25}/l_5 0.880   0.994
     (iii) l_{30}/l_{10} 0.866   0.994
     (iv) $(l_{15} - l_{35})/l_{35}$ 0.158   0.009
     (v) $(l_{20} - l_{30})/l_{10}$ 0.079   0.004
     (vi) $\left(\dfrac{l_{15} - l_{25}}{l_{15}}\right)^2$ 0.005   0.00001

3.4 $900\left(\dfrac{l_{25} - l_{30}}{l_{15}}\right)$, 38 and 2

3.5   (i)   225,367
     (ii)   1,066

3.7 $\sum \dfrac{1000}{l_{30}}(T_{30} - T_{60}) = 24,947 + 29,321 = 54,268$

3.8   (i)   42.8   75.4
     (ii)   60.2   77.0
     (iii) 66.7   77.6
     (iv) 73.5   79.3

3.9   50.9   52.6

3.11 (i) $(T_{20} - T_{60})/l_{20}$
     (ii) l_{60}/l_{20}
     (iii) $(T_{50} - T_{60})/(T_{20} - T_{60})$
     (iv) $T_{60}/(T_{20} - T_{60})$
     (v) $l_{60}/(l_{20} - l_{60})$

3.12 (i) l_{60}/l_{20}
     (ii) d_{45}/l_{20}
     (iii) $(l_{40} - l_{60})/l_{30}$
     (iv) l_{70}/l_{20}
     (v) l_{30}/l_{20}
     (vi) d_{35}/l_{30}
     (vii) l_{20}
     (viii) $l_{20} - l_{51}$
     (ix) l_{41}
     (x) $50{,}000\, l_{18}/T_{18}$
     (xi) $50{,}000\, T_{80}/T_{18}$
     (xii) $\mathring{e}_{18}$
     (xiii) $50{,}000\, l_{18}/(T_{18} - T_{80})$
     (xiv) $(T_{18} - T_{80})/l_{18}$
     (xv) $50{,}000\, l_{80}/(T_{18} - T_{80})$
     (xvi) $(T_{65} - T_{80})/(T_{18} - T_{80})$

3.13 .000875; .033507

3.14 (i)   .0358
     (ii)   .0508

4.1   (i) $100 \times \dfrac{1000}{l_{20}} \times (l_{20} - l_{50})$

     (ii) $\dfrac{100}{l_{18}} \times (T_{18} - T_{60})$

     (iii) $\dfrac{100}{l_{18}} \times T_{60}$

     (iv) $\dfrac{100}{l_{18}} \times (T_{40} - T_{60})$

     (v) $\dfrac{100}{l_{18}} \times l_{60}$

     (vi) $\dfrac{100}{l_{18}} \times (l_{18} - l_{60})$

     (vii) $\dfrac{100}{l_{18}} \times l_{60}$

     (viii) $\dfrac{100}{l_{18}} \times (l_{70} - l_{80})$

     (ix) $\dfrac{100}{l_{18}} \times l_{43}$

     (x) $\dfrac{100}{l_{18}} \times [(T_{18} - T_{21}) + 0.9(T_{21} - T_{25}) + 0.9 \times 0.95(T_{25} - T_{60})]$

     (xi) $\dfrac{T_{69}}{l_{40}}$

     (xii) $\dfrac{1000}{l_{30}} \times (T_{50} - T_{70})$

     (xiii) $3000 \times l_{18}/(T_{18} - T_{60})$

4.2   (a) $\dfrac{1000}{l_{20}} \times [(T_{20} - T_{23}) + 0.9(T_{23} - T_{26}) + 0.9 \times 0.95(T_{26} - T_{60}) + 0.9 \times 0.95 \times 0.6(T_{60} - T_{65})]$

     (b) $\dfrac{1000}{l_{20}} \times 0.9 \times 0.95 \times (0.4T_{60} + 0.6T_{65})$

     (c) $\dfrac{1000}{l_{20}} \times 0.9 \times 0.95 \times 0.4(T_{60} - T_{65})$

(d) $\dfrac{1000}{l_{20}} \times [0.9L_{25} + 0.9 \times 0.95(T_{26} - T_{40})]$

(e) $\dfrac{1000}{l_{20}} \times [0.9 \times 0.95(0.4l_{60} + 0.6l_{65})]$

(f) $\dfrac{1000}{l_{20}} \times [(l_{20} - l_{23}) + 0.9(l_{23} - l_{26}) + 0.9 \times 0.95(l_{26} - l_{60}) + 0.9 \times 0.95 \times 0.6(l_{60} - l_{65})]$

(g) $[(T_{20} - T_{23}) + 0.9(T_{23} - T_{26}) + 0.9 \times 0.95(T_{26} - T_{60}) + 0.9 \times 0.95 \times 0.6(T_{60} - T_{65})] \div l_{20}$

(h) $[0.95(T_{40} - T_{60}) + 0.95 \times 0.6(T_{60} - T_{65})] \div l_{25}$

(i) $0.95 \times 0.6 \times \dfrac{l_{63}}{l_{25}}$

4.3   (i) $\dfrac{1,500}{l_0} \times T_0 = 4,091$

(ii) $\dfrac{1,500}{l_0} \times (T_1 - T_4) = 2,453$

(iii) $\left(1,500 \times \dfrac{5,000}{T_0}\right) - 1,500 = 333$

4.4   \$722,869

4.5   (a) (i) l_x column

(ii) d_x column

(b) (i) l_5/l_0

(ii) l_6/l_3

(iii) $(l_4 - l_6)/l_1$

(c) (i) $\dfrac{1,000}{l_0} \times T_0$

(ii) $\dfrac{1,000}{l_0} \times L_x$ column

(d) (i) $\dfrac{1,000}{l_0}(T_2 - T_5)$

(ii) $\dfrac{1,000}{l_0} \times 10 \times l_5$

(e) (i) T_0/l_0

(ii) T_3/l_3

(f) (i) $\dfrac{400}{l_0} \times 500 \times (l_0 - l_2)$

(ii) $\dfrac{400}{l_0} \times 10 \times [2(l_0 + l_4) + (l_2 + l_6 + l_8)]$

4.6   (i) $300,000 \times l_{20}/[(T_{20} - T_{25}) + 0.05(T_{25} - T_{55}) + 0.05 \times 0.6(T_{55} - T_{60})]$
  $= 300,000 \times l_{20}/Z$ (say)

(ii) $\dfrac{300,000}{Z}[0.95(T_{25} - T_{32})]$

(iii) $\dfrac{300,000}{Z} \times [0.05(0.4T_{55} + 0.6T_{60})] \times 15,000$

(iv) $\dfrac{300,000}{Z}\left[9,000T_{20} + 600\sum_{21}^{24} T_x - 11,400T_{25} + 0.05\left(15,000T_{25} + 300\sum_{26}^{45} T_x - 21,000T_{55}\right)\right.$

$\left. + 0.05 \times 0.6 \times 21,000\,(T_{55} - T_{60})\right]$

(v) $0.05 \times 0.6 \times l_{60}/l_{20}$

4.7   Reduction factor $(R) = 300/[(T_{18} - T_{23}) + 0.9(T_{23} - T_{38}) + 0.9 \times 0.95(T_{38} - T_{60})]$

(i) $R\left[6,900T_{18} + 300\sum_{19}^{22} T_x - 8,100T_{23} + 0.9\left(8,400T_{23} + 300\sum_{24}^{37} T_x - 12,600T_{38}\right)\right.$

$\left. + 0.9 \times 0.95\left(12,900T_{38} + 300\sum_{39}^{45} T_x - 15,000T_{60}\right)\right]$

(ii) $R[0.9 \times 0.95 \times l_{60}]$

(iii) $R[0.9 \times 0.95 \times T_{60}]$

5.1   (a)   139.0; 96.6
      (b)   134.5; 77.2
      (c)   136.7; 86.9

5.2   28 and 29 deaths per 1,000 population
      (i)   1.176
      (ii)   34 deaths per 1,000
      (iii) 33 deaths per 1,000

5.4   100; 108; 110.

6.6   1.519; 1.481; 1.473; 1.206; 1.090

6.7   (i)   6
      (ii) 2.8

6.10 58.7; 67.8

8.2   1.46% p.a.; 6.90% p.a.
      14,968,000; 283,900
      19,747,000; 1,009,300
      2057

8.3   36,520; 39,460; 42,600; 45,860; 49,270

10.2 0.761

10.3 4.48%

10.6 (i)   1.152
      (ii)   (a) 57.7
             (b) 47.5
      (iii) (a) 40.2
             (b) 63.4

10.10 (i)   .86561
      (ii)   .00403
      (iii) .12474

10.11 0.0958

11.1 4.86

11.2 1 − 5
      Digital preference for 1 − 5 = 50.02%

11.3 14.1; 15.2; 17.4; 81.6

11.5 Males   Females
      118,871   112,985
      114,577   109,255
      112,250   107,474
      110,670   105,615
      108,457   102,613

11.6 2,936

Index